COMMUNITY AND TRADITION

COMMUNITY AND TRADITION

Conservative Perspectives on the American Experience

Edited by
George W. Carey
and
Bruce Frohnen

ROWMAN & LITTLEFIELD PUBLISHERS, INC.
Lanham • Boulder • New York • Oxford

ROWMAN & LITTLEFIELD PUBLISHERS, INC.

Published in the United States of America
by Rowman and Littlefield Publishers, Inc.
4720 Boston Way, Lanham, Maryland 20706

12 Hid's Copse Road
Cumnor Hill, Oxford OX2 9JJ, England

British Library Cataloguing in Publication Information Available

Library of Congress Cataloging-in-Publication Data

Community and tradition : conservative perspectives on the American
experience / edited by George W. Carey and Bruce Frohnen.
p. cm.
Includes bibliographical references and index.
ISBN 0-8476-8660-4 (cloth : alk. paper). — ISBN 0-8476-8661-2
(pbk. : alk. paper)
1. Community. 2. Conservatism. I. Carey, George Wescott, 1933– .
II.Frohnen, Bruce.
HM131.0637 1998
307—DC21 98-23398
CIP

Printed in the United States of America

™ The paper used in this publication meets the minimum requirements of American National Standard for Information Sciences—Permanence of Paper for Printed Library Materials, ANSI Z39.48—1984.

Contents

Acknowledgments vii

Introduction 1

1 Contemporary Communitarianism, the Lure of the State, and the Modern Quest for Community 17
Kenneth L. Grasso

2 American Community 39
Barry Alan Shain

3 The Constitution and Community 63
George W. Carey

4 Mr. Emerson's Tombstone 85
Wilfred M. McClay

5 Charles Taylor on Multiculturalism and the Politics of Recognition 103
Norman Barry

6 On the Extent of Community: Civil Society, Civil Religion, and the State 125
Brad Lowell Stone

7 Is William Galston Really a Liberal? 143
Peter Augustine Lawler

8 Commitment and Obligation 165
Bruce Frohnen

Notes 187

Index 201

About the Contributors 205

Acknowledgments

The editors wish to thank Liberty Fund, Inc., for hosting a colloquium on "Liberty and Community" in April 1996, from which much of this work grew.

Introduction

Where there is man there is community. The individual, as contemporary scholars like to call him, is born of the union between a man and a woman. He comes into the world as part of a family. He is educated in communal schools. And he lives out his life in associations from the parish to the workplace to the local glee club. In former times, a man died surrounded by his family. Today he is more likely to die in an antiseptic hospital ward—but still surrounded by people, as even his lifeless body will be surrounded by others in the graveyard.

But if man always and everywhere is in community, why the need for a book on community, particularly one such as this that seeks to examine the recent "rebirth" of that concept? Because not all communities are alike. Because not all communities live up to their name. Because our communities are disappearing as we forget what we are losing.

To say that man is always in some form of community is merely to note that we are all by nature social beings. We seek out the company of others in our work and in what we rightly term our "social" lives—our pursuit of entertainment and companionship. But not every chance encounter produces community. Politics involves "social" interaction, but its results—laws and programs—can hardly be called communities. Some relations produce only conflict. Others produce only the satisfaction of material wants-of-the-moment. Even lasting relationships may lack the essential bonds of shared thought, feeling, and experience of which true community is made.

A word's origins can tell us much about its deeper meaning. The origins in effect show us what people were thinking when they coined the word. The Latin roots of the word "community" are *communis*—which means "common"—and *communitas*—which means "fellowship," a term itself close to the Greek *philia,* or friendship. Thus a true community, one that lives up to its name, is one in which the members share something in common—something important enough to give rise to fellowship or friendship and to sustain it. There may be many kinds of communities with varying ends or goals. But each must form around characteristics, experiences, practices, and beliefs that are important enough to bind the members to one another, such that they are willing to sacrifice for one another as "fellows" or sharers of a common fate.

To truly bind men to one another, that which they hold in common must be important to them. Daily life, consisting of numerous repetitious acts necessary for survival, encapsulates many ties that bind. That is why a community generally is depicted as being relatively small and geographically compact. The world is not a community. But the typical American small town of the 1950s, the subject of nostalgia for many Americans and of contempt for most intellectuals, continues to be seen as exemplifying community. In them individuals lived together in meaningful ways. Neighbors shared more than a property line: they shared a way of life characterized by common values, common habits, and a common culture.

It is the term "culture" that perhaps best sums up the commonality of a shared life. For culture is rooted in Latin words for "cult," as in a religious group, and "cultivation," as in farming and other routinized practices intended to produce fruit. When people share a culture, they share common beliefs and practices and cultivate the same land. They cultivate their own characters in roughly the same way, with ends in mind that their fellows would recognize as good and proper. A man cultivating himself through primitive rituals and the casting out of evil spirits to produce the character of a shaman would be out of place in present-day New York City. One cultivating himself through attention to theoretical science and logic to become a physicist in the wilds of the Amazon would be equally out of place.

Common culture is in disrepute because many believe our Western tradition has promoted uniquely oppressive and imperialistic attitudes and practices. But it remains the case that no community can exist unless the people in it share important aspects of their lives in common. As Alexis de Tocqueville observed, centralized governments seek to make people's lives more "fair" and equal by taking over the functions of local associations and leaving neighbors with no reason to interact. The result is a loss of common conditions, practices, and feelings—a loss of community.

During the early nineteenth century, the United States maintained its communities by providing its localities with many "local liberties." As Tocqueville argued,

> The general business of a county keeps only the leading citizens occupied. It is only occasionally that they come together in the same places, and since they often lose sight of one another, no lasting bonds form between them. But when the people who live there have to look after the particular affairs

> of a district, the same people are always meeting, and they are forced, in a manner, to know and adapt themselves to one another. Local liberties, then, which induce a great number of citizens to value the affection of their kindred and neighbors, bring men constantly into contact . . . and force them to help one another.[1]

When men must constantly interact, they want this interaction to be pleasant. One is more likely to want peace and mutual respect to rule one's relations with a constant companion or helpmate than with a stranger. Over time, individuals come to see helping their neighbors as a necessary part of daily life, and they work to gain esteem in those neighbors' eyes. Again, as Tocqueville put it, "To gain the affection and respect of your immediate neighbors, a long succession of little services rendered and of obscure good deeds, a constant habit of kindness and an established reputation for disinterestedness, are required."[2] The result is a habit of mutual assistance that can be called fellowship or friendship.

Tocqueville saw the model of community in the medieval towns of his native France. He argued that the French king's insistence on enhancing and centralizing his own power destroyed local communities in France. Meanwhile, the more decentralized governments in Great Britain and the United States kept their communities intact.

Medieval towns had order and freedom. Order was maintained by a variety of associations, from craft guilds to religious orders to municipal government. Each of these associations had its own prerogatives and duties; its members cooperated with one another to promote the common good. Because each represented a different aspect of the common good (e.g., religious, economic, or political) each served as a check on the others. For example, municipal leaders were held in check not only by a widespread local suffrage but also by concern that local church leaders not be offended by heavy-handed practices. After all, offended church leaders might speak out publicly against municipal leaders or even refuse them the sacraments, causing their authority and public reputation to plummet. This variety of social powers protected the people against oppression, thereby according them significant freedom to go about their lives unmolested.

To be sure, the local landlord or "seigneur" could compel the peasants in the area to labor on his lands. But he also had the legal duty to care for his peasants, supplying food and other goods in time of need while fulfilling a number of administrative functions on their behalf. And the seigneur was not the only authority in the locality.

> During the Middle Ages the inhabitants of each French village formed a commonality independent in many ways of the seigneur. No doubt he requi-

> sitioned their services, watched over and governed them; but the village held property in common and had exclusive ownership of it. The villagers elected their own officials and governed themselves on democratic lines.[3]

French villagers during the Middle Ages could defend themselves against potential tyrants because they held property, political control, and other essential interests in common. Unfortunately, this made them obstacles to the French kings' lust for power, and as the Middle Ages waned they imposed increasing burdens on the townspeople, for example, taking away their right to elect their own local rulers and then selling it back to them again and again. Louis XIV gave the death blow to local liberty by cajoling and coercing local landlords to live at his court as his dependents. The peasants found themselves abandoned, dependent on the landlords' agents, who treated them as sources of income rather than fellow members of a community who had claims on their aid and goodwill.

Thus the French monarchy eliminated the power of the town to limit its powers. It took five hundred years, but by the time of the French Revolution of 1789, France had become a thoroughly centralized, modern government. Bureaucrats based in Paris oversaw even the most minute local issues. As Tocqueville observed, the French Revolutionary tyranny changed the rulers but not the form of rule when it overthrew the monarchy. Having lost any control over their destiny, people in the localities lost any reason to cooperate with one another, and their communities broke down and eventually disappeared.

Across the channel in Great Britain, however, the story was different. For several centuries, villages and townships maintained their prerogatives, often encapsulated in local charters, against monarchs' efforts to destroy them. Charles I lost his head in part because he trespassed too greatly on the chartered rights of villages and towns. When Charles's son, James II, set about systematically to revoke these charters by packing Parliament with his favorites, he too was chased from the throne, in the popular and nearly bloodless Glorious Revolution of 1689.

And it was from Great Britain that American local government sprang. Great Britain at the time of America's colonization maintained its medieval village structure, thus allowing the Americans to transfer, maintain, and develop townships in the freedom and isolation of the New World. The result, as Tocqueville put it, was that "the French and the American systems resembled each other in so far as a dead creature can be said to resemble one that is very much alive."[4]

From the days of the earliest settlements, during the early seventeenth century until the end of the nineteenth century, America was a country of decentralized power in which townships thrived.

It is against this backdrop that we can appreciate the magnitude of the decline of communities in the United States during the course of the twentieth century. It is not at all uncommon nowadays to hear the word "atomistic" used with reference to individuals, not only to characterize their separation or detachment from one another but also to indicate their lack of relationships with meaningful associations. In the political realm we easily see additional evidence of this isolation. The individual increasingly finds himself alone, having to deal with a centralized government that, presumably, speaks for the collective whole, or "society." In this individual/sovereign relationship, the individual lacks the resources and support of intermediate associations that citizens once possessed.

Indeed, today's political institutions, built as they are around the principle "one person, one vote," both reinforce and reflect this conceptual understanding of the individual's relationship to the state. In this framework, individuals and government act directly on one another, neither recognizing nor paying attention to the role of traditional mediating structures such as church, family, or voluntary associations in the composition of public life. The representative institutions of modern democracies, particularly in the United States, are increasingly instituted and defended on an understanding of individuals as constituent parts or "atoms" of an undifferentiated mass, forming the basic units of representation.

Pluralists, who seek to explain our politics in terms of interest groups doing "battle" with one another, might take exception to this analysis. They would point out that our Founders expected conflict between various interests and that the Constitution they adopted anticipated a multiplicity and diversity of interests in an extended republic. Today, pluralists would point out, we find literally thousands of interest groups, most of them well represented in legislative halls—national, state, and local. They also would point out that these interest groups represent individuals with the same or similar interests. And, to a limited degree, they have a point.

But these pluralist groups are not substitutes for the traditional intermediate associations that once stood between the people and their government. In the first place, modern interest groups do not have the qualities or characteristics of the traditional associations Tocqueville and others identify as essential for genuine communities. They certainly are not noted for their face-to-face meetings and activities, for providing their members with a sense of belonging or accomplishment, for upholding norms and ways of life. Although many of these groups certainly do have important objectives, at least for their members, they are still built around narrow concerns. Moreover, the purposes of these groups are generally self-centered or self-regarding. Most of them are organized precisely because we now have a highly centralized and far-reaching government that can and does touch upon their affairs and concerns. As a consequence, the textbooks tell us, they seek either to advance their own interests through legislation or to protect the advantages and benefits they enjoy from encroachment or diminishment by securing favorable laws and policies.

What the pluralists show us, to give them their due, is that individuals find it advantageous to unite around particular, well-defined interests to influence government action. As government expands and as it begins to assume more and more of the functions once regarded as the province of communities or state and local governments, the number of pluralist groups grows. The growth of modern pluralism is a barometer of the degree to which individuals find it necessary to protect and advance their interests through government. The growth is a reaction to the vulnerability of individuals confronting the powers of the modern state, scarcely an indication of the growth of organic mediating institutions as traditionally conceived.

We cannot, at least in quantitative terms, prove that the relationship between the individual and the state has changed over the last century in the manner we have suggested. But we have every reason to believe it has. One very significant piece of evidence is the fact that, in contrast to the whole of the nineteenth century and the first decades of the twentieth, today we find a goodly portion of our political conversation and debate centering on individual rights. We are constantly debating whether this or that policy or action of government accords with or contravenes individual rights presumably derived from the language of the Constitution.

The changes in our thinking about the individual and the state in the second half of the twentieth century are revealed in the mushrooming number of cases before the Supreme Court involving claims of individual rights. Politicians, academics, and the media frequently remind us that the most precious legacy of the founding generation is the Bill of Rights. Indeed, the mere existence of the Bill of Rights has been interpreted by many, if not most, as recognition of the centrality of individual rights in our political tradition.

In modern times we have witnessed two major developments: a gradual but pronounced weakening of communities, intermediate groups, and associations, accompanied by the evolution of a political environment that extols individual rights; and the simultaneous expansion and centralization of political power. We shall see that these two developments are highly interrelated, each feeding on the other.

The individual/sovereign framework, which leads to the reliance on "rights," is little more than the conceptual framework within which social contract theorists, increasingly since the Enlightenment, discuss the origins of the state. From these theories emerges the image of atomistic individuals coming together to constitute a state through the medium of a contract. Such theories are, in the main, ahistorical and highly deductive in nature. It is hardly surprising, then, that they totally ignore all intermediate groups—communities, the family, voluntary associations—in their picture of the state and society.

Another feature of social contract thought is the view that the state is sovereign or supreme, vested with the final say at least on issues that arise in the public arena. The logic of social contract thinking is simple enough: the sovereign within the state—whether it be one, the few, or the many—has complete control over all matters that have been placed in its care. In the language of modern liberal theory, this means that the government created by the compact between individuals is responsible for these same individuals, or a majority thereof.

As philosopher Bertrand de Jouvenal has noted, popular government based on the fiction of a social contract can expand its powers more readily and with less resistance than governments with monarchical or aristocratic roots. Indeed, the powers of such popular governments—the scope of their sovereignty and control over society in all aspects—is far greater in practice than that enjoyed by monarchies or aristocracies of the past.[5] In times past, for example, the expansion of royal authority was looked on (and often resisted by large sectors of the population) as an unwarranted imposition by an "impersonal master" akin to a foreign power. Other major groups within the society, e.g., church, aristocrats, and guilds, could appeal to a wider audience in targeting the excesses of a single individual whose authority they could also bring into question. In liberal democracies, when the government encroaches, it does so presumably in the name of the people, whose authority and status are difficult to challenge, particularly given the doctrine of consent. Even those who may not subscribe to the social contract origins of the state have come to accept, perhaps through a process of osmosis, its essential framework and the conception of democracy that flows from it.

Conservatives are deeply concerned about almost every aspect of the social contract mode of thought, particularly that which has produced the dominant individual/sovereign paradigm so fashionable today. Conservatives would agree, of course, that the state may rightly be regarded as the largest association, but this does not necessarily render it the most important in all spheres of life. Important to conservative thought is the belief that in most respects intermediate groups and associations are far more important than the state in the daily lives of individuals, as well as for their understanding of the world about them. To ignore or to minimize their role cannot help but lead to a distorted and highly fragmentary picture of the state and society. Thus, to allow a highly centralized national government to replace or to undercut subsidiary groups and associations is to cut off prospects for individuals to fulfill themselves as human beings and to reach their potential as productive and responsible citizens. It is also, as we have intimated (and for reasons we will spell out in some detail in what follows) highly dangerous.

If conservative views are only partially correct concerning the dangers and drawbacks that arise from the weakening of intermediate associations, certain crucial questions arise: How did centralization come to pass in the United States? Why is it that we continue to have such a highly centralized regime, given that our system increasingly exhibits the debilitating effects associated with the individual/sovereign paradigm? What can be done to arrest this process?

The essays that follow will tackle these and similar questions. We can, however, offer some understanding of the theoretical arguments that helped pave the way for this acceptance of a highly centralized state. We can do this best by exploring the thought of the acknowledged father of the New Deal and perhaps the foremost progressive theoretician of the twentieth century, Herbert Croly.

Croly, founder of the highly influential progressive magazine the *New Republic,* published his major work, *The Promise of American Life,* in 1909. Certain portions of this work, particularly those dealing with specific problems and policy concerns, are dated. But its approach, assumptions, principles, and goals provided the foundations for Franklin Roosevelt's New Deal of the 1930s—a program that drastically altered the character of our social and political landscape. Over the decades since the New Deal—decades marked by a continuous expansion and centralization of the welfare state—the core elements of Croly's thought have become so much a part of our political discourse that most Americans are unaware of their origins, much less their meaning in the context of broader progressive theory. *The Promise of American Life* merits our close examination because it, as no other single volume, provides a comprehensive overview of the progressive theory that has been a dominant and persistent force in reshaping our policies and institutions for most of the twentieth century.

Croly believed that the promise of American life in large part consisted of "improving popular economic condition[s]," moral and social betterment, "democratic political institutions," and among other goods the "opportunity for self-improvement." This promise, in Croly's view, could no longer be taken for granted. On the contrary, he wrote, the achievement of this national promise was now highly problematic due to an "undesirable distribution of wealth."[6] Croly's specific plan for the attainment of our national promise called for political centralization, in large part to regulate the economy and the distribution of wealth.

But Croly was interested in a much wider variety of social concerns and problems that he thought only a centralized regime could handle. He was quick to argue that economic freedom had to be curtailed "by a certain measure of discipline" that individuals heretofore had not demonstrated, that henceforth individuals would have to moderate or even subordinate their desires through "self-denial," particularly in their pursuit of wealth. As Croly proceeds to elaborate his program, we come to see that he has an expansive vision of the national interest that he believes is being thwarted and even perverted by selfish interests. In the final analysis, on his showing, the achievement of the national promise he conceived calls for measures to perfect human nature ("democracy cannot be disentangled from an aspiration toward human perfectibility") as well as efforts toward "individual emancipation," including "disinterested motives" and a recognition of the primacy of "national purpose." In Croly's words, each individual must be taught "to sacrifice his recognized private interest to the welfare of his countrymen."[7]

It is beyond our purpose here to detail Croly's ambitious program. But it is important to note how strongly his approach, his view of society, and his proposed "reforms" all indicate his acceptance of the state/individual framework. This conception tacitly permeates his entire discourse. He writes, in the space of just two pages, about a "collective purpose" and a "collective responsibility" that can be fulfilled only by a "collective organization" with able individuals exercising the "collective power" to bring about or induce "collective action." All these "collectives" are not metaphysical abstractions. For Croly they are very real, albeit largely potential, entities that play an indispensable role in directing, controlling, and improving individual citizens.

Croly does not shy away from placing the responsibility for producing a political, social, and economic environment conducive to the realization of his national promise in the hands of a central government; only at this level can his "collectives" operate in the fashion he wants. Thus at one point he writes that "the arduous and responsible political task which a nation in its collective capacity must seek to perform is that of selecting among the various prevailing ways of exercising individual rights those which contribute to national perpetuity and integrity." Agonizing over the tension between the democratic ideal of equality and the need for distinction and leadership that requires "political, economic, and social discriminations," Croly observes: "It is the function of a [democratic] state to represent the whole community; and the whole community includes the individual as well as the mass, the many as well as the few." It is "community, and nothing less than the whole community," he continues, that must establish the legitimate grounds for allowing individuals or the few to distinguish themselves from the masses. Likewise it is the whole community, for now Croly writes of the state or nation as coterminous with "community," that determines when such "discriminations show any tendency to excessive endurance."[8]

Virtually all of Croly's discussions are cast in terms of a collective authority—the national government or the community understood as the "national" community—exercising power directly on an undifferentiated mass of individuals. No mention is made of what contributions the excluded intermediate groups—family, church, neighborhood, associations—might make to the achievement of his goals. The reconstruction of society proceeds from the top down, as if nothing of worth or consideration stood between the individuals and the central government.

Throughout his discourse Croly unmistakably incorporates and employs the assumptions and values associated with what Robert Nisbet has dubbed the "monistic state."[9] On Nisbet's showing, Rousseau's dream of uniting state and society by eliminating or subordinating all associations standing between the individual and the state illustrates the enormous dangers associated with the monistic state. Under Rousseau's plan, individuals would be compelled to use the powers of a supreme central government for them to advance or realize their personal goals and wants. Rousseau's state, then, would not only serve the traditional function of providing for the "protection and security" of its inhabitants from foreign enemies but it would also become the only agency with the means to provide for their security and well-being—economic, social, and cultural. It would be, as well, the only agency through which the pursuit of higher ends such as liberty, equality, virtue, and fraternity could be undertaken. The powers of this state, as its advocates would have it, are never repressive, so long as individuals are free from the selfish and destructive influences fostered by partial associations and interests. They further contend that it is only when individuals are free from these destructive influences that the people can be trusted to pursue the common good and their true interests.[10]

Bearing in mind this aspect of the monistic state, we can better understand Croly's deep concern to emancipate individuals; they must be liberated from their selfishness and acquisitiveness so that they can think and act on the basis of disinterested motives to perceive more clearly the national purpose. This point is driven home in (among other places) Croly's discussion of popular sovereignty and its compatibility with the "constructive democratic ideal" that he seeks to advance. He acknowledges that to accept majority rule as an expression of popular sovereignty is "a necessary constituent of any practicable democratic organization."[11] But not all majorities should enjoy such a status. Some popular majorities exhibit "arbitrary and dangerous tendencies." These majorities can be effectually checked by "the cherishing of a tradition," partly expressed in some body of fundamental law, that the true people are, as Bismarck declared, in some measure an invisible multitude of spirits—the nation of yesterday and tomorrow, organized for its national historical mission.

Put another way, Croly holds that individuals "even when united into a majority . . . are not Sovereign in reason and morals." "They become Sovereign" to the extent "they succeed in reaching and expressing a collective purpose," or when, "they are united in spirit and purpose . . . are loyal to one another, to their joint past, to the Promise of their future."[12] At another juncture, Croly puts the matter even more forcefully in terms reminiscent of Rousseau's General Will: "In the complete democracy a man must in some way be made to serve the nation in the very act of contributing to his own individual fulfillment"; "his personal action" should be "dictated by disinterested motives" so that there might be a "harmony between private and public interest." This might be an impossible demand, but "just such a continual sacrifice is apparently required of an individual in a democratic state."[13]

The monistic state, the outlines of which appear in Croly's quest for institutions that will fulfill our "national promise," is anathema to conservatives. Their concerns emphasize both the internal and external harm and abuse that befall individuals in such a state. To begin with, as Nisbet points out, individuals instinctively seek goods and values such as "purpose, membership, status, and continuity" that can only be realized through communities and associations. Individuals, to put this somewhat otherwise, want to feel a sense of belonging; they seek the warmth of friendships and the sense of unity and fellowship that come from the pursuit of common goals, overcoming shared obstacles, or in simply meeting the challenges of everyday life. They appreciate certainty and predictability in their lives, and these derive from an understanding of their role, functions, and responsibilities toward their fellow man. But these, along with other like sentiments and goods serving to satisfy and give meaning to man's social nature, can only be had in smaller, human-sized communities; they cannot be realized, say, in any large-scale "national" community such as that envisioned by Croly and leading contemporary progressive politicians.

Nisbet himself, in reflecting on the status of community and political trends after the completion of his classic *The Quest for Community,* made this point in unequivocal terms: "It should be the prime business of any serious conservative party or other faction to expose the fraudulence of such a phrase as 'national community.' Do we dare suppose that any actual national community, with headquarters of course in Washington, D.C., might have in its cabinet a Secretary of Love and another of Intimacy? It is . . . the serious business of any conservative group to recognize 'national community' for what it is and to oppose it at every turn." Nisbet goes on to deplore a practice that, following Croly's theoretical design, has become commonplace: "The favorite strategy of proponents of national community, is to draw up a purportedly heartrending account of the disappearance of all the traditional communities such as kinship, neighborhood, church, and voluntary association of every kind, and then with majestic finality declare the national community to be our only salvation."[14]

The loss of intermediate institutions leads to dependence on a highly centralized, omnipotent state. The central government either assumes the functions of the intermediate associations or directs and controls their activities. Under these circumstances, individuals grow accustomed to relying on the central government for the fulfillment of their wants and needs. In this "nanny state," we find a "soft" tyranny, or what Tocqueville so dramatically pictures as a "species of oppression" unique to democratic nations. Tocqueville writes of "an immense and tutelary power" hovering over the citizens, "which takes upon itself alone to secure their gratification and to watch over their fate." This power he describes as "absolute, minute, regular, provident and mild"—a power unlike that of the father because it seeks to "keep" the citizens "in a perpetual state of childhood." For the "happiness" of its citizens, he continues, "such a government willingly labors, but it chooses to be the sole agent and the only arbiter of that happiness; it provides for their security, foresees and supplies their necessities, facilitates their pleasures, manages their principal concerns, directs their industry, regulates the descent of property, and subdivides their inheritances." He asks, rhetorically, "What remains, but to spare them all the care of thinking and all the trouble of living?"[15]

Thus, as Tocqueville sees it—and his observations have been borne out in modern times—the debilitating effects of the nanny state on individual citizens are enormous. Though hard to measure in concrete terms, there is an inevitable loss of individual incentive and initiative with demands, particularly in democratic political systems, that government "solve" problems, including those arising out of irresponsible individual behavior. And, as Tocqueville intimates, the process feeds on itself. As the "compassionate" welfare state develops, matters once handled through private initiatives within communities or by local governments become the responsibility of the central government. Its powers, in Tocqueville's words, eventually reduce the people "to nothing better than a flock of timid and industrious animals of which the government is the shepherd."[16]

Other serious consequences flow from this dependence. High taxes must be imposed and, as it turns out, a crushing debt incurred to meet these commitments and burdens. This serves to weaken the private economic sector that provides the wherewithal for this state in the first place. Most importantly, the state must be granted enormous powers. Even with these powers, it cannot establish a national "community" that can approximate the companionship, warmth, and sense of belonging that are found in small, intimate communities. Nevertheless, the state needs the willing cooperation and assistance of the masses, a conglomeration of isolated individuals now totally disconnected from the associations that previously had fulfilled their human need for association. Rulers are constrained to provide a new focus, meaning, and purpose to replace what has been lost. "Totalitarianism," as Nisbet points out, involves not only the tearing down of traditional institutions and intermediate associations, but "their replacement by new ones, each deriving its meaning and sanction from the central structure of the state."[17]

Moreover, each of these new associations takes its purpose, its reason for being, from the state. Sometimes, particularly in the twentieth century, these purposes may be wicked or evil. But totalitarianism does not always assume this character. Its purposes may be cloaked in righteousness as an endeavor to create the redemptive state. "Its success," as Nisbet notes, "depends on incorporating into new structures of power those values with the widest appeal to a population."[18] It may be able to accomplish this rapidly, thereby obviating the need for physical coercion. In any event, to go no further, the growth of an omnipotent central state, the loss, for whatever reason, of the associations, communities, and groups that stand between the state and the individual opens up the possibilities of "hard" totalitarianism such as we have witnessed in the Soviet Union, Communist China, and Nazi Germany.

By way of contrast, Croly places a good deal of trust in the modern nation-state, "particularly . . . as it is constructively democratic." Such a state, he writes, "constitutes the best machinery as yet developed for raising the level of human association." He goes so far as to maintain that "it really teaches men how they must feel, what they must think, and what they must do, in order that they may live together amicably and profitably."[19]

Whereas conservatives fear a powerful state, particularly one in which there are no countervailing powers that can check abuses and oppression, Croly looks upon it with approbation. He recognizes that the achievement of his ideals requires the use of force. He remarks, for example, that "unregenerate individuals" may compel the state to use its powers to ensure the widest possible association necessary for a genuine national community. He exhibits no concern about the use of this power. On the contrary, he seems to hold that, at least with respect to "constructively democratic" government, there is no longer any need for countervailing institutions to check or control it. As if answering his conservative critics, he observes that "just as formerly the irresponsible and meaningless use of political power created the need of special religious associations independent of the state, so now the responsible, the purposeful, and the efficient use of physical force, characteristic of modern nations, has in its turn made such independence less necessary, and tends to attach a different function to the church."[20]

In Croly's view churches, like all other intermediate institutions, are no longer needed to check governmental power. Their sole function today is to help impose the will of the state on the mass of individuals it seeks to shape. Community, in this view, exists between a caring nanny state and its individual charges.

This book is in large measure an attempt to answer Croly and to counter the ideological program of modern liberal communitarians who owe so much to Croly's initial efforts. One of our basic concerns is that these modern communitarians, following in the footsteps of Rousseau and Croly, would destroy the possibility for real communities in their drive to force human nature into an ill-fitting mold of their own devising. To date they have not succeeded in making man "unselfish," but they have greatly damaged the local communal institutions that tame man's selfishness and focus his attention on the interests and welfare of those around him. Accordingly, as we see it, our first task is to set forth a fuller and deeper understanding of the true nature of community and its place in our tradition. In this way we can better ascertain what is necessary to rebuild what the centralized state has torn down.

The first chapter of this book, by Kenneth Grasso, discusses the origins and goals of contemporary thinkers who present themselves as partisans of community. Broadly speaking, these partisans fall into two camps—those who see the nation as the locus of communal feeling and those who insist that decentralization and the primacy of local associations are crucial in making any true community possible. Most who go by the name "communitarian" today fall into the former category; traditional conservatives like those represented in this volume belong to the latter.

The three chapters that follow focus on the American experience with local communities from a variety of perspectives. These chapters point to the fact that our tradition, far from being one of individual rights and centralized control, is one marked by a high degree of local autonomy in which small communities, as well as intermediate groups and associations, flourished.

As Barry Shain argues in chapter 2, a shared vision of man's nature, purpose, and duties in this world and the next served to hold traditional American communities together. Early America was a land of many small, local communities, often differing greatly from one another. But within each community there was a shared vision of man's nature and proper ends. It was to defend these self-governing communities, dedicated to pursuit of a godly life in common, that our war for independence was fought. The growing power of political definitions of the good life helped undermine the moral structure that once bound individuals to their communities, but the habits and traditions of communalism remain to this day.

The forces of politicization were intended by our Founders to be held in check by a written constitution. At this constitutional level, as George Carey points out in chapter 3, our tradition is one of leaving sufficient room or space in the structures and delegation of authority for the emergence and development of local communities. Thus in early America it was crucial that our Constitution left the bulk of governmental power at the state and local level, where it could be hedged and even taken over by local townships and other associations. The result was a community of communities held together by a Constitution that intentionally failed to provide the moral basis for society—instead protecting such bases as already had been formed in local communities.

Still another dimension of our tradition is emphasized by Wilfred McClay in chapter 4. McClay emphasizes the extent to which early American Protestantism promoted and eventually succumbed to an overemphasis on the independence of the individual self. As religious belief waned in America, individual judgment, so much a part of Puritan biblical tradition, was set free from the moorings of religion, the force of tradition, and the constraints of preexisting elites. American intellectuals soon succeeded in turning authority itself upside down, claiming for artistic temperaments the right and ability to create their own meanings. Thus current attempts to restore community on the basis of humanly created meanings can do nothing to reverse the increasing anarchy of our age. Only a return to religious belief and the authority of moral principles and tradition can again bind us to one another.

The second step in our effort to confront the communitarianism of modern liberalism involves an undertaking of a different order. Here our end is to point up the strains and elements of modern liberal communitarian thought that reinforce, rather than diminish, the tendency toward greater centralization in our modern welfare and administrative state. Our goal is to indicate on what issues and concerns these communitarians propose measures that are contrary to our traditions or are counterproductive to the emergence and development of genuine communities by the standards of traditional conservatism.

But this task is not as easy as it might at first appear. As we shall see, modern liberal communitarians have appropriated a good deal of the language that leading conservatives have customarily used in addressing the problems associated with communities and intermediate associations. Indeed, the mere fact that modern liberals profess a concern about the health and vibrancy of communities and intermediate associations indicates the extent to which they have seemingly embraced a conservative orientation. In many ways, then, these liberal communitarians seem conservative. But the operative word in this context is "seem." The similarities between their thinking and the core tenets of conservatism is only paper-thin, and masks profound differences.

We have chosen the theories of Charles Taylor, Robert Bellah, and William Galston for extended analysis, not only to highlight the differences between traditional conservative thought and modern liberal communitarian thinking but to indicate as well the conceptual continuity of liberal thought that strives, albeit with a terminology different from that of the early progressives, to correct for past failures by the further centralization of political power. Few would criticize our selection of the works of these individuals for intensive examination. They are all prominent practitioners, each with a significant following, whose works have received considerable praise. Nevertheless, as Norman Barry, Brad Stone, and Peter Lawler show in chapters 5, 6, and 7, the theories of these leading liberal communitarians lack the essential elements of community present in the American tradition, and their implementation would, by extending the sphere of central governmental powers still further, exacerbate the current individual/sovereign dichotomy to which we have referred above. Modern communitarian programs, by nationalizing and politicizing all attachments, would render the right to exit an uncongenial locality meaningless, reduce religious obligation to a sham political loyalty, and leave the individual engaged in the lonely pursuit of his material wants of the moment.

The third and final step in our attempt to answer Croly and his followers is necessarily short and more suggestive than definitive. It is a chapter by Bruce Frohnen seeking to point the way back toward true community in our atomistic era. Frohnen argues that the central element missing in contemporary debates over the decline of community is the sense of sacred obligation. The state undermines such a conception by politicizing it, in effect undermining religious and moral force through its threat of brute coercion. More importantly, it is the government's determination to break down competing, local associations that makes such coercion necessary by destroying the individual's ability to see that he owes his existence, and thus his loyalty, to those who have nurtured him and helped shape his character.

Individuals can be bound to one another by neither faceless bureaucracies nor force. They form lasting attachments only on the basis of moral obligations—obligations formed by common recognition of man's fundamentally religious duty to love his neighbor as himself. Such an understanding cannot be taught by the state. It must grow from experience in family, church, and local association. It must grow within the local communities that decent, fitting governments protect in all their natural vigor.

1

Contemporary Communitarianism, the Lure of the State, and the Modern Quest for Community

Kenneth L. Grasso

"It is by now a familiar lament," Jean Bethke Elshtain recently observed, "that all is not well with us; that something has gone terribly awry with the North American version of market-modernity."[1] At the same time, it has come to be widely recognized that the difficulties besetting us today have their roots in a sharp decline in "civic solidarity" and "social connectedness"[2] and the increasing domination of our public discourse by a highly individualistic vision of man and society. Emerging from the liberal intellectual tradition, at the heart of this vision is a conception of human beings as, in Michael Sandel's words, "free and independent selves unclaimed by moral ties antecedent to choice." The self is thus "installed as sovereign, cast as the author of the only obligations that constrain."[3]

One of the most visible signs of this recognition has been the emergence of "communitarianism." The thinkers commonly associated with this movement are a heterogeneous lot. They are united less by a shared model of man and society than a common conviction as to the inadequacy of the radically individualistic variety of liberalism that has come to hold sway over our political culture and a common desire to forge a new public philosophy recognizing man's social nature and setting the stage for the revitalization of community in America.

Its heterogeneous character makes communitarianism difficult to access. The label "communitarian" itself is the subject of considerable controversy. Alasdair MacIntyre, often considered the leading exponent of contemporary communitarianism, explicitly rejects both the label and the movement. MacIntyre's problem with contemporary communitarianism concerns the locus of community. The thinkers whose work has come to shape communitarianism as an organized intellectual movement, he argues, "have insisted that the nation itself through the institutions of the nation-state ought to be constituted to some significant degree as a community."[4] This effort, MacIntyre believes, is both misconceived and dangerous. It is misconceived because the communities in which men can pursue a common vision of the good "are always, and could not but be, small-scale and local." It is dangerous because the vision of "the nation-state as [an] all-embracing community" generates "totalitarian and other evils."[5]

MacIntyre's total rejection of the communitarian label indicates the deep divide separating those "communitarians" who see the nation-state as the locus of community from those (like MacIntyre) who seek to defend, often against the nation-state, the institutions that compose what we have come to call civil society, in particular family, church, and neighborhood. It also indicates the degree to which the proponents of the former variety of communitarianism have come to dominate communitarianism as an organized intellectual movement.

Our goals here are essentially threefold. First, we will attempt to situate these varieties of communitarianism in historical context. As we shall see, neither the understanding of community MacIntyre rejects nor the understanding he embraces is a purely contemporary phenomenon. Whereas the former grew from the dissolution of medieval society and crystallized in the revolution-inspiring thought of Jean Jacques Rousseau, the latter received expression in the work of thinkers like Johannes Althusius, Alexis de Tocqueville, Emile Durkheim, and, perhaps above all, Edmund Burke.

Second, without attempting to place every conceivable partisan of community into any particular category, we will seek to explore how and why contemporary communitarianism, despite its recognition of local, small-scale forms of community, has nevertheless made the nation-state the locus of community. Finally, we will briefly examine how contemporary communitarianism's focus on the nation-state as the locus of community affects its ability to resolve the crisis of community that besets us today.

Our analysis will take Robert A. Nisbet's seminal work on the problem of community in the modern world as its point of departure. His penetrating analysis of the modern crisis of community and the perils inherent in the quest for community will set the stage for our examination of contemporary communitarian thought.

Society, the State, and the Quest for Community in the Modern World

"One may paraphrase the famous words of Karl Marx," Nisbet writes,

> and say that a specter is haunting the modern mind, the specter of insecurity. Surely the outstanding characteristic of contemporary thought on man and

> society is the preoccupation with personal alienation and cultural disintegration. The fears of the nineteenth-century conservatives in Western Europe, expressed against a backdrop of increasing individualism, secularism, and social dislocation, have become, to an extraordinary degree, the insights and hypotheses of present-day students of man and society.[6]

In the face of this state of affairs "the concern for community, its values, properties, and means of access" has become "the major intellectual fact of the present age" (QC 30).

Nisbet makes clear that the concern for community that finds expression in modern communitarianism is nothing new. Indeed, its roots go back to the dissolution of the medieval world. One of the defining features of medieval society, Nisbet observes, was "the pre-eminence . . . in its economy, religion and morality . . . of the small social group." In the world of the Middle Ages both the "autonomous individual" and the "centralized political power" were "subordinated to the immense range of associations that lay intermediate to the individual and ruler and that included such groups as the patriarchal family, the gild, the Church, feudal class, and the village community" (QC 80).

As the center of the social order these groups not only enjoyed an "immense range of legal autonomy" vis-à-vis the state (QC 10) and exercised a far-reaching "authority" over the lives of individuals, they also provided the matrix "within which innumerable, indispensable functions were performed" (QC 80–81). If the primacy of these groups and their status as "the irreducible unit of the social system at large" (QC 81) derived in part from the organic and communitarian character" of the dominant philosophies (QC 81), it stemmed primarily from "the indispensable functions" they "performed in the lives" of their "members" (QC 83–84).

"By the sixteenth century," however, "many of the communalisms of the Middle Ages had declined sharply" (QC 85). "Socially," Nisbet remarks, "the Renaissance was in large degree a time of institutional dislocation, breakdown and collapse" (TA 245). The result was the emancipation of the individual from the social bonds of the Middle Ages and the inception of modern man's quest for community.

It is no accident, Nisbet argues, that the demise of the "medieval forms of community" has been followed by a pervasive and often frenzied search for "new forms of community" (QC viii). "The quest for community will not be denied," he writes, "for it springs from some of the powerful needs of human nature—needs for a clear sense of cultural purpose, membership, status and continuity" (QC 73). Humans are by nature social beings. "Man," Nisbet notes, "does not live merely as one of a vast aggregate of arithmetically equal, socially undifferentiated, individuals" (QC 267). "Nowhere do we in fact find [such] aggregates of 'individuals.' What we find are human beings bound, in one or another degree, by ties of work, friendship, recreation, learning, faith, love, and mutual aid" (TA 277).

Since human nature "cannot tolerate a moral and social vacuum" (TA 160), the disintegration of the medieval world gave man's "timeless and universal" need for community a peculiar urgency and "intensity" (QC 47). This quest, in turn, came to focus on the one social institution that not only had survived the disintegration of the medieval world but was strengthened by it: the state. The political community absorbed "the powers and responsibilities formerly resident" (QC 104) in intermediary groups and simultaneously became the subject of the "emotional loyalties and identifications" previously directed toward them (QC 164). In the process, the state emerges as "the successor to the Church in its inclusion of all human needs, desires and hopes" (QC 166). Thus, between the isolated individual in search of community and the modern state

> there developed a bond, an affinity, which . . . made the political community the most luminous of all visions. In it lay salvation from economic misery and oppression. In it lay a new kind of liberty, equality and fraternity. In it lay right and justice. And in it, above all else, lay community. (QC 187)

The Ideology of the Political Community

The progressive absorption of the functions and emotional loyalties of small groups by the state coincided with the emergence of what Nisbet terms the "ideology of the political community" (QC 175). By the nineteenth century this ideology had come to decisively influence the Western mind, providing the context (QC 156) from which the century's most important political movements emerged. It decisively shaped not only socialism (QC 156) and nationalism (QC 164) but also modern popular democracy (QC 156) and liberalism (QC 267) as well. Indeed, all of the major political movements of the past two centuries must ultimately be viewed as variant expressions of its vision. Existing in both strong and weak versions, pure and diluted forms, the ideology of political community, Nisbet believes, receives its most concentrated and hence clearest expression in the thought of Rousseau.

"Two entities," he remarks, "dominate Rousseau's thought: the individual and the state" (QC 141). Its starting point is a radical individualism. Man, Rousseau lamented, was born free but is everywhere in chains. The chains are "those of traditional society—class, church, school, and patriarchal family" (QC 106). In fact, "Rousseau's passionate" individualism "arises out of his opposition to the forms and observances of society" (QC 142). But his hostility toward traditional society does not extend to the state. For Rousseau, the rightly ordered state is "the most exalted of all forms of moral community." Indeed, outside of it "there is no morality, no freedom, no community" (QC 140). The state, in Rousseau's thought, "is the means by which the individual can be freed of the restrictive tyrannies that compose society." Its function is nothing less than the "emancipation" of the individual from "the oppressions and corruptions of society" (QC 142–43).

Ordered by the force of the general will, the most striking features of Rousseau's vision of the rightly ordered polis are its monism and statism. "The mystic solidarity that Rousseau preaches," Nisbet writes,

> is not . . . the solidarity of the community existing by custom and unwritten law. The social community, as it existed in the thought of Thomas Aquinas or, later, in the theory of Althusius, is a community of communities, an assemblage of morally integrated minor groups. The solidarity of this community arises out of the moral and social observances of the minor groups. Its unity does not result from being permeated with sovereign law, extending from the top through all individual components, of the structure. Rousseau's community however is a *political* community, one indistinguishable from the State and sharing all the uniformitarian qualities of the State. It is, in his mind, a moral unity, but it is a unity conferred by the sovereign will of the State and directed by the political government. (QC 144)

The monism and statism that pervade Rousseau's thought manifest themselves in his treatment of intermediary groups. Inasmuch as there must exist "no bond of loyalty, no social affiliation, no interdependence save what is symbolized by the general will," such groups must be proscribed. Society is thus transformed into "an aggregate of atoms held rigidly together by the sovereign will of the State alone" (QC 147). Rousseau's hostility to intermediary groups can be seen in his treatment of the family and the church. The state assumes "the traditional educative function of the family," which is "broken into the atoms of its individuals" and "coalesced afresh into the single unity of the state" (QC 150–51). Likewise, Rousseau rejects not only Christianity but the very idea of "a socially independent Church" because such an autonomous spiritual authority "like any form of nonpolitical loyalty, would constitute an interference with the functioning of the general will" (QC 147). The independent spiritual authority of the Church must be supplanted by an established civil religion which will instill "respect for the sovereign, allegiance to the State alone, and subordination of all interests to the law of the realm" (QC 149).

Between the rights of individuals and the powers of the state, intermediary groups tend to be ground "into dust" (QC 157). From the perspective of this ideology, intermediary groups are inherently "suspect" on account of "their fettering influence upon the individual and their divisive consequences" for the state (QC 253). Even where these groups are not absorbed outright by the state, they are reduced to mere creatures of the state having no "legal existence, [no] legal reality . . . except insofar as this existence and reality had been conceded by the sovereign" (TA 170), thus being "made dependent upon the will of the State for the exercise of their functions and authorities" (QC 113). The "plurality of authorities and functions" that had hitherto characterized society ends up being "supplanted by a unity of authority and function arising from the monistic state" (QC 156). Absorbing the responsibilities and loyalties previously commanded by such institutions, the state becomes "the context of the realization of all man's aspirations, even as the Church formed this context in the Middle Ages" (QC 155–56).

Ersatz Community

Far from constituting the basis for a satisfactory resolution of modern man's search for community, the mixture of the "search for community" with "the apparatus of political power" embodied in the ideology of the political community represents "a very dangerous combination" (QC viii). To appreciate why, it is necessary to understand both the precise source of the modern world's crisis of community and the indispensable role of intermediary associations in the overall economy of social life.

"Historically," writes Nisbet, the modern crisis of community

> must be seen in terms of the decline in functional and psychological significance of such groups as the family, the small local community and the various other traditional relationships that have immemorially mediated between the individual and society. These are the groups that have been morally decisive in the concrete lives of individuals. Other and more powerful forms of association have existed, but the major moral and psychological influences on the individual's life have emanated from the family and local community and the church. (QC 50)

Nor is this an accident. These groups play an indispensable role in the overall scheme of human social life. Although their forms may vary, writes Nisbet,

> there must be in any stable culture . . . functionally significant and psychologically meaningful groups and associations lying intermediate to the individual and the larger values and purposes of his society. For these are the small areas of association within which alone such values and purposes can take on clear meaning in personal life and become the vital roots of the larger culture. (QC 70)

The source of "the dislocations and the deprivations that have driven so many men in this age of economic abundance and political welfare, to the quest for community" lies "in the realm of the small, primary, personal relationships of society," in the realm of intermediary groups (QC 49).

The decline of these groups, in turn, has its origins in the fact that they "have manifestly become detached from positions of functional relevance to the larger economic and political decisions in our society" (QC 54). In fact, these groups "have become functionally irrelevant to our state and economy" (QC 49). Inasmuch as "social groups thrive only when they possess significant functions and authorities in the lives of their members" (QC 247), intermediary groups' progressive loss of function has inevitably precipitated their decline and has thereby left individuals "precariously exposed to . . . chilling currents of anonymity and isolation" (TA 85).

Seen in the context of the decline of intermediary groups, the ideology of the political community must be understood as an effort "to find" in a "large-scale" organization—the state—"the values of status and security which were formerly gained" in such groups as "the family, neighborhood and church" (QC 49). This effort, however, is doomed to failure. To begin with, by virtue of its vast size, bureaucratic structure, and impersonal character, the political community is incapable of either supplying the sense of intimacy and belonging formerly supplied by intermediary associations or effectively mediating between the individual and larger groups. Substituting ersatz community for the real community supplied by intermediary groups, the political community is ultimately incapable of satisfying man's need for community.

At the same time, the ideology of the political community can only foster the further decline of intermediary associations and thus intensify the very crisis of community it seeks to address. Perhaps "the single most decisive influence" (QC 948) in the decline of these institutions, Nisbet argues, has been "the structure of the Western political state." Starkly "monistic" (QC 103), the modern state has progressively deprived intermediary groups of their autonomy and has "consolidated" their "functions and authorities" in itself. Indeed, "the real conflict in modern political history has not been . . . between state and individual, but between state and social groups" (QC 109). The modern state has grown "on what it" has taken "from competing social relationships—family, labor union, profession, local community, and church" (QC 256).

The ideology of the political community is "dangerous" not merely because it misdirects modern man's search for community but also because it unleashes a wide array of political pathologies. Ironically, by devitalizing intermediary groups the ideology of the political community actually undermines the very institution it wishes to strengthen: the state.

Inasmuch as an entity as large and impersonal as the modern state can never "generate for more than a short time the kind of loyalty that is given naturally to family or to neighborhood" (TA 69), Nisbet contends, it follows that "citizenship must be rooted in the groups and communities within which human beings actually live" (TA 287). The decline of intermediary groups (combined with the state's inability to perform effectively the myriad functions once discharged by these groups) thus erodes citizenship and public-spiritedness, and ultimately alienates citizens from the body politic.

Furthermore, as the state becomes "swollen by the economic and social responsibilities" once discharged by intermediary groups, it will gradually lose its capacity to discharge both these responsibilities and those that are properly its own (TA 71). It thus engenders what Nisbet, echoing Lamennais, terms "apoplexy at the center and anemia at the extremities" (QC 256).

This ideology also endangers freedom and representative government. To begin with, the "real barriers" to despotism "are not individual rights so much as the kinds of rights associated with autonomy of local community, voluntary association, political party. These are the real measures of the degree to which political power is limited in a society" (TA 228). Indeed, "the sole possibility of personal freedom and cultural autonomy lies in the maintenance of a plurality of authorities in . . . society" because, as Montesquieu maintained, "the only safeguard against power . . . is rival power" (QC 269–70).

Likewise, intermediary institutions play an indispensable role in promoting moral values (TA 77)—the moral affirmations and virtues—on which a free society depends for its vitality. "Genuine freedom," writes Nisbet, is not based on the negative psychology of release. Its roots are in positive acts of dedication to ends and values. Freedom presupposes the autonomous existence of values that men wish to follow and live up to" (QC 269).

It simultaneously presupposes a citizenry who have internalized "such cultural and social values as objective reason, the discipline of language, self-restraint, [and] the work ethic" (TA 76). Inasmuch as the "values" in which a free society is rooted "arise out of, and are nurtured by" (QC 269) intermediary groups, "social atomization" necessarily issues in "a diminution of intensity and a final flickering out of [the] political values that interpose themselves between freedom and despotism" (QC 202). Indeed, far from providing a secure foundation for political freedom, the ideology of the political community finds its "full realization" in "the twentieth century totalitarian state" (QC 155).

The Pluralist Tradition

The ideology of the political community, however, was not the only response to modern man's search for community. Nisbet also directs our attention to what he terms the pluralist tradition. Although less influential than political ideology in shaping modern political life and social philosophy, the pluralist tradition nevertheless finds expression in the thought of a number of the modern world's most perceptive social theorists, including Althusius, Burke, Tocqueville, Proudhon, and Durkheim. At the heart of this tradition is found "a recovery of the social with its implication of the diversity of social membership" and "the liberation of the idea of the social from the political" (TA 241).

In sharp contrast to the atomistic individualism and political monism that inform the ideology of the political community, the pluralist tradition insists that

> man does not live merely as one of a vast aggregate of arithmetically equal, socially undifferentiated, individuals. He does not live his life merely in terms of the procedures and techniques of the administrative State. . . . As a concrete *person* he is inseparable from the plurality of social allegiances and memberships which characterize his social organization. (QC 267)

Society is a *communitas communitatum,* a community of communities and, as such, possesses a pluralist structure.

This vision of society has far-reaching implications for our understanding of the place of the state in the overall economy of social life. To begin with, it issues in a recognition that the state must share the stage of social life with a wide array of other institutional actors with their own distinctive functions and responsibilities. The state, in this view, is "but one of the associations" (QC 250) to which man's social nature gives rise. "Equally important" from its perspective are "the whole plurality of other associations in society." Indeed, in the pluralist tradition "intermediary associations . . . rather than atomized political particles, become the prime units of theoretical and practical consideration" (QC 250).

At the same time, the pluralist conception of society issues in the recognition that "state and society must be sharply distinguished" (QC 99). Implicit in this distinction, moreover, is a view of the state as a limited order of action for limited purposes, and thus a commitment to the idea of limited government. The state, in this view, exists not to supplant other social institutions or to absorb their functions but to complement and assist them. "The major objective" of the state according to the pluralist tradition is "that of making harmonious and effective the various group allegiances which exist in society, not sterilizing them in the interest of a monistic political community" (QC 250).

From these foundations emerge four principles that inform the pluralist tradition's view of a rightly ordered society. The first is what Nisbet terms the principle of "functional autonomy." This principle demands that the various social groups that issue from man's nature as a social being be allowed to enjoy a broad autonomy and to discharge the responsibilities that are properly theirs. "What characterizes the pluralist view of autonomy," writes Nisbet,

> can best be thought of in terms of the ability of each major function in the social order to work with the maximum possible freedom. What applies to the school or university should apply also to economy, to family, to religion and to each of the great spheres of society. Everything must be done to avoid intrusion by some one great institution, such as the political state, into the spheres of other institutions. (TA 237)

The second principle, decentralization, requires the "dispersion" of power in society. As far as the state is concerned, this means that political power should not be concentrated in a single central government but should be dispersed among local governments possessing a considerable degree of autonomy. More importantly, it means that the amount of power "wielded by government" must be sharply circumscribed. Power "must be distributed into as many hands as possible—not abstract, desocialized *political* hands but those we actually see in the social order, those of workers, enterprisers, professionals, families, and neighborhoods." Nor is this principle limited in application to the state. It applies to "all large institutions" (TA 237).

Finally, there are the principles of hierarchy and tradition. The former flows "from the very functional requirements of the social bond." Since community necessarily involves "the stratification of function" (TA 238), it necessarily involves authority. Indeed, inasmuch as "apart from authority there can be no really vital social relationships in society" (QC xiv), the rejection of authority necessarily destroys authentic community and creates a vacuum into which political power must move.

The principle of tradition, on the other hand, is rooted in the realization that although "formal, statute law" plays a "vital" role in social life, "when every relationship in society becomes a potentially legal relationship, expressed in adversary fashion, the very juices of the social bond dry up, the social impulse atrophies." Pluralism thus demands that society be ordered "in the largest possible measure, not [by] formal law, ordinance, or administrative regulation" but instead by the "informal" and "spontaneous" mechanisms of custom, folkway, and tradition (TA 239–40).

Pluralism and the Revitalization of Community

If the pluralist tradition has been less influential in shaping the modern world than the ideology of the political community, Nisbet nevertheless maintains that it is simultaneously "far more interesting and valuable" (TA 245) and "far more relevant to the needs of our time" (TA 246). Its value and relevance stem from its capacity to play a pivotal role in bringing modern man's quest for community to a successful conclusion.

As we have seen, one of the major causes of the decline of intermediary groups has been "the gradual absorption" by the modern state of "the powers and responsibilities" (QC 104) formerly exercised by them, a process justified and intensified by the ideology of the political community. The state has gradually transformed "the basic needs of education, recreation, welfare, economic production, distribution, and consumption, health, spiritual and physical, and all other services of society" into "aspects of the administrative structure of the political government" (QC 282). In the process, the modern state has not only undermined traditional intermediary groups but has prevented "the establishment of new forms" of intermediary associations, "forms which are relevant to contemporary life" (QC viii).

Inasmuch as a solution to modern man's crisis of community requires the revitalization of intermediary groups, it thus necessarily presupposes the comprehensive rethinking of the whole "problem of the relation of political government to the plurality of cultural associations which form the intermediate authorities in society" (QC 265). The pluralist tradition, Nisbet maintains, gives us the conceptual resources necessary to escape from the monism that has defined the modern state. By taking the "social group" rather than the autonomous individual as its "basic unit" (QC 278), it enables us to envision a type of state that differs fundamentally from that which has dominated the modern political landscape.

A state inspired by the pluralist vision would emphatically reject "the political absorption of the institutional functions" of intermediary groups, but "without sacrificing its legitimate sovereignty." It would instead seek "to maintain a pluralism of functions and loyalties in the lives of its people." Accordingly, it would seek "to diversify and decentralize its own administrative operations and to relate these as closely as possible to the forms of spontaneous association which are the outgrowth of human needs and desires and which have relevance to the economic, educational and religious ends of a culture." Although not spurning "the demands of human security," such a state would "seek means by which such demands can be met through" intermediary groups "rather than through [the] bureaucratic rigidities of formal law and administration" (QC 283).

A state inspired by the pluralist tradition would thus "create conditions within which autonomous groups may prosper" (QC 279) by establishing "a setting" in which such groups can simultaneously possess "social authority" and exercise a "significant function or role in the larger society" (TA 276). Such a state would lay the groundwork for the revitalization of intermediary institutions and thus for the successful resolution of modern man's quest for community.

Contemporary Communitarianism and the Lure of the State

Against the backdrop of Nisbet's work, we can distinguish between two distinct types of communitarianism embodying two very different responses to the modern crisis of community, and rooted, respectively, in what he terms the ideology of the political community and the pluralist tradition. For what might be called "unitary" or "political" communitarianism, the basic units of analysis are "the citizen" and "the nation as a whole" (QC 108). For it, society and the state are "synonymous" (QC 155), and community means the political community, which, in turn, "is indistinguishable from the state" and shares the latter's "uniformitarian qualities" (QC 144). In political communitarianism, the state becomes the center of social life and the context for the realization of man's deepest aspirations. Indeed, from its perspective, the "principal problem" is "the discovery of means" by which the citizens can be "brought ever closer . . . in their political wholeness" (QC 250).

Whereas this variety of communitarianism is informed by the philosophy of the political community, the second variety emerges from the tradition of social pluralism. From its perspective, the political community is not the only nor even the primary form of community. Insisting on clearly distinguishing between state and society, pluralist communitarianism believes the proper role of the state in the overall economy of social life to be a limited one. Indeed, for it, the institutions of civil social (in particular, the family and what Mary Ann Glendon terms "the communities of memory and mutual aid" that surround it[7]) rather than the state are the center of social gravity. Whereas unitary communitarianism affirms the primacy of the political, pluralist communitarianism insists on the primacy of the social.

Civil Society, the State, and the Communitarian Project

Nisbet's analysis suggests that the ability of contemporary communitarianism to contribute to a resolution of our difficulties will depend on where it fits in this typology. It is clear that modern communitarianism has sought to avoid the type of monistic statism that characterizes what we have termed unitary communitarianism. If the theoreticians of contemporary communitarianism are critical of those who would entrust the promotion of the human and social good to the workings of the market, they are also critical of those who would entrust their promotion primarily to the power of the state. "Where libertarian liberals defend the private economy and egalitarian liberals the welfare state," Sandel observes, "communitarians worry about the concentration of power in both the corporate economy and bureaucratic state, and the erosion of those intermediate forms of community that have at times sustained a more vital public life."[8]

Indeed, communitarians have sought to transcend the individual-state-market grid that informs our public argument, attributing our difficulties to the devitalization of our intermediary institutions. Rejecting "both the market and the welfare state in pursuit of a third way," as Christopher Lasch notes, they have called for "a political program designed to strengthen civil society."[9] The theorists of today's communitarianism have thus sought to forge what we have termed a pluralist communitarianism—a communitarianism rooted in a vision of society as a *communitas communitatum*.

It is by no means clear, however, that they have succeeded. Lasch, for example, has persuasively argued that although communitarians like Alan Wolfe and Robert Bellah acknowledge the importance of civil society's institutions to the well-being of our polity and recognize the ways in which both market and welfare state can act to undermine them, their work is ultimately "more an attack on the market than an attack on the welfare state." If Wolfe, for example "condemns the market, he is merely 'ambivalent' about the state." Although Wolfe admits that the welfare state may not be, in his own words, "completely satisfactory" and recognizes the ways in which it undermines intermediary institutions, he nevertheless insists, Lasch writes, that "it is clearly preferable to the market." In the final analysis, he concludes, "Wolfe's book does not live up to its promise. What began as a case for a 'third way' ends up with a qualified endorsement of the welfare state."[10]

The Good Society, Lasch maintains, is open to the same basic criticism. Their concerns about the ways in which the welfare state can undermine civil society notwithstanding, Bellah and his collaborators "explicitly call for a 'global New Deal.' " Likewise, although they "have a great deal to say about responsibility," the responsibility they seek to foster is primarily "a broad 'social responsibility,' not the responsibility of individuals." The "communitarianism" championed by Wolfe and the authors of *The Good Society*, he concludes, "is difficult to distinguish from social democracy."[11]

A survey of the literature of contemporary communitarianism supports Lasch's analysis. If theorists of modern communitarianism are critical of both market and state, they nevertheless are far more hostile toward the former than the latter. "Most of our problems in America," Bellah insists, "come from the market economy."[12] In sharp contrast to their posture toward the market, they seem surprisingly willing to make their peace with the modern welfare state. Indeed, in the final analysis, their primary criticism of America's welfare state seems to be that it is not large enough. Despite the statist character of the vision animating it and their recognition of its corrosive effects on the institutions of civil society, these thinkers do not fundamentally challenge the structure of the modern welfare state.

Its aspirations notwithstanding, contemporary communitarianism simply seems incapable of resisting the siren song of the modern state. Beginning as an effort to articulate a pluralist vision of society, modern communitarianism seems to move rapidly toward what we have called a political communitarianism in which the state rather than civil society emerges as the center of social gravity. How can this ironic turn of events be explained? At least part of the answer is to be found in the model of man and society that informs contemporary communitarian thought.

Liberalism and Communitarianism

One of the central themes of contemporary communitarian thought is the inadequacy of what Bellah and his collaborators term "philosophical liberalism."[13] Nevertheless, when communitarian theorists seek to articulate an alternative to the hyperindividualism of contemporary liberal theory with its vision of the sovereign self, they turn for assistance to the liberal tradition itself, the very tradition in which the political theory they reject has its roots. The work of Michael Sandel and William Sullivan—two of the most philosophically astute of modern communitarian thinkers—illustrates the essential point. When Sandel seeks to formulate an alternative approach to the whole problem of religion and public life that issues from today's liberalism of the encumbered choice, he begins with the work of Jefferson, Madison, and Locke.[14] Similarly, in seeking to forge a theory of politics embodying a richer appreciation of the social dimensions of human life than the theory found in contemporary liberalism, Sullivan draws on the work of "social liberals" such as John Dewey and T. H. Green.[15] Implicit in their choice of sources would seem to be the belief that the liberal tradition contains within itself the resources to generate the new and better public philosophy, the alternative to today's liberalism of the unencumbered self, that they seek.

The dependence of contemporary communitarian theory on the very tradition whose manifestations it criticizes has not gone unnoticed. Michael Walzer, for instance, has observed that the liberal conception of community is the only type of community most communitarians actually know and that communitarians rarely advocate the curtailment of the rights associated with contemporary liberalism.[16] Occasional suggestions by communitarian thinkers to the contrary notwithstanding, contemporary communitarianism, he argues, is best seen not as a fundamental challenge to liberalism but as a "correction" of it, as "a selective reinforcement" of "liberal values" and "a pursuit of the intimations of community within liberalism." When all is said and done, he concludes, communitarianism must be seen as a particular sort of liberalism, as a liberalism that defends a distinctively liberal vision of community against the disintegrative effects of liberalism's own individualism.[17]

Similarly, Bruce Frohnen has argued that modern communitarianism seeks "to save liberalism from itself by solving its core cultural problem."[18] This problem consists in "an inability to discuss, let alone foster, the kinds of behavior necessary if liberalism itself is to survive."[19] Communitarianism seeks "to reinvigorate liberal society" by providing "the coherent theory of virtue" that liberalism has hitherto failed to develop. "Communitarians," in short, "are liberals who want to reestablish a common sense among the people of what the nation is for, of what its people share in their history, and what they should strive to accomplish," to foster a common commitment to liberal values and to the virtues on which a society dedicated to those values depends for its vitality. Communitarians thus find themselves "in the awkward position of decrying liberalism's actual effects while lauding its theoretical goals."[20]

Liberalism and the Individual-State-Market Grid

To appreciate the implications of this for contemporary communitarian thought, it is necessary to grasp the nature of the liberal tradition, the core premises that define it as a distinct intellectual tradition. One of liberalism's most striking features is its individualism. It insists, as two recent authors have noted, that "politics is justifiable only by appeal to the well-being, rights or claims of individuals."[21] Yet to grasp what is distinctive about the type of individualism that informs the liberal tradition, this individualism must be seen against the backdrop of the nominalism and rationalism that inform liberalism's metaphysics of the person. This nominalism and rationalism, in turn, ultimately entail "the rejection of teleology," of "the claim that there is a discoverable excellence or optimal condition . . . which characterizes human beings" as such.[22]

This vision of man has far-reaching implications for liberalism's understanding of social and political life. To begin with, it causes liberalism to move inexorably in the direction of a progressively deeper, more radical individualism. Indeed, the history of liberal thought is largely the story of the triumph of the will—the triumph of the subjective will of the individual over those elements in the political theories of earlier generations of liberal thinkers that had originally acted to restrain it. Liberalism, as Walzer writes,

> seems continually to undercut itself . . . and to produce in each generation renewed hopes for a more absolute freedom from history and society alike. Much of liberal political theory, from Locke to Rawls, is an effort to fix and stabilize the doctrine in order to end the endlessness of liberal liberation. But beyond every version of liberalism, there is always a super liberalism, which, as Roberto Unger says of his own doctrine, "pushes liberal premises about state and society, about freedom from dependence and governance of social relations by the will, to the point at which they merge into a larger ambition: the building of a social world less alien to a self that can always violate the generative rules of its own mental or social constructs.[23]

Far from being an aberration, the thoroughgoing individualism of contemporary liberalism with its vision of human beings as sovereign selves, as Francis Canavan has written, "is the direction in which the inner dynamism of liberal thought has moved it from the beginning."[24]

The source of this "inner dynamism," he continues, "is liberalism's nominalism" which reduces "the world . . . to a collection of individual substances only externally related to each other."[25] Liberalism's nominalist metaphysics thus "makes it difficult for it to entertain the notion of relations as natural." For liberalism, "relations are external, accidental and adventitious, not the consequences of the natures of things."[26]

Under the influence of its metaphysics of the person, liberalism therefore moves inexorably toward an "understanding of relations among human beings as external and voluntary" and of "the individual human being" as "an atom, motivated by self-interest, to whom violence is done if he is subjected to a relationship with other human beings that he has not chosen."[27] Social relationships come to be understood not as the natural product of man's dynamic orientation toward his own perfection, toward the realization of his natural good, but as, in Canavan's words, the "essentially contractual"[28] products of the subjective preferences (the self-chosen goals) of naturally autonomous individuals. Liberalism thus ends up viewing all social relations through the prism of market models. Understood in this fashion, a community is reduced to what Carl Schneider describes as "a collection of individuals united temporarily for their mutual convenience and armed with rights against each other."[29]

Since, furthermore, communities are nothing more than, in Unger's words, the "products of the will and interests of individuals," they lack a determinate nature, a natural structure. As the conventional product of the arbitrary preferences of individuals, such institutions are simply what individuals choose to make of them. Inasmuch, moreover, as "the interests of their members are unstable, groups themselves are precarious associations constantly destroyed and reborn in new forms."[30] From this perspective, for example, one must speak of "families" rather "the family" because the institution of the family has no determinate structure; it is simply a creation of naturally free individuals who are at liberty to create whatever form of "family" they desire.

As far as the scope of the state is concerned, liberal theory moves in two basic directions. The first is toward what is called "classical liberalism" or "libertarianism." The proponents of this approach seek to radically circumscribe the role of the state in the overall economy of human social life. The second is toward what is generally termed "reform" or "egalitarian" liberalism. In sharp contrast to classical liberalism, the proponents of reform liberalism embrace a large interventionist state charged with the establishment of a more egalitarian social order. Whereas the proponents of the former liberalism embrace what is sometimes called the "night watchman" state, the proponents of the latter liberalism embrace the welfare state.

Their disagreement on the proper scope of the state, however, must not be allowed to obscure the underlying agreement between the two schools. Both classical and egalitarian liberalism agree that the political community exists simply to provide a framework of order within which individuals can pursue their self-chosen ends. Both likewise acknowledge only a single limitation on the scope of the state, namely, the rights of individuals.

They also share a common social ontology. As a result of its utterly voluntarist conception of social relations, liberalism moves toward a vision of social life revolving around three poles: the sovereign individual, the sovereign state (understood as the guardian of the autonomy of the individual and the provider of the framework of order within which individuals can pursue their self-chosen activity), and the market (understood as a realm of free individual action in accordance with a utilitarian calculus of self-interest and thus the institutional embodiment of the sovereignty of the individual). Liberalism thus operates within the horizon of what Glendon has aptly termed the individual-state-market grid.[31]

Liberalism, as Elshtain observes, has "no robust way to thematize entities intermediate between the state and the individual."[32] Its radically voluntarist view of social relations simply makes liberalism incapable of doing justice to these groups. More specifically, what Canavan describes as its inability "to entertain the notion of relations as natural" makes liberalism incapable of fully appreciating the nature and ontological density of these communities, compelling it to understand them as no more than collections of individuals temporarily united for reasons of mutual convenience. Liberal presuppositions thus distort what Stanley Hauerwas describes as "the moral reality" of the family and other communities of memory and mutual aid that lie at the heart of civil society.[33]

A culture informed by the liberal vision of man and society will thus be profoundly inhospitable to these groups. Liberalism's "absolutizing of choice and its celebration of radical autonomy," as Elshtain remarks, "cast suspicion on ties of reciprocal obligation or mutual interdependence and help to erode the traditional bases of personal identity and authority in families and civil society alike."[34] In fact, liberalism's elevation of individual choice to the status of the highest human good will cause a liberal society to view these institutions with considerable suspicion as potential obstacles to the autonomy of the individual.

Such a cultural environment will weaken these institutions precisely by causing them to understand themselves as what liberalism claims them to be: mere aggregations of individuals temporally united for utilitarian reasons. To the extent that the self-understanding of these institutions comes to coincide with the liberal understanding of them, they will become progressively less stable. The whole liberal ethos of the sovereign self is thus ultimately subversive of these groups.

A state informed by the liberal vision of man and society will be no more supportive of these institutions than a culture animated by it. The individual-state-market grid, through which liberalism views social life, acts, as Glendon notes, to preclude "a well-developed discourse" about the institutions of civil society, to prevent us from "bringing into focus" the "various networks of relationships, beginning with emotionally and economically interdependent households, and fanning outwards" that compose civil society.[35] Indeed, liberalism's social ontology and commitment to the maximization of individual autonomy combine to preclude efforts on the part of the state to nurture and safeguard intermediary institutions, to create conditions conducive to their flourishing.

In the case of classical liberalism, the night watchman state simply leaves the institutions of civil society to fend for themselves in the face of the market. Market forces, in turn, take a profound toll on these institutions. "The market," as Lasch writes,

> notoriously tends to universalize itself. It does not easily coexist with institutions that operate according to principles antithetical to itself: schools and universities, newspapers and magazines, charities, families. Sooner or later the market tends to absorb them all. It puts an almost irresistible pressure on every activity to justify itself in the only terms it recognizes: to become a

> business proposition, to pay its own way, to show black ink on the bottom line. It turns news into entertainment, scholarship into professional careerism, social work into the scientific management of poverty. Inexorably it remodels every institution in its own image.[36]

The relentless pressures generated by the market will act to reinforce the atomizing effects of liberal culture. Specifically, these forces will weaken intermediary institutions both by depriving them of the social environment they require to flourish and by refashioning them in a way that brings them into conformity with market models of social relations.

The welfare state of egalitarian liberalism exacts its own cost on the institutions of civil society. In essence, reform liberalism undermines these institutions in two ways. On the one hand, the internal dynamic of the liberal model of man and society drives it to attempt to remake these institutions in accordance with liberal values. Liberalism's true goal is not limited government per se but rather the maximization of individual autonomy. Driven by the internal logic of this commitment, the liberal welfare state will aggressively intervene in the internal affairs of intermediary institutions to remake them in accordance with its individualistic and egalitarian ethos. As Hauerwas points out, "the very means used [by liberalism] to insure that the democratic state be a limited state—namely, the rights of the individual—turn out to be no less destructive for intermediary institutions than the monistic state of Marxism."[37]

These institutions also are weakened by the omnicompetent nanny state's absorption of the responsibilities they had traditionally discharged. Even as liberalism celebrates the liberation of individuals from the social ties that historically bound them, it cannot but notice the social costs involved. The progressive disabling of these institutions under the impact of the market and liberal culture leaves them incapable of discharging their traditional functions, and by doing so unleashes a whole array of social pathologies.

It thus becomes painfully obvious that society cannot be organized in a satisfactory fashion by the market alone. At the same time, inasmuch as its thinking is imprisoned in the horizon of the individual-state-market grid, liberalism is forced to turn to the state as the only possible counterweight to the very forces that it itself unleashed. The state thus ends up being empowered both to restrain the market and to undertake the functions that had traditionally been performed by intermediary groups.

The transition from the night watchman state of classical liberalism to the welfare state of modern reform liberalism thus hardly creates a more favorable environment for intermediary groups. What is involved here, in essence, is the transition from a regime of libertarian individualism to one of statist individualism. By using law and public policy to remake intermediary institutions in accordance with liberalism's voluntarist vision of community and by stripping them of their functions, the liberal welfare state only intensifies the atomizing effects of the market and liberal ethos. Intermediary institutions thus confront not only a hostile culture but a state that is at best indifferent to them and the conditions they require to flourish. Under the liberal dispensation, intermediary associations are, in Glendon's words, "caught in a pincer between individual rights on the one hand, and reasons of state on the other,"[38] between the sovereign individual and the sovereign state.

The Failure of Contemporary Communitarianism

At this point, we are in a position to appreciate why the efforts of what might be termed liberal communitarianism to forge a pluralist theory of society have failed. In essence, liberal communitarianism has tried to construct an alternative to the contemporary liberal theory of the unencumbered self while not breaking fundamentally with the liberal model of man and society. Liberal communitarianism has operated on the implicit assumption that the liberal tradition itself contains the resources to remedy the crisis besetting contemporary liberal theory. The difficulties that have beset contemporary communitarian theory attest to the untenable character of this assumption.

Its failure to break decisively with liberalism explains, to begin with, contemporary communitarianism's inability to formulate anything like a comprehensive theory of politics to challenge that contained in today's liberalism of the sovereign self. Although modern communitarianism has offered us an incisive critique of today's liberalism of the unencumbered self, "when it comes to providing a constructive and affirmative philosophical foundation for the communitarian viewpoint," as Thomas A. Spragens Jr. has noted, "we find rather thin fare."[39] Even at this late date, what communitarianism rejects is far clearer than what it embraces.

Its failure to break decisively with liberalism also explains what Clarke E. Cochran has aptly described as the "thinness" of modern communitarianism's vision of community itself. As Cochran has shown, if contemporary communitarianism embraces "community," it nevertheless offers us nothing like a full-fledged theory of community, and its fragmentary explorations of the subject give short shrift to a whole array of subjects such as character, authority, loyalty, commitment, obedience, law, coercion, tradition, ritual, and common good that are essential to any "thick" conception of community.[40] Although thick "communities," Cochran observes, "cannot exist" without these elements and a thick theory of community necessarily involves "the description of these concepts and of the relationship between them and the distinctions among them," nevertheless, "none of the communitarians has provided this description."[41]

The thinness of communitarianism's theory of community is a product of the intellectual tradition within whose horizon it has chosen to operate. A "thick" theory of community is simply unsustainable on the premises of the liberal model of man and society. Indeed, insofar as this model forces us to conceive of all human social relations in an utterly voluntarist fashion, it is incapable of doing justice to thicker and richer forms of community, and ultimately it renders such forms of community unintelligible.

Finally, and most importantly for our purposes here, it explains why contemporary communitarianism's efforts to forge a pluralist theory of society have veered toward what we have termed political communitarianism. If communitarianism has sought to restrain both the state and market and to protect what Sandel terms "intermediate forms of community" in a way that fosters "a more vital public life," when all is said and done, its conception of the role of the state ends up being virtually indistinguishable from that which informs egalitarian liberalism. At the end of the day, the communitarian state turns out to be nothing more than a fine-tuned version of the liberal welfare state.

Conclusion: The Unrealized Promise of Communitarianism

Nisbet's analysis indicates that revitalizing the institutions of civil society requires a radical transformation of the relation between the state and these institutions. Such a transformation presupposes a new public philosophy embodying the vision of what we have labeled pluralist communitarianism. The promise of modern communitarianism lay in its commitment to the fashioning of just such a public philosophy. Although one can only applaud its powerful critique of today's liberalism of the sovereign self and its role in reinjecting an awareness of the dangers of individualism and a concern for community and the vitality of civil society into our national consciousness, communitarianism has nevertheless failed to fulfill this promise.

On the one hand, it has simply failed to provide the new public philosophy it sought to articulate. Rhetorical appeals to community, the common good, and solidarity, however powerful, do not in themselves constitute such a philosophy. On the other hand, the fragmentary efforts by communitarian thinkers to formulate such a philosophy and to unpack its implications at the level of law and public policy display little if any sign of the type of comprehensive rethinking of the relation of the state to the institutions and associations of civil society that an authentically pluralist theory of society demands. In fact, these efforts suggest that the attempts of liberal communitarian thinkers to forge a communitarianism rooted in such a vision of society quickly derail into what we have termed political communitarianism.

Contemporary communitarianism's attempts to articulate a pluralist public philosophy have been frustrated by a tragic failure of intellectual and political imagination. Indeed, intellectually speaking, one of communitarianism's most striking (and disappointing) features is its timidity, which finds expression in a resolute refusal to move beyond the familiar confines of the horizon within which the mainstream of modern political thought has operated.

Admittedly, the formulation of the new public philosophy we need will be no simple matter. Requiring as it does the comprehensive rethinking of the relation of the state to the institutions of civil society, such a philosophy will involve a drastic break with the vision of state and society embodied in both the modern state and the dominant political theories of the modern era. Indeed, it presupposes nothing less than the wholesale reconstruction of the intellectual foundations of modern political life—a reconstruction that looks to traditions and historical arrangements currently out of favor with most contemporary communitarians. Obviously this will involve an intellectual project of extraordinary magnitude, one for which the work of earlier thinkers in the pluralist tradition can be no more than a prelude. To date, communitarianism has displayed little real interest in such a bold undertaking. Until it does so, however, its promise will remain unrealized.

2

American Community

Barry Alan Shain

Contemporary communitarians, who at their core are liberal, find themselves defending imagined communities. Real communities, with the exception of certain short-lived utopian ones, have invariably been illiberal. American conservatives, however, confront no such dilemma; they can turn to American history and uncover a rich inheritance that is at once conservative and communal. This salient feature of American social, religious, and political history is found in almost all epochs and locations of our past. Because of the importance we Americans attach to the birth of the nation, the years surrounding the Declaration of Independence and the founding of the republic, 1765–1785, are of great interest. Revolutionary-era Americans held to a political theory that awarded priority to the needs of the public over those of the individual and believed that the individual best flourishes when living with others in locally controlled political and social units. This conservative understanding of the human good legitimated authoritative group intrusion into the moral choices made by individuals. Eighteenth-century Americans' lived experience continued to conform, though with increasing tension by the end of the century, to their theoretical expectations about the communal requirements for a good life.

Early American Conservatism

Before going any further, let me briefly outline the essential features of a political theory like that held by our American forebears, which we now describe as conservative. Eighteenth-century Americans were conservative even before the term took on its current philosophical meaning in the 1830s. Seven general principles can be isolated from this long tradition of American de facto conservatism, communalism being one of the most important. These principles include a recognition that the needs and good of the public must be awarded priority over those of any particular individual—the priority of the public good. Conservatives defend a theory of the good, *communalism,* which holds that individual human flourishing is best pursued through familial and communal shaping of individual character (as opposed to both collectivism of the left and right, and individualism) through the active inculcation of corporately agreed-upon virtues. This sanctioned formation of individual character by intermediate social and political institutions is guided by an underlying moral, invariably religious, conception of a well-lived human life. This necessitates a common morality that rests on universal and absolute truth claims and by contemporary liberal sensibilities must be judged intrusive. In effect, the quest after personal virtue is not a fully private or even wholly familial project but rather a corporate and public one that involves political, social, and usually theological elements.

Conservatism, in union with classical liberalism, understands human nature as innately selfish, passionately unruly (particularly that of males), and, in a sense, deformed. This pessimistic view of human nature in the language of Christianity is known as the dogma of original sin. This, in essence, may be the core principle that distinguishes both conservatism and classical liberalism from more optimistic political theories. Conservatism, because it recognizes the complexity of society, also views attempts at rapidly transforming society as likely to lead to numerous unexpected and undesired consequences. This supports a willingness to prefer inherited social, political, and cultural patterns, *traditionalism,* to the greater hubris and dangers that accord with the Enlightenment's confidence in man's ability to reconstruct an intact society. This conservative position is not an unreasonable bias in favor of the old but a reflection of reasonable epistemological doubt concerning any human ability to create anew a remarkably complex societal inheritance.

These three latter elements when combined, particularly in American conservatism, have resulted in a reliance and confidence in local and intermediate social and political institutions. These usually include an extended family, the neighborhood, religious congregations, fraternal organizations, occupational groupings, and locally controlled schools and governments. All human beings, conservatives believe, suffer from selfishness and a limited ability to comprehend fully the dense fabric of social and cultural life that surrounds them. People must therefore live together intimately and help each other live virtuously and achieve, as well as possible given human limits, a good life. Accordingly, long chains of hierarchy, distant political control, and bureaucratic centralization have traditionally been viewed by Americans with great suspicion. In adhering to traditional and Christian patterns of social and political thought, American conservatism rejects the conceits of the late Enlightenment.

American conservatives thus hold a strong preference for a religiously based (in America, traditionally Protestant) local communalism in which each individual is enmeshed in overlapping circles of communal integration through intermediate institutions, most importantly family, congregation, and local social and governmental bodies. The late Russell Kirk, the dean of American conservatism, observed that "the family, religious association, and local community—these, the conservatives insisted, cannot be regarded as the external products of man's thought and behavior; they are essentially prior to the individual and are the indispensable supports of belief and conduct."[1] Rejected, then, are the individualistic, secular, nationalistic, and central bureaucratic aspirations of contemporary liberalism. It is to the conservative and communal vision of human flourishing—social constraint and the shaping of individual moral character through local intermediate institutions—that our American forebears were committed and to which they dedicated their lives and new federal political structure. Only the limitations of space will prevent us from showing that each and every element of the conservative vision, like communalism, was similarly embraced by colonial and Revolutionary-era Americans.

Communalism in the Revolutionary Era

Communal political theory had for centuries described two interconnected features of social thought and life. True to this tradition and in keeping with its first demand, Americans were stridently dedicated in theory and practice to local rather than central and national political, religious, and economic authority and organization. They insisted that local institutions must shape and make possible their members' moral existences. As Aristotle had taught, a political community "must devote itself to the end of encouraging goodness." Otherwise it sinks into being "a mere alliance."[2] Edmund Burke, the father of modern conservatism, reminded his readers that the political community was more than "a partnership agreement in a trade of pepper and coffee." Instead, it is "to be looked on with other reverence, because it is not a partnership in things subservient only to the gross animal existence of a temporary and perishable nature."[3] In such an understanding of the good life, individual moral ends were publicly defined as only achievable through local communal existence. These two key facets of communalism, localism and corporately shaped moral existence, formed the core of eighteenth-century American moral, social, religious, and local political life.

Americans' dedication to serving the public good, although an important component of conservative thought, is not unique to it. Awarding priority to the public good over that of the individual does not demand that a polity embrace a communal understanding of human flourishing. Accordingly, corporate moral intrusiveness (one of the two central elements of communalism) and an overarching preference for the public good necessarily reinforce each other but remain distinct social ideals.

Imagine, therefore, a society of moderate individualists, in which serving the collective good is the precondition for the exercise of a measured amount of autonomous individual freedom. In such a society there would be limited public intervention in the moral formation of each individual. This scenario is probably familiar to most Americans who grew to maturity in the middle years of the twentieth century (before the beginning of the Vietnam War). Serving the public good in this way demands no concomitant devotion to communalism. Therefore, the priority that colonial and Revolutionary-era Americans surely awarded the public—its rights and its good—need not have demanded that the individual be seen as radically incomplete outside an enveloping and ethically invasive community.

Serving the public good also need not be localist (the second of communalism's key features); it does not demand that appropriate corporate decisions be made by the smallest possible viable polity in an extended political system. In fact, awarding priority to the public's needs is compatible with localism and with various forms of nationalism, and possibly even internationalism. Defense of the public's welfare is usually claimed by each level of political aggregation and sovereignty to be its particular preserve. As Publius would claim of the central government in *The Federalist* and Marx would claim for an international proletariat, it was their preferred level of government and their controlling elite that best understood the needs of the people. There are sound analytical reasons, therefore, for distinguishing between the important preeminence Americans awarded to the public good and their supplemental embrace of a communal rather than an individualistic approach to a well-lived human life.

Revolutionary-era Americans awarded preeminence to the public's needs, but most expected more from themselves and fellow members of town and congregation, for they were a communal and conservative people. They believed that local intermediate (familial, social, religious, and governmental) institutions must play a prominent role in defining the moral life of individuals, most importantly by placing strict limits on individual autonomy and inculcating virtuous behavior. Without such barriers to human licentious passions, in particular for men, a well-lived human life was believed impossible.

The truth of this claim does not rest solely on what Americans wrote and said, however, for recent research by social historians has done much to reconstruct a portrait of the social, economic, and political lives of eighteenth-century Americans. Their empirically based portraits of eighteenth-century American life offer insight into otherwise undiscoverable lived American political and social norms. Americans' political and social thought is "inferred from ordinary daily behavior, rather than formal ideas."[4] The less articulate agrarian majority adhered to an understanding of a virtuous human life that was public centered, conservative, and communal. Americans were local communalists who "did not espouse the ethic of individualism" but instead backed a localism in which freedom "was possible only within a community of like-minded men."[5] The research findings of most social historians, then, largely corroborate my characterization of Americans as conservative, largely Protestant, local communalists.

The localism of seventeenth- and eighteenth-century Americans is undisputed. The geographical isolation of their villages almost demanded it. At the time of the Revolution, 95 percent of Americans lived in rural, largely agricultural communities. Most Americans were proud of living in such communities, many of which had their own parochial and idiosyncratic standards. Often their central corporate aspiration was to be left alone in their secluded villages to shape their lives as they collectively saw fit. Indeed, in the most rural areas, the settlers "were so local-minded . . . that to get them to become loyal to the state and conscious of its problems would have constituted a vast broadening of their horizons."[6] Localism was an inescapable and enduring feature of American political life.

Thomas Jefferson was a witness to the strength of American localism. Late in his life he stood in particular awe of the democratic power of the New England villages' local autonomy. He claimed that these little hamlets had shaken the very foundations of government under his feet during his administration's embargo on American trade with the European warring powers, and thereby "overrule[d] the Union." Jefferson, however, defended such localism and argued that "generalizing and concentrating all cares and powers" in the central state was the death knell of liberty.[7] He added that "these wards, called townships in New England, are the vital principle of their governments, and have proved themselves the wisest invention ever devised by the wit of man for the perfect exercise of self-government, and for its preservation."[8] Localism in politics and religion continued to be, even late in Jefferson's life, so central to the American experience that it might well have formed the essence of lived American political and religious traditions.

Nor is it by accident that religion and politics in America were thus connected. American political localism found great support in the thought and practices of reformed Protestantism and its insistent covenantalism, for it demanded local political and religious autonomy to support and foster individual salvation as well as godly and neighborly service. From the reformed Protestant perspective, only "local resistance to social hierarchy and to religious and political centralization" allowed the community to remain free to effect moral discipline and thus aid the individual in living a godly life and the community in appropriately honoring God.[9] As was true in Europe as well, "the town even considered itself as a kind of intermediary through which the individual found his salvation."[10] Only within the compass of a small community could the visible saints be known—those principally responsible for subjecting "the damned to the divine supervision of the Church" in a manner "consistent with the glory of God."[11] From the reformed Protestant perspective, any loss of corporate autonomy to extralocal religious, social, or governmental power would have made their divinely ordained duties and functions more difficult to fulfill.

Americans derived from their reformed Protestant theology and its associated political institutions, then, a marked distrust of elites who were not locally situated. They believed that it was the responsibility of a local community, not distant authorities, to define the ethical ends to be pursued by its members. Commenting on the unequaled local control exercised by village and congregation in America, a British minister, after a fourteen-month visit to America in 1807, observed that "whether Anglican or separatist, we [the English] have a notion of Church and nation. In the American states, even Anglicans speak only of village and congregation."[12] An absence of nationalism in America, however, did not for most of two centuries foster individualism but instead a restrictive local and conservative communalism that offered little protection to deviant individuals and ethnic or religious minorities (with the exception of the right to leave and go elsewhere). The exclusive right to enact and enforce moral legislation, known at the time as police power, was at the most general level reserved for states or more immediately, localities.

Another reflection of Americans' reformed Protestant and covenant-inspired insistence on local communal control, as well as their hostility to the centralization of authority, was their powerful embrace of federalism. In the political sphere, Americans believed that a confederated form of government would allow them to benefit from the collective military and economic strength of a large number of small republics, while preserving local moral oversight and religious establishments. Most importantly, this entailed control over police powers, which allowed a community to shape the moral lives of individuals, including "the rules for daily life; rules concerning the production and distribution of wealth, personal conduct, the worship of God."[13] If such powers were not retained, the citizens of different states would lose any sense of themselves as particular peoples. Revolutionary-era Americans envisioned as their preferred polity a confederation in which the needs and ethical ends of the local community (already coming to be despised in Enlightenment Europe as particularistic) would continue to shape the lives of their individual members.

Similarly, in defending local communalism and traditional federalism, an anonymous opponent of the federal Constitution observed that the people should "convene in their local assemblies, for local purposes, and for managing their internal concerns" and that "the essential characteristic of a confederated republic" is "that this head be dependent on, and kept within limited bounds by the local governments."[14] Twentieth-century progressive nationalist Herbert Croly later commented that "behind the opposition to a centralized government were the interests and the prejudices of the mass of the American people."[15] Here, then, was the ground on which authentic federalism, in contrast to centralization and nationalization, had been initially supported: local communalism. In the tradition of his great nationalist predecessor Publius, Croly found nothing of value in either authentic federalism or its localist-preserving foundations.

Indeed, nationalist supporters of the Constitution early on wished to end or greatly weaken American localism in order to promote a more rational market-dominated economy and individualistic social and political practices. Like the imperial elite and many of their Loyalist followers before them, nationalists zealously opposed America's rich tradition of local communalism that, in the words of Gouverneur Morris, was "one of our greatest misfortunes" because "the great objects of the nation had been sacrificed constantly to local views." As Hamilton noted, "The small good ought never to oppose the great one."[16] Luther Martin, a member of the convention who refused to sign or support the Constitution, angrily observed of his peers, however, that "a majority of the convention hastily and inconsiderably [had] . . . decided that a kind of government, which a Montesquieu and a Price have declared the best calculated of any to preserve internal liberty, and to enjoy external strength," a federated republic, was for America "totally impracticable; and they acted accordingly."[17] The dozen or so modernizing state builders, who are celebrated in contemporary history books and in the commentaries of many so-called conservative students of the period, were resolutely opposed to "those who preferred local" political advantages.[18]

Their contempt for parochialism was not the only factor that led the nationalizing and liberalizing elite to oppose local communalism. Another was the corporate public moralism of American communalism, the conservative vision of human flourishing guided by family and community that so troubled some of the celebrated nationalists at the end of the eighteenth century. Forrest McDonald points out that the local community traditionally exercised nearly absolute power over the lives of its members. From the perspective of localists, the local community needed such controls because it served as the front line of defense against the encroachment of undesirable individuals, groups, and ideas. For our eighteenth-century forebears, then, community demanded a relatively high level of exclusivity.

With something like a robust protective barrier erected around them, local and county officials in the seventeenth and eighteenth centuries guarded their neighbors against physical, social, and religious pathologies, internal as well as external, that might draw the weak away from their God-appointed duties. Local communities were, therefore, little concerned about a loss of personal freedom for individuals with "communicable" diseases. Public officials and their constituencies did not doubt that it was their legitimate responsibility to prevent the spread of all manner of pathology. For example, they believed that stopping the spread of "smallpox was more important than the right of victims to wander" into their midst.[19] But it was not physical diseases alone that they sought to isolate. The Handlins, highly respected colonial historians, note that "the corporate community bred intolerance of every form of deviant behavior," primarily "out of fear that wrong behavior by some would destroy the health of all."[20]

In the seventeenth century, Americans had insisted that the community was not "an aggregation of individuals" but "an organism, functioning for a definite purpose, with all parts subordinate to the whole."[21] Individual sacrifice, to the point of self-abnegation, was for them therefore not a heroic act but a moral obligation. In the eighteenth century, such corporatist, almost collectivist thinking was still present in America, although in a more nuanced form. For example, Abraham Williams, preaching in 1762 before the Massachusetts legislature, held that "the natural Body consists of various Members, connected and subservient one to the other, each serving some valuable purpose and the most perfect and happy State of the Body results from all the Members regularly performing their natural Offices; so collective Bodies, or Societies, are composed of various Individuals connected together, related and subservient to each other."[22] Society was thus seen, at least by respected New Englanders, as an organic whole, a community, within which each member found meaning and ultimately the means to achieve his or her true, everlasting welfare.

This corporate view of society continued to be defended in the sermon literature of Revolutionary America which regularly rehearsed and defended the necessarily ethical intrusiveness of communal life. On one such occasion, the future Vermont Supreme Court judge and U.S. Congressman Nathaniel Niles excoriated materialism and the foundations of liberalism. In a lengthy note, Niles explains what he meant in his sermon when he argued that "originally, there were no private interests." From a common eighteenth-century perspective he held that "a compact formed with a particular design to secure and advance the private interests of those by whom the compact was made" is indeed "the maxim on which pirates and gangs of robbers live in a kind of unity." After denouncing materialist and liberal contractual foundations for civil society, he argues in favor of an ethically demanding communal one in which "every individual is to have his part assigned him . . . but he is not to have any separate interest consigned to him, for this would tend to detach him from the community. . . . Thus each individual is to take care of the community, and the community in its turn, is to make provision for the individuals."[23] The individual in this communal view is not without ethical standing but is radically incomplete outside a defining, nurturing, and morally invasive communal environment.

A close student of early modern political thought, Father Francis Canavan, describes this communal aspect of the eighteenth-century mind and its critical role in moral and political thought. He finds that for such a people,

> man is designed by God and nature for life in civil society, without which he cannot arrive at the full development of which his nature is capable. The potential for that development sets the goals of human life. The goals of human life, in turn, are the source of moral obligation, both individual and political, because man is morally obliged to consent to his nature's goals and to the necessary means of achieving them.[24]

Offering prior support to this assessment, prominent eighteenth-century author John Brown noted that the "solitary and wretched State is strictly *unnatural;* because it prevents the Exertion of those Powers, which his *Nature* is *capable* of *attaining:* But those *Powers Society* alone can *call forth* into *Action*. Man is therefore formed for Society."[25] Community life was foremost a shared moral existence in which accepted moral ends must concur with man's elevated status. Man's unique ethical standing thus demanded restrictive, not liberating, local public involvement in the moral lives of its members.

For most colonial Americans, then, serving God and leading a fulfilled human life depended on membership in a hierarchically structured household (normally with a male head of house) and a locally controlled congregation and community. In turn, each community was to be guided by appropriate transcendent morality (usually guided by Protestant-revealed theology) that, in effect, defined it as a community. One anonymous author drew attention to the centrality of such a shared ethical vision, noting "in the solitary state of nature" the most elevated motive that man is able to produce is a "*natural affection* towards one's offspring." But it is only in an environment of shared morality, "supported with the joint advice and affections of his fellow creatures," that man is able to reach his highest development by sustaining "a common relation to the same moral system or community." For this author, it was Americans' inherited Protestant ethical framework and English legal system that defined them as a people. He continued that "*love of our country* does not import an attachment to any particular soil, climate, or spot of earth, where perhaps we first drew our breath," but "it imports an affection to that *moral system*, or *community which is governed by the same laws*."[26] A common morality and community were for him, as for any defender of authentic community, not separable.

At the end of the Revolutionary years, the considered opinion of the politically active, much-published, and theologically liberal pastor of the Congregational church in West Springfield, Massachusetts, Joseph Lathrop, was still that "government is a combination of the whole community against the vices of each particular member" so that it might "exercise a controul over each member, to restrain him from wrong and compel him to right."[27] Michael Zuckerman observes that "the community they desired was an enclave of common believers, and to the best of their ability they secured such a society, rooted not only in ethnic and cultural homogeneity but also in common moral and economic ideas and practices."[28] Even Pennsylvania, in many ways the most progressive state, in its Declaration of Rights gave absolute protection only to the right of religious conscience. Outside this hallowed sphere, the state was to enact "laws for the encouragement of virtue, and prevention of vice and immorality." Such laws were to be "constantly kept in force, and provision shall be made for their due execution."[29] Only within a restricted enclave of unified believers was a virtuous human life, a life of sanctioned limits guided by tradition and custom, possible.

This vision demanded that little protection be awarded the potential source of discord—Thoreau's nonconforming individual. In such communities, "narrow but consensual norms might be necessary for any clear sense of communal purpose and unity."[30] Their shared commitment to a fixed and objective end for individual members demanded some measure of intolerance, for toleration "led neither to improvement nor to regeneration."[31] Men and women standing outside the circle of agreed-upon ethical precepts were without antecedent inalienable individual rights (except that of religious conscience). Moral "pariahs" either reconciled themselves with the community or were expelled by villages that "had efficient ways of driving out strangers and disciplining and humbling individual deviants within its own fold."[32] Although "individual dissidents were always free to pull up stakes and depart to other places,"[33] during the Revolutionary years and the 150 years of American history preceding them, what they could not choose was self-defined individual autonomy.

The early nineteenth century was not much different in this regard, at least at the level of public opinion. As Alexis de Tocqueville wrote of early nineteenth-century America, "the multitude requires no laws to coerce those who do not think like themselves: public disapprobation is enough; a sense of their loneliness and impotence overtakes them and drives them to despair."[34] At the midpoint of the nineteenth century, American ethical intolerance and communalism was still strident. Consider the words of Senator Stephen Douglas, employing political language that would have been equally familiar in the late eighteenth century. "If there is any one principle dearer and more sacred than all others in free governments . . . it is that which asserts the exclusive right of a free people to form and adopt their own fundamental law, and to manage and regulate their own internal affairs and domestic institutions." Daniel Rodgers clarifies that "Douglas's people was a patchwork of local peoples, each clutching to its vested rights, its fraternal exclusion."[35] Nevertheless, American communalism in the nineteenth century, like almost everything else in American cultural, social, economic, and religious life, had changed greatly from what it had been in the eighteenth century, to say nothing of the seventeenth century.

The change in the character of communalism was not precipitated, as one might expect, by the rapid spread of tolerance of individual deviance among American communities or by a desire among the people for enlightened individualism. Rather, toward the end of the eighteenth century, with the ascendance of a new national liberal elite, American communalism increasingly began to lose leadership and, with it, its demanding moral dimension. Village self-direction and order "without reference to the saving of souls or the building of God's kingdom on earth" became increasingly the goal of communal life.[36] It was localism, the deeply traditional Anglo-American desire of a people "to be left alone in their villages,"[37] that began to emerge, stripped of some of its defining ethical moorings, from the eighteenth century. Although deference to the public good and the existence of localism would long remain, something of the legitimating moral force supporting the corporate shaping of ethical lives had already been lost.

Ironically, then, this new national elite of "founding fathers," often credited with preserving America's inherited ways was, in reality, composed of anything but conservatives who sought to maintain the moral intrusiveness of local communal life. It was the classical liberal and skeptical democratic "founders" who sought to foster and protect an emerging liberal bourgeois world by reducing the local community's ability to interfere in private-regarding individual behavior. For these enlightened men, local communalism was necessarily to be hedged by an overriding concern with protecting the individual, even morally obnoxious ones. It is this concern, so unrepresentative of eighteenth-century Americans, that became the cornerstone of a political vision that began to dominate American elite political discourse during the last decade of the eighteenth century. But it is folly to suggest that these men represented the political vision that obtained in America during the first half of its history (up to and including the conclusion of its war of liberation). Even at the end of the eighteenth century the rural citizenry, not the urban elite, was most representative of Americans—those who continued, long after the revolution, to remain true to the conservative communal vision that had guided the founding of the colonies and had sparked resistance to a modernizing Britain.

Roots of Communalism

Recently, intensive research by social historians into the lives of colonial and early national Americans has unseated many previously well regarded beliefs about American individualistic social and political practices. Social historian Christine Heyrman captures the essence of their findings when she describes the norms of a challenging test case, an eighteenth-century commercial center. She finds that even the men and women engaged in modern economic activities such as international maritime trade, were conservative communalists committed to "localism, insularity, [and] intolerance towards outsiders" and had "an aversion to risk and an attachment to tradition."[38] Only a handful of social historians today question whether colonial American society was, in the main, communalistic in the essential two senses described above.

Some social historians have even argued that before English settlers were "Americans," they were already committed local communalists. Timothy Breen writes that "having to resist Stuart centralization, a resistance that pitted small congregations against meddling bishops," English settlers in America were "determined to maintain their local attachments against outside interference, and to a large extent the Congregational churches and self-contained towns of Massachusetts" were demonstrable evidence of their success.[39] Kenneth Lockridge finds that "long before the migration to New England, Puritanism had begun to serve as a weapon in the hands of men and women who resented the erosion of local customs and local power by the evolving central state" and that, in particular, their "Puritanism was characterized by a passionate devotion to the authority of the local congregation."[40] Thus Americans were able to realize traditional European communal ideals (though not of hierarchy) in their locally autonomous and unusually democratic peasantlike villages. From the moment of settlement, in an almost reactionary stance, then, the communal village (northern colonies), township (middle), or county (southern) sought to be the center of Americans' self-directing political, religious, and social lives.

Throughout the colonies in the seventeenth century, American communities guarded their ability to be largely autonomous, as they "did not want the individualistic, competitive, commercialized, ruthlessly hierarchical social world or the centralized state characteristic of the Renaissance England whence they fled."[41] The freedom they sought reflected a deep and rich reformed Protestant communalism, described in possibly exaggerated fashion by Lockridge as a "Christian Utopian Closed Corporate Community,"[42] which the early colonists hoped would flourish in America.

And this was true beyond the northern plantations. David Hackett Fischer shows that "the founders of Virginia shared the religious obsessions of their age" so much so that in Virginia each individual was also expected to join in common religious practices.[43] Darrett and Anita Rutman, after years of studying and writing about New England, found that a communal form of life was similarly sought in Virginia. They noted that the scattered entry of initial immigrants into the region was more a response to the riverine geography than the result of an individualist political vision. Once installed, Virginians, like their neighbors to the north, structured their lives around families, neighborhoods, congregations, counties, and regarding anything else as "anathema, even sinful."[44] John Waters concludes that the collective portrait emerging from town studies in the middle colonies also finds a conservative and communal people who "lived in nucleated villages just as they had in the old country."[45] According to the research of the majority of social historians, then, the seventeenth century must be understood as the religious, social, and political foundation on which an American commitment to local communalism was built. Even in the unusually tolerant colony of Pennsylvania, ethnic and religious solidarity and attendant intolerance, rather than enlightened individualism, provided the atmosphere in which this localism flourished.

Eighteenth-Century Communalism

Scholars and theorists have been forced to turn to eighteenth-century American life and politics in their search for evidence of individualism at America's European founding. Yet social historians have demonstrated that throughout most of that century, too, political, social, and religious existence in the British north American colonies continued along largely local communal lines. For instance, Gregory Nobles in his innovative work on Hampshire County, Massachusetts, finds that in the eighteenth century this region was still communal, but that there were two different forms of conservative communalism in conflict. He contends that during the first half of the eighteenth century the county elite had successfully wrested power from the towns. This change would be contested in the second half of the century by a resurgent reactionary wave of local communalism that challenged the county elite's usurpation of power. By the mid-eighteenth century, then, "there emerged a widespread movement among common people to maintain—or regain—local control of their political and religious affairs. . . . A growing number of people sought to establish their own independent churches and towns, to recreate the traditional patterns of town life, and in the end to separate themselves from the dominance of the county leadership. This second sort of conservatism, with its emphasis on localism and in many cases on strict religious practices, was almost reactionary in nature, looking back to standards of an idealized past."[46] We must keep in mind that both groups were localists who were unwilling to cede power to either centralized provincial or imperial authority.

Intense localism should be expected, as Alfred Chandler reminds us, because even in 1790 America was still overwhelmingly rural. It was a country in which only "202,000 out of 3,930,000 Americans lived in towns and villages of more than 2,500."[47] Among the relatively urbanized areas, there were twelve with about forty-five hundred people, seven towns of about seven thousand, three of about sixteen thousand (Boston, Albany, and Charleston, South Carolina), and two (New York and Philadelphia) with about twenty-five thousand inhabitants each.[48] The modal population for the villages where the other 95 percent of the population lived was five hundred to one thousand residents![49] So the vast majority of Americans lived in rural environments, including those living in the even more sparsely populated frontier regions of the larger states. It is often forgotten that as late as 1870, "fewer than one-in-four Americans lived in places of twenty-five hundred or more."[50]

The pervasiveness of the communal character of life in the eighteenth century is further displayed by Heyrman. She demonstrates that even exposure to the modernizing effects of urbanization and commercialization did not erode the communal character of northern town life. She writes that searching in the late eighteenth century for "stereotypical 'Yankees' of boundless initiative and ambition, restive under the restraints of established institutions and inherited values, turns up instead Puritan traditionalists." She finds that, throughout the century, the residents of Gloucester, an international trading center, "remained committed to corporatism" and "to localism and conservative Calvinist orthodoxy," despite their cosmopolitan connections.[51]

Americans' commitment to local communalism is ironically evident in cases where goodwill and comity had broken down. Those who argue that the numerous town divisions experienced in the Northern colonies in the late eighteenth century evidence an increased individualism among the inhabitant misinterpret this phenomenon. In fact, the communalist assumptions of American political thinking were most conspicuous precisely when an older town was torn by religious strife and when ill feelings ran highest. It demonstrates that for common American farmers, a town (or its principal divisions) was to be ethically, religiously, and preferably ethnically one people. When significant ethical or religious differences developed between divergent groups, "separation was often seen as the only solution. The communities of the province simply could not conceive of successfully maintaining structural diversity. Harmony required homogeneity."[52] It was not individual freedom, then, that these "wreckers of corporate harmony" were seeking but traditional local communalism with its attendant ethical, religious, and ethnic homogeneity and limited tolerance.

Current research on the southern colonies has begun to show that local communalism was not unique to the eighteenth-century north. Historians of the southern colonies have noted that "politically the attitude of the southern planters was neither national or imperial, but intensely local, dominated by a fierce suspicion of any active central government."[53] Rossiter finds that autonomous county self-government in the South was "as typically colonial as the towns of New England."[54] Charles Sydnor charges that southern county governments were almost beyond colonial (and later state) control.[55]

More adamantly, Donald Lutz holds that these governments were not just communal in the localist sense but were corporately intrusive and thus fully met the twin standards of communalism. He writes that "in Virginia, the Carolinas, Georgia, and Maryland, local government was centered in the county due to the absence of population concentrations . . . they involved themselves in every aspect of economic, social, and political life. . . . If a government today were to have such complete powers, it would be termed totalitarian."[56] Carl Bridenbaugh adds that in the back settlements of the South, these relatively intolerant communities were organized along overlapping ethnic and religious lines. "The toleration born of the Enlightenment and voiced by some liberal Tidewater Anglican gentlemen had no interior echoes before 1775."[57] As social historical research on local communities in the colonial South proceeds, it should continue to yield a communalistic portrait of eighteenth-century American life that is centered geographically on the county rather than the more intimate northern village.

Communalism in the Middle States: An Exception?

Largely because of their internal diversity, the people of the middle colonies, unlike the more ethnically and religiously homogeneous colonies to the north and the south, are often seen as the first in America to reject communalism and embrace an incipient form of individualism. It is widely recognized that the middle colonies and states lacked the religious and ethnic homogeneity and other communal characteristics often found at the provincial level in the colonies to the south and, to a lesser degree, to the north with their local-level establishments. Thus statewide commitments to particular ethical systems (beyond a vague Christianity) in the middle colonies and states are not to be expected. But evidence of such broad commitments is not necessary to argue that eighteenth-century Americans, including those living in the middle colonies and states, were local and ethical communalists.

There is good reason to hold that communalism was as descriptive of towns in the middle states as elsewhere in America with the anomalous exception of the chartered corporate city of Philadelphia, whose urban government, "in striking contrast to the New England town," was closed "to full or even meaningful citizen participation."[58] Thomas Bender has it right when he argues that Revolutionary-era Americans sorted themselves ethnically and religiously and that "the same thing occurred, in more obvious ways, in the middle colonies, where the differences among towns were sharper. Men and women sharing particular cultural values came together to form the small, intensely parochial, local units of life that made up the kaleidoscopic American social landscape."[59] It seems particularly apt, then, to view the middle colonies and states as a sea of tolerance dotted with large and small communal islands of intolerance.

The localism bequeathed to us from the middle states might form the essence of America's particular political genius. Patricia Bonomi suggests as much. She holds that in New York State it may well have been its "very parochialism—its very narrowness of view, its suspiciousness, its jealous attachment to local prerogatives—that furnished the vital ingredient" of its political institutions.[60] If one excludes New York City, her conclusions seem difficult to dispute. One-fourth of New York's population was composed of deeply religious New Englanders living on Long Island; another large percentage were Dutch members of their reformed church, who until the 1780s were highly suspicious of any form of extralocal English intrusion.

Possibly much of the confusion regarding the middle colonies and states stems from a conflation of two kinds of pluralism. One form groups together, in a common political body, individuals in competition with each other or with diverse groups, and takes this assemblage to be the basic local unit. Another form sees a relatively homogeneous and self-governing community as the essential building block in a pluralistic environment. The former is consistent with a system of pluralism that accommodates populations of ethnically and religiously distinct peoples living together in a specific geographical area and common political grouping; it is most often associated with liberal or individualistic political philosophies. The latter creates a plural system that exists between divergent local populations and allows for local communal self-government and an understanding of human flourishing that defends the active intervention of intermediate institutions in the shaping of individual moral character. They are distinct, and the presence of one does not necessitate the presence of the other. In truth, these two forms of pluralism are closer to being antithetical than not. In Pennsylvania and the other middle colonies, especially in the backcountry, the form of pluralism that existed most often was the corporate variety that defined itself through ethnic and religious exclusivity. Fundamental forms of group identity such as ethnicity and religion were not weakened by this form of pluralism; indeed, they were likely strengthened.

Evidence that addresses how various ethnically homogeneous communities coexisted in the middle states shows that each group attempted to adhere to traditional European patterns of local intolerance in seeking to separate itself from its ethnically or religiously distinct provincial neighbors. This was particularly true in New York and Pennsylvania, with large minority enclaves of traditionally communalistic Dutch, reformed Protestant Swiss, separatist German Pietists (a third of Pennsylvania's population), and Quakers. Even one of the most powerful defenders of an individualistic America, geographer James Lemon, finds that the Pennsylvania countryside was filled with separatist settlements of Welsh, Scotch-Irish, Quakers, and Mennonites that were both ethnically and religiously exclusive.

John Waters in detailing the ways of the Protestant Scotch-Irish (also a third of Pennsylvania's population), writes that they had not come to America "either to compromise or to assimilate." Instead, as they had in Ulster, "these Scotch-Irish 'did not intermarry to any extent with the other settlers who came from the English settlements' . . . [and they retained] Old Country ethnic-cultural and religious values. . . . When they assembled with blackened faces . . . and rode on a rail a wife beater, it was to enforce collectively by this 'rough music' the mores of their community."[61] The residents of the middle colonies and states seem, in fact, to have had much more in common with the highly polarized, ethnically exclusive, lower-middle class neighborhoods of contemporary Brooklyn and the Bronx than with the cosmopolitan elite sections of Manhattan. At their core, then, one finds in these ethnically and religiously exclusive enclaves of the eighteenth century a vision of human virtue that rested on local self-government and an active role for intermediate institutions in the corporate shaping of the individual's moral character.

The exception to this norm in the Middle colonies, however, might be the Quakers. An important minority religious group predominantly located in Delaware, West Jersey, and Pennsylvania, its members saw themselves as "an organized segment of the population which kept morality and good order in its own ranks, expected no special favor from the government, and thought other elements should do likewise."[62] Their religious exclusivity, therefore, did not demand, as it did for most other religious or ethnic communities, geographical separation, corporate homogeneity, or local political autonomy. Because of their voluntaristic religious, social, and political views, they were content to live as a morally closed cell in close proximity with others. But in spite of their own corporate exclusivity and communally imposed moral strictures, they likely played a critical role in introducing benevolent, voluntaristic, and individualistic social and political arrangements into Philadelphia.

The key to these innovations was the Quakers' pietistic embrace of social and political voluntarism. But, if they were directly or indirectly responsible for progressive social and political changes, this was largely unintentional. Such changes occurred in spite of their richly fraternal organization, the public spirit they encouraged in Philadelphia, their intrusive regulation of their members' personal lives at quarterly meetings, their extreme sexual repressiveness, and the morally severe laws they helped enact in Pennsylvania. The Quakers' commitment to voluntarism and a certain kind of individualism followed, then, from reasons that were pietistic rather than secular, reactionary rather than modern. From such foundations they fostered a precocious hostility toward local political communalism wherever they were politically important. Their devout religious sectarianism, when conjoined to secular political power and promulgated as political doctrine, was destructive to communities dedicated to the larger public's shaping of individual morality.

Quakers were translocalists (as well as transnationalists), with little commitment to a local community (or a nation) and its corporate morals, concerns, and constraints. It was this particular Quaker trait that the majority of Americans found so repugnant (as many in central Europe found separatist Jews threatening). David Hackett Fischer writes that almost the only thing that all other eighteenth-century Americans could agree on was their genuine hatred of the Quakers, whom they saw "as dangerous radicals" and "pious frauds and hypocrites."[63] For many Americans, their cosmopolitan sectarianism smacked of conspiracy and bordered on treason. Thus the Quakers might be justly seen as having championed values and as having been the creators of social structures that eventually proved to be effective solvents of American local communalism. Yet the anomalous nature of the Society of Friends and its hostility to traditional communal political mores, as well as Americans' reciprocal loathing of the Quakers, indirectly confirm the overall communalist nature of late-eighteenth-century America.

It was not until the nineteenth century, though, that others began to join the Quakers in viewing morality as a primarily private concern, even though, as with the Quakers, it was often still a voluntary morality that was nevertheless directed by religious and corporate guidelines rather than secular and individualist ones. A perverse result of these innovations, when they were adopted, was that publicly directed and seemingly communal activities such as voluntary and fraternal associations "served to set neighbors off from one another, [and] to nurture attachments separate from the whole community." Accordingly, the community "lost a certain moral unity."[64] Robert Hine, a historian of American communalism, explains that many laudatory public-spirited activities championed by Quakers, such as charity, are in truth "individualistic, and [their] arena may more realistically be called the neighborhood than the community."[65] Again, as we noted earlier in this essay, attentiveness to public needs does not necessitate an adherence to a communal political and social theory of human flourishing.

Communalism and the Revolution

The important exception represented by the Quakers notwithstanding, local communalism emerges from the work of historians as one of the most pervasive forces in eighteenth-century American social, political, and religious life. And it was above all this commitment to local communalism, not a new, abstract theory of individual rights, that may have led many Americans in April 1775 to take up arms against Britain. David Hackett Fischer recounts a conversation between George Bancroft and an aged veteran that is particularly telling. The old man was asked whether it was the writings of Locke and Paine that had moved him and his friends to revolt. He answered that he had never heard of Locke and had to admit that he had not read Paine. But then he explained that "New Englanders had always managed their own affairs, and Britain tried to stop them, and so the war began."[66] Similarly, Samuel Morison tells of a young man in 1842 interviewing Captain Preston, who was then an aged veteran of the battle at Concord. The twenty-one-year old began by asking whether it had been oppression or taxes that had led Americans to revolt. The old man responded that he had neither felt oppressed nor ever seen any evidence of the stamp or tea taxes. The young man continued, "Then I suppose you had been reading Harrington or Sidney and Locke about the eternal principles of liberty?" The veteran responded, "Never heard of 'em. We read only the Bible, the Catechism, Watts' Psalms and Hymns, and the Almanac." The interviewer followed up, "Well, then, what was the matter? And what did you mean in going to the fight?" The ninety-one-year-old man retorted, "Young man, what we meant in going for those redcoats was this: *We always had governed ourselves, and we always meant to. They didn't mean we should.*"[67] An attachment to local self-government was, by their account, still alive and well in late-eighteenth-century America.

The aged veteran's memories and the evidence presented by social historians of a communalist people interested primarily in local control of their lives agrees with articulate Americans' arguments in newspapers, pamphlets, and from the pulpit. Social historians have thus helped us recognize that American communalism was not uniquely a product of elite intellectual concerns, quite to the contrary. The near congruence of the communal norms of the political class, those of many of the true elite, and those of popular forces during the Revolutionary period were less the result of shared secular texts and more the result of shared religious and social experiences. Especially important was their having grown to maturity in a reformed Protestant communal environment of local political and social institutions that had blossomed in the luxurious soil of America. Edward Everett, the famous nineteenth-century orator, Unitarian pastor, and Harvard professor of classics, argued as much in 1828. He reminded his auditors that "it was no refinement of philosophical statesmen to which we are indebted for our republican institutions of government. They grew up, as it were, by accident, on the . . . simple foundation" of ordinary English communal practices.[68] Indeed, for our democratic foundations, Americans owe an enormous debt of gratitude to the English crown for its chartering the colonial experiment in Massachusetts as a joint-stock commercial enterprise rather than a subordinate political entity.

America at the end of the eighteenth century, however, had begun to change. There is persuasive evidence that preceding the Revolution, economic and social practices had already begun to conflict with most Americans' communal normative precepts. Americans were beginning to be torn between dynamic demographic, economic, religious, and social material forces and their static ideational communal norms and expectations. In many ways, Americans, in resisting their changing material conditions and in trying to preserve their traditional patterns of thought, were replicating the wrenching changes that had begun two centuries earlier in England. Of special interest, then, is Keith Thomas's claim that the rising number of witchcraft accusations at the beginning of the seventeenth century in England had resulted from "an unresolved conflict between the neighborly conduct required by the ethical code of the old village community, and the increasingly individualistic forms of behavior which accompanied" the beginnings of modern economic relationships.[69] In each instance, a conservative people was trying to resist disruptive social, religious, and economic changes while integrating them into an unyielding communalistic public philosophy.

Yet even historians who emphasize the individualistic character of the new social and economic forces in the late eighteenth century continue to insist on the communalism of American political thought. For example, Jack Greene, one of the most aggressive defenders of individualistic eighteenth-century American practices, admits that "the revolution in behavior suggested by growing evidence of increasing individuation had not yet been accompanied by a revolution in values." Most importantly, new social and economic patterns were unable to challenge "the old system of values that deplored" individualistic behavior. Thus, in the Revolutionary era, "the fear that excessively atomistic behavior would lead to social chaos and loss of control and the belief that man could not tolerate freedom without strong societal restraints were still too deeply embedded in cultural consciousness and too easily activated to permit the development of an alternative morality that would more accurately reflect the modes of behavior."[70] Still more recently, Oxford historian Daniel Walker Howe, in opposition to his classical liberal preferences, also concludes that

> in eighteenth-century North America many, probably most, people still thought of themselves less as autonomous individuals than as members of small communities—families, towns, gathered churches. . . . Jonathan Edwards, deploring self-interest and exalting the corporate interest of the village community, spoke for the traditional and predominant view; Benjamin Franklin, in advocating a more positive view of self, was conscious of having to fight against the cultural hegemony of Reformed Protestantism and the doctrine of original sin.[71]

Another historian favored by liberal theorists, Joyce Appleby, suggests that the very persistence of communal norms, in the face of rapid social and economic change, attests to their continued power to shape the American consciousness.

Without conceding that the overall landscape of social practices had given up its communal character, it must be admitted that an emerging tension between communal norms and evolving individualistic practices had developed. Indeed, this disjunction helped preciptate the desperate attempt mounted by Revolutionary-era Americans to preserve traditional norms. In the face of unplanned and little understood destabilizing institutional and structural changes represented by changing production, marketing, and consumption patterns, they were trying to preserve, both in practice and in thought, Western communal injunctions against what came to be called liberal individualism in the nineteenth century. Heyrman concludes that Americans "clung to the past, relinquished their hold on it reluctantly, tried to recapture it, and gave no thanks to those who would wrest it from them."[72]

In some ways, then, the War of Independence itself must be seen as an oddly reactionary communalist effort to resolve the tension between new structural demands and old ideational goals confronting eighteenth-century Americans. They had sought to delay cultural, economic, and political secular changes that could not be reversed or readily stopped. As Robert Gross puts it, "In 1774 the townspeople had set out only to protect their traditional community life against outside attack. But in the course of the resistance to Britain their goal had become a revival of the community itself. Concordians sought not revolution but regeneration: an end to the bickering and fighting . . . and a rebirth of the virtue and public-mindedness that infused the ideal New England town."[73] To the extent that these goals were widely shared, as most evidence suggests they were, the Revolution clearly was a perverse failure that only exacerbated the problems it was meant to solve.

These changes, whose roots were already solidly established in the prewar period, came fully to fruition during neither the Revolution nor its immediate aftermath, but only some years later, in the last decade of the eighteenth century or, possibly still later, in the early nineteenth century. As Robert Wiebe observes, "The immediate effects of the war were decentralization and diffusion [as] liberty for most Americans remained a local matter."[74] Thomas Bender and Henry May even argue that "for two decades following the ratification of the Constitution, American society seems to have regressed into a stolid communalism."[75] Thus, it might be said that Americans' commitment to local communalism led them both into and out of the Revolutionary War, even if the war itself did much to undermine the lived and philosophical foundations on which communalism had flourished for over a century in much of British America.

Although communalism did lose many of its articulate adherents by the end of the imperial and constitutional crises (1790), it continued to describe the lives and aspirations of most Americans during the nineteenth century. Late in the century (1888), James Bryce observed that the long tradition of American communalism was still powerful, noting that "the autonomy of communities . . . has been the watchword of the Democratic party."[76] Indeed, writing some twenty years later, still in the period before American life had become radically transformed in the aftermath of the World War I, Herbert Croly observed that the "local democracies" in America still "disliked the idea of a centralized Federal government . . . which could interfere with the freedom of local public opinion and thwart its will . . . the kind of freedom they wanted, was freedom from anything but local interference,"[77] the very stuff of American communalism. And such sentiments sound remarkably similar to Storing's description of the communalist core at the heart of the Anti-Federalist opposition to the Constitution some one hundred years earlier.

Apparently American local communalism, even if its commitment to an intrusive moralism had been slowly diminished, continued to enjoy a history well beyond the demise of its eighteenth-century defenders. Some argue that although elite spokesmen largely abandoned communalism at the end of the eighteenth century, they rediscovered it in the nineteenth century with a vengeance—this time in various forms of states rights, Hegelian organicism, or ethno-nativistic nationalism. Examination of local communal life in America at the end of the nineteenth century might show that many of its basic features had remained constant since its European founding nearly three centuries earlier. According to John Roche, "In the United States there existed both a weak and decentralized governmental apparatus and a fundamental absence of individual freedom for those to whom it was important: those who differed on basic issues with the rural white, predominantly Anglo-Saxon Protestant majority."[78] But this was the same communally defined and publicly intrusive understanding of liberty for which the Revolution had been fought and, apparently, in spite of the best efforts and intentions of the eighteenth-century elite proponents of a national state and individual liberty, it continued to define the localistic and conservative practices of the common citizens of America during much of the nineteenth century.

In the American hinterlands, the death of communalism must have been slow. Even in the early twentieth century, America's rural inhabitants continued to be primarily concerned with local farm life, and their morals were shaped by their local churches and affected by "gossip and the fear of gossip." The local community thus continued to exercise great control over the individual's moral conduct, at least, until the advent of Roosevelt's social reforms.[79] And far more irksome to many of the cosmopolitan elite, the communal values "of community autonomy and states rights" have continued to survive even late into the twentieth century.[80] Without the support of cultural elites and the most prominent national political leaders, traditional communal values have remained important to persistent sectors of "the lower levels of twentieth-century society."[81] In opposition to Jefferson's hopes and fears, American local communalism and reformed Protestantism has been unexpectedly slow to die, at least among America's working and lower-middle classes.

American communalism is structurally, politically, and intellectually under attack today. If this inheritance is worthy, for one reason or another, of being preserved, scholars must now resist highlighting only part of the American historical inheritance. The Founding moment (or more accurately moments) will have to be recast more broadly. Indeed, this needs to be done now so that American local communalism, silently lived for much of the last two centuries, might be made fully articulate once again. Only by giving voice anew to this otherwise prevalent but overlooked seminal Founding vision can Americans possibly recover the balance previously maintained between it and the moderate individualism articulated in *The Federalist.* What must be reasserted, then, is a coherent vision of man as an ethical being with a divine nature that understands the importance of family, congregation, and local community in the public shaping of a moral existence. In effect, what is needed is the recovery of an older articulate American conservative and communal understanding of man and his subordinate place in the universe to stand in opposition to the ubiquitous and seductive appeal of moral relativism, hedonism, individualism, and bourgeois materialism.

Certain groups may be mildly advantaged in their search for political legitimacy by the recognition of this vision's enduring presence in the sometimes hidden crevices of the American political and social psyche. But the nation as a whole will also benefit as it is realized that regnant in Revolutionary America was an understanding of the community, the individual, and the moral universe (the cosmos) that was radically different from that held by today's best-educated Americans. All will profit from the Founding generation's understanding of the importance of what we have come to call intermediate institutions as it enriches contemporary American social and political thought by expanding what is authentically American. Americans' current range of political options cannot but be broadened, since various alternatives to individualism, particularly strongly democratic, familial, and conservative communal ones, will no longer be readily denigrated and dismissed as being un-American.

3

The Constitution and Community

George W. Carey

Conservatives recognize that constitutions play a limited role in fostering and nourishing communities. This role, moreover, is largely passive. Genuine communities evolve naturally; they are complexes of voluntary associations bound together by ties of loyalty, affection, and purpose. Consequently, constitutions, no matter how well crafted, play little, if any, role in their origins and growth. Communities are by nature fragile; they are profoundly affected, as we have come to recognize, by the dynamics of society, particularly by technological developments and economic changes, in ways that are impossible to anticipate. Constitutions and even legislation provide at best a frail protection against these underlying powerful and complex forces. This realization, in turn, means that all communities, to one degree or another, are continuously in the process of change and adaptation.

The fragile and changing character of communities also means that they cannot be viewed (as seems to be the wont of social "scientists" who have fallen prey to the more radical strains of Enlightenment thought) merely as parts of a machine (society) that can be created or manipulated to advance some noble purpose. To be sure, communities can be created, but to be vital and functional, and to operate in conformance with their goals, they must have their origins in some shared and genuine human interest or need, not the dreams or aspirations of social planners.

These considerations, as obvious as they may seem, point to one vital relationship between a constitution and the growth, persistence, and health of communities that for some seems self-evident; namely, communities fare best and enjoy free and spontaneous development under political constitutions that allow "space" or "room" for their functioning and development, as well as for their adjustments to the social, economic, and technological factors that affect them. In the modern nation-state, particularly one with an extensive territory with an endless variety of functional and geographic interests such as ours, this space is a function of the scope of powers vested in government and the degree to which these powers are centralized or dispersed. Put in more concrete terms, a highly centralized government with extensive and virtually unlimited powers to provide for the general welfare subordinates local governments, associations, and communities in contrast to decentralized regimes with limited authority. The reasons for this seem clear enough: the more confined the scope of the central government, the greater the need and opportunity for the spontaneous growth of communities and associations at the local level—the only place, after all, where they can grow.

In what follows I want to survey briefly our experiences from colonial times to the present with respect to the allocation of authority among levels of government. The survey provides the background for examining certain critical questions and concerns: What principle (or principles) seemed to dictate the terms and substance of the allocation of powers? What importance, if any, did our Founders attach to allowing sufficient "space" for families, communities, private associations, and local governments? What dangers or difficulties do we face today in maintaining this "space"? What might be done constitutionally to protect against further harmful centralization? In this fashion I hope to show that whereas constitutions cannot do much to create communities or to determine their character, communities and other local institutions and organizations, both private and public, do have a decided impact on the form and nature of constitutions.

The Colonial Experience

There can be no question that up to a relatively recent date in our history not only was there ample room for community development but most political activity was centered at the state and local levels. Unlike the situation today, the role of the central government was circumscribed. As Tocqueville remarks in the opening sections of his *Democracy in America,* the "incomplete" national government provided for in the Constitution meant that most of the day-to-day concerns of individuals were handled by voluntary associations or local governments.[1] As Tocqueville also emphasizes—in part by taking up the role of townships and municipalities first in his survey of the American political institutions—this division of authority resulted from the organic growth and development of the colonies. Indeed, one might go so far as to say the original settlements of the seventeenth century form the "seeds" of our national development; that is, the Constitution represents the culmination of a process in which these basic units united into ever larger political associations, thereby creating the layers of government that are with us today. At every step of this process toward a larger political union certain crucial questions arose, not the least of them relating to the distribution of authority between central and local governments.

This organic view of our political development differs fundamentally from that which is set forth in most accounts of our national development that focus almost exclusively on the "Founding period"—a period that even broadly defined, constitutes a relatively narrow time frame that excludes all, or the major portion, of our colonial experience. From this vantage point, the resolution of the issue over state/national powers, the outgrowth of which we call "federalism," is usually discussed in terms of a compromise at the Constitutional Convention, that is, as a compromise between those who wanted a unitary or centralized government and those who sought to preserve states' rights and sovereignty. Over the course of history, according to the typical textbook account, the forces of nationalism, never really content with the compromise achieved at Philadelphia, sought to expand the powers of the national government, largely through liberal interpretations of the Constitution's more nebulous provisions such as "necessary and proper" and "general welfare." Aided by the Civil War, the Fourteenth Amendment, and an astonishingly broad interpretation of the commerce clause, the nationalists, after decades of conflict, finally emerge victorious in the 1930s with the coming of the New Deal.

This account is essentially correct in indicating how a centralized or unitary system has come into being. Yet it lacks any orientation, any sense of history or understanding of what can be termed the "organic" development of our nation that would serve to put the origins of federalism and the original relationship between central and local political authorities into a coherent historical context in the manner, say, that marks Tocqueville's account. This rendition, in other words, would have us believe that federalism was born out of political compromise and that it was the product of political necessity, representing something virtually unheard of in the annals of our political thought and practice.

As we intend to show, however, our constitutional federalism arose naturally out of America's unique political landscape, its roots firmly planted in colonial experiences. The colonies, we do well to remember, consisted of towns, settlements, and plantations, and each, regardless of the nature of its charter (proprietary, royal, or charter) had to provide a framework that would simultaneously fulfill the needs or purposes for which they were united, while allowing the colonists to handle their more immediate needs within their communities or within the smaller political/administrative units such as counties or townships. The only government most colonists came in contact with was local.

The framework of government varied in the colonies, but the similarities can be said to outweigh the differences. To begin with, representation in the central councils, legislatures, or assemblies of the colonies was territorial and was not based on population. This form of representation not only reflected their decentralized nature, it also recognized that towns, settlements, or the basic political subdivisions were central to the concerns, political and otherwise, of the colonists. Generally speaking, parishes and counties emerged as the basic units for government in the South mainly because the population was thinly dispersed and the daily life of most inhabitants centered around plantations. Towns or townships composed the basic units of local governance in the Northern colonies. Here, in contrast to the southern colonies, the units of local governance, the towns, were the constituent parts of the colony that had emerged in the natural course of its founding and growth. The northern colonies also enjoyed greater democracy at the local level than their counterparts in the South, where control was confined largely to elites in the parishes. In the middle colonies both forms, to one degree or another, could be found even within the same colony. In all sections there was a recognition that certain commercial centers with large populations, for example, Charlestown, Philadelphia, New York, required a special status to meet their needs effectively.

Perhaps, as Tocqueville intimates, the political associations in New England provide the best parallels to our later experiences in seeking to unify the thirteen colonies and states. The Fundamental Orders of Connecticut (1638–39) created our first confederation by uniting the "inhabitants and residents of Windsor, Hartford, and Wethersfield" into "one public state or commonwealth" for the ordering and disposition "of the affairs of the people at all seasons as occasion shall require."[2] Although the institutions of the newly created government are spelled out in the Fundamental Orders, its powers are not. Instead what we find are the general goals of union, such as the maintenance or preservation of "peace and union," "the liberty and purity of the gospel," "the discipline of the churches"—goals that could not be accomplished by the settlements singly and on which there seemed to be a collective consensus.[3] Clearly, under the terms of the Fundamental Orders, the towns were left with considerable authority to conduct their affairs free from the control of the central authority that they had created.

Developments in Massachusetts were somewhat the reverse of those in Connecticut. Five years after the founding of Massachusetts, the existing central authority (the General Court) bestowed authority on the towns, already multiplying at a rapid rate. Recognizing that "particular towns have many things which concern only themselves," the General Court provided that they should have authority to "make such orders as may concern the well-ordering of their own towns."[4] Over the years, the towns acquired a high degree of independence. The central authority, in the main, performed functions such as settling boundary disputes or providing aid in emergencies that lay beyond the capacity of the towns to fulfill individually.

We gain further insight into early thinking about the division of authority in confederations by looking at the New England Confederation (1643), a union between the independent Puritan governments of Massachusetts, New Plymouth, Connecticut, and New Haven. To begin with, we should note that despite the high degree of commonality among these settlements, Connecticut rejected the initial proposal for union offered by Massachusetts that called for decision making by simple majorities in the confederation's single legislative chamber. The plan finally agreed to stopped short of calling for unanimity by providing that at least six of the eight representatives, two from each settlement, would be necessary for any action by the confederation. More significantly, the powers of the Confederation were quite limited. Indeed, its overall purpose was primarily one of protecting the members of the confederation. "The said colonies," according to the Second Article of the Confederation, "for themselves and their posterity, do jointly and severally hereby enter into a firm and perpetual league of friendship and amity for offence and defence, mutual advice and succor upon all just occasion both for preserving and propagating the truth and liberty of the Gospel and for their own mutual safety and welfare."[5] The Articles also provided that the commissioners from the settlements might also "endeavor to frame and establish agreements and orders in general cases of a civil nature, wherein all the plantations are interested." But Article 3 of the agreement made clear that "the peculiar jurisdiction and government" of the settlements were beyond change or control by the confederation. Article 6 emphasized the nature and limits of the confederation by pointing out that the purposes of the confederation were "amity, offence, and defence; not intermeddling with the government of any of the Jurisdictions."[6] Each jurisdiction, moreover, bore responsibility for meeting the requisitions that might be placed on it by the confederation, the confederacy itself lacking any means to force compliance.

Benjamin Franklin's Albany Plan, proposed in 1754, offers an interesting parallel to the New England Confederation. Two differences are immediately apparent. First, the union suggested in Franklin's plan is far more extensive than that envisioned by the New England Confederation. Second, it is entirely secular, making no appeal to common religious beliefs and purposes. Nevertheless, the documents share one overriding purpose, the protection or defense of their members. As Franklin put the matter, the proposed union would overcome the difficulties that had been experienced in securing the united and coordinated support of the colonies in resisting French aggression. Indeed, Franklin believed that the union might well prevent further invasions, perceiving that "one principal encouragement to the French . . . was their knowledge of disunited states, and of our weakness arising from such want of union." In addition to this, the government created by the Albany Plan would be better able than individual colonies to conclude effective commercial treaties with the Indians, as well as to "make Peace and declare War" with the various Indian tribes. As in the New England Confederation, there was an understanding of the limited powers of the Albany Union. Its powers, as Franklin makes clear, "*are such only* as shall be necessary for the government of the settlements; the raising, regulating and paying soldiers for the general service; the regulating of Indian trade, and laying and collecting the general duties and taxes [for these purposes]. . . . It is not intended," he continues, "that they [the agencies of the Union] may interfere with the constitution and government of the particular colonies; who are left to their own laws, and to lay, levy, and apply their own taxes as before."[7] Finally, in order to overcome the hurdles attendant on obtaining the consent of each colony and to ensure that colonies might not withdraw from the union, the plan called upon parliament to establish the union through a legislative act.

Two major problems that subsequently arose with respect to the Articles and the Constitution reveal themselves in these early efforts. The first involved assuring the constituent units that the central authority would confine itself to its stated missions. This, in turn, emanated from a concern to preserve local prerogatives and powers from interference by the new general authority. At the same time there was an awareness of centripetal forces that could disrupt the union or cause difficulties in securing compliance with the legitimate demands of union by the constituent units.

The Articles and the Constitution

For decades, until the end of the French and Indian War (1763), the colonies enjoyed a high degree of self-government due to the British the policy of "salutary neglect." This arrangement included a tacit federalism. The colonies were largely free to handle their own local affairs, although external or foreign affairs were handled by England. The arrangement, for reasons we need not go into here, changed markedly after the French and Indian War. Indeed, the efforts of England to control certain aspects of the internal affairs of the colonies were among the colonists' basic grievances.

In light of the colonial experiences, it is scarcely surprising that our first attempt at national union, the Articles of Confederation, resulted in a weak confederacy that, in effect, allowed the states to retain sovereignty. But viewed from a wider perspective, the Articles reflect a tension that has manifested itself in various ways throughout our nation's history. On one side, it called for a "perpetual union," throughout pointing to the desirability and need for a central authority to handle such matters as disputes between the states, defense, and diplomatic relations. The third article refers to the government as a "firm league of friendship" among the states instituted "for their common defense, the security of their Liberties, and their mutual and general welfare."[8] The last article stipulates that "Every state shall abide by the determinations of the united states in congress assembled, on all questions which by this confederation are submitted to them."[9] Yet, as we know, the government under the Articles did not operate as originally envisioned because, lacking adequate means to enforce its will, the central government proved no match for the state governments that wanted to go their separate ways. The failure of a number of states to meet their financial obligations by ignoring the requisitions placed on them by Congress is, perhaps, the most telling sign of the need for a stronger central government. In sum, under the Articles the centripetal forces and interests were too strong for the centrifugal impulses.

The Articles in some respects reflected the tension between unity and separateness evident in the Declaration of Independence, wherein we find reference to "one people" and to "these United Colonies" alongside the affirmation that they "ought to be . . . Free and Independent States" with the authority to "levy War, conclude Peace, contract Alliance, establish Commerce, and to do all other Acts and Things which INDEPENDENT STATES may of right do."[10] In any event, the operations of the government under the Articles clearly revealed that an effective and lasting union of states would require a stronger central government, which in turn would require the states to relinquish control over certain concerns and activities. The essence of the difficulty, however, was not over what powers or authority the states had to relinquish but how the decisions of the national government could be made in order to secure the states against national encroachment. On this point, as Madison remarks at various points in *The Federalist,* the proposed constitution is similar to the Articles. It recognizes the states as independent and sovereign bodies, and the powers it confers on the central government, save principally for control over commerce, are essentially the same.

This point may be put another way: In arguments for a "stronger" national government the basic concern was to secure the compliance of the component units, not to add powers, except power over commerce, which was regarded on all sides to be essential. Thus, in the Philadelphia

Convention the major issue confronting our Founding Fathers was never over whether the states would have to surrender portions of sovereignty to the central government. That much was taken for granted, with an understanding as well as to what the portions would be. To appreciate this, we need only look to the New Jersey (Paterson or "small state") Plan that was offered as an alternative to the Virginia Plan by delegates who were the most concerned about protecting the independence of the states. Under the terms of this plan the new national government would possess all the powers provided for in the Articles plus the powers to raise revenues and control commerce. The differences between the Virginia and New Jersey Plans were significant, the structure of government in the New Jersey Plan, for example, a unicameral legislature with states represented equally, designed to protect the states against unwarranted intrusions by the national government into their internal affairs. On the matter of powers to be vested in the national government, however, the plans were not far apart.

In an important sense the Constitutional Convention can be viewed as an effort to find the proper balance between the states and national authority, between the need for unity and the interests and loyalties supporting independence for the states. In this regard one of the major and essential differences centered on the nature of the states: Were the states to be considered, as the nationalists were wont to do, as artificial political units within a large national society? Or were they, in reality, political societies in their own right that should be treated as equals? These different perspectives were at the heart of the bitter debate over representation in the Senate—an issue that almost led to the breakup of the convention in mid-July. William Johnson, a delegate to the Constitutional Convention from Connecticut and a supporter of equal representation of the states in the Senate, put the basic issue between the two sides in perspective in his remarks on 29 June. "The controversy must be endless," he maintained, "whilst Gentlemen differ in the grounds of their arguments; Those on one side considering the States as districts of people composing one political society; those on the other considering them as so many political societies."[11] Johnson and others who shared his view of the states wanted equal state representation in recognition of the fact that the states were political societies and to provide some defense for the states against encroachments by the national government.

What we see at the Philadelphia Convention are the same kinds of concerns that were evident with respect to the more limited unions of the New England Confederation and the Albany Plan, chief among these providing some assurances that the central authority would not overstep its bounds. To a significant degree this was provided for by equality of state representation in the Senate, with senators elected by the state legislatures. Once the equality of states was provided for in the Senate, many of those most fearful of new and stronger national government threw their support behind it, largely because they felt this mode of representation provided sufficient protection against a meddlesome national government.

The Constitution and Centralization

Since the major problems associated with union were known from earlier experiences, there would seem to have been a consensus on the proper division of powers between the central authority and the constituent units. But if this assessment is essentially correct, we must view the issue of federalism—the division of authority between the states and national government—from a perspective that is different from the currently prevailing one in regard to its origins. In the first place, the mainline nationalist position at the Philadelphia Convention was never to concentrate all powers in the hands of the central government or to vest the national government with authority over the affairs handled by states, local governments, or communities. The nationalist would have allowed the room or space to which we have referred that is necessary for the existence and growth of communities. With regard to extent of national powers, the nationalists seemed to be guided by the basic principle embodied in their Virginia Plan; that is, the national legislature would have the powers vested in the congress of the confederation plus the authority "to legislate in all cases to which the Separate States are incompetent, or in which the harmony of the United States may be interrupted by the exercise of individual legislation."[12] We see that this formulation was expanded somewhat after the Great Compromise to grant the national legislature power "to legislate in all cases for the general interests of the Union." This broadening of the scope of national concern was defended on grounds that only the central government, not an individual state, was competent "to legislate for the *general interest* of the Union."[13] Finally, as we know, the convention enumerated the powers of the national government, an enumeration that seems in accord with the more general formulations.

Whereas federalism today is frequently pictured in terms of a compromise between competing forces at the Philadelphia Convention, our view suggests that the division of authority by itself was never a matter of substantial controversy. The very terms of the Virginia Plan, as well as the experiences of wider political union to that point in time, indicate that there was a consensus surrounding the purposes of such unions. From this vantage point, our modern understanding of federalism was tacitly assumed by the Founders to be the proper division of powers and authority; that is, consonant with the general formulations in the convention, a division that enabled the central government to do that which the states singly were unable to do or could do only with difficulty. To put this still another way, we are inclined to impose theoretical symmetry on the Framers' handiwork by picturing it as a compromise between a consolidated, national, or unitary form and the confederate form. This in-between status, what we today call federalism, is not without its difficulties, which have served to undermine the very idea in the eyes of many modern commentators. Perhaps the most serious difficulty is that federalism raises the specter of divided sovereignty, which seems to pose insoluble problems. Yet the division of powers set forth in the Constitution conformed with existential reality, as well as with the prevailing understanding of how powers should be distributed and exercised. This understanding was the outgrowth of an organic process, not a theoretical dialectic, so that what seems impossible in theory was, in fact, a reality for the Founders. This perhaps explains why Alexander Hamilton, certainly one of the most ardent nationalists, could describe the proposed system in *Federalist* 9 as one that leaves the states with "certain exclusive and very important portions of sovereign power."[14] Or why Madison pictured the new government in essentially the same terms in *Federalist* 39, where he observes that the jurisdiction of the national government "extends to certain enumerated objects only, and leaves to the several States a residuary and inviolable sovereignty over all other objects."[15]

Viewing federalism as a division of powers and purposes that accorded with the common sense and sensibilities of the Founders and ratifiers alike, we come to understand the controversies surrounding it in a different light. For instance, during the ratification process, the anti-Federalists sought to reinforce the barriers against any intrusion of the national government into the internal affairs of the states, ultimately leading to the adoption of the first ten amendments (the Bill of Rights). Of particular interest in this respect, of course, is the Tenth Amendment, which makes explicit the implicit understanding with regard to the constitutional division of powers, that is, those powers not delegated to the national government are reserved to the states or to the people. This amendment, combined with the Ninth Amendment, was intended to mark out explicitly the barriers to national authority, and to ensure that the national government would be confined to the general ends for which it was established.

Over the decades the effect of the Tenth Amendment has been to treat federalism largely as a legal or constitutional issue usually without an awareness of the evolutionary process and the underlying rationale that originally produced this division of power. Because, as a practical matter, the Supreme Court has come to be regarded as the logical institution to settle controversies surrounding the proper boundaries of state/national powers, it is not difficult to see why federalism probably receives its most serious treatment today in courses on constitutional law, albeit from a perspective that is not likely to yield any durable principles. We can also understand why, today, federalism is widely held to be little more than an "inert legalism" or, if not that, an anachronism.[16]

Federalism and the Principle of Subsidiarity

As our discussion to this point indicates, however, there is another way of looking at the development of our federal system that places the role of communities and local governments relative to the national government in perspective and, at the same time, provides us with guidelines and criteria, distinctly nonlegal, by which to judge whether this relationship is out of kilter or not. We refer here to the principle of subsidiarity, at least the dimension of it that deals with the distribution of powers. This principle seems to go a long way toward explaining the basis for the division of powers in the New England Confederation, the Albany Plan, the Articles of Confederation, the Constitution, as well as in the colonies and states.

Although the principle of subsidiarity has it roots in Catholic social teachings, it embodies practical and functional principles with regard to the distribution of authority that would seem to be universally applicable.[17] In the context of our political system it holds that the national government ought not to assume functions that can be performed at "lower" levels, that is, by state and local governments or by nongovernmental associations such as communities and intermediate groups. Put otherwise, according to this principle, the responsibility for the performance of a given function ought to be vested in the lowest level in a hierarchy—stretching from the lowest or more basic levels (the individual and family) through intermediate associations (e.g., voluntary groups, local communities) up to the highest level (the national government)—that is capable of performing that function. As a corollary, the principle would also dictate that if a task can be accomplished through private, voluntary efforts, it should not be undertaken by public or governmental agencies.

That the Founders thought in terms of the subsidiary principle, although they did not articulate it as such, is seen in the general formula, first set forth in the Virginia Plan, for determining what powers the central government ought to possess. It is also evident in their understanding of the character of the division of powers provided for in the Constitution. Perhaps the best overview we have of this division of authority is Madison's statement in *Federalist* 45: "The Powers delegated by the proposed Constitution to the Federal Government are few and defined.

Those which are to remain in the State Governments," he continues, "are numerous and indefinite." He perceived that the national powers were concerned primarily with "external objects, as war, peace, negotiation, and foreign commerce"; whereas those remaining with the "several States" would "extend to all the objects, which, in the ordinary course of affairs, concern the lives, liberties, and properties of the people; and the internal order, improvement, and prosperity of the State."[18] Hamilton's understanding of what was provided for by the Constitution was virtually the same. His formulation set forth in *Federalist* 23 stressed the ends of the national government as providing for the "common defense," securing the "public peace," regulating "commerce with other nations and between the States," and conducting foreign relations; that is, ends of a scope and nature that could be achieved effectively and efficiently only through a central government.[19]

Normative elements of the subsidiary principle come into play when we ask why functions should devolve upon the lowest level capable of fulfilling them. What are the costs involved in a central authority, such as our national government, gathering all functions to itself, even those that can adequately be performed at lower levels by constituent organizations? The answers to this question proceed from an understanding that society is the natural state, that man is by nature a social being. In the end, centralization in violation of the subsidiary principle not only leads to the degeneration of society but also eventually weakens (if not destroys) the individual's inherent and distinctive capacities as a human being. Specifically, unnecessary centralization deprives the individual of meaningful participation at those levels most important for developing a sense of initiative, obligation, and responsibility. The feelings of achievement, the sense of reward or accomplishment, would not be his, nor would he develop friendships through cooperative enterprises. His growth as a human being with creative potential, free choice, and dignity would be stunted. The situation, in sum, would not be unlike that of children whose parents have continually protected and coddled them at every turn throughout their lives, making all decisions for them, providing for their every want, thereby depriving them of the opportunity to develop and assume the responsibility of adults. Another analogy is to be found in individuals who, after having been liberated from the grips of highly centralized regimes, find themselves at a loss in exercising liberty, incapable even of making decisions over the simplest concerns.

But realizing obvious goods such as individual fulfillment; a sense of duty, obligation, and responsibility; a feeling of efficacy; a refined sense of justice—in sum, the goods that are associated with the subsidiarity principle—is problematic even in a political system whose constitution closely conforms with the subsidiarity principle. Subsidiarity, more exactly, is a necessary but not sufficient condition for the growth and full development of an individual's character and capabilities in the sense we have spoken of them. The goods that subsidiarity promises can only come when the citizens are virtuous; they do not come as a matter of course. As experience teaches us, following the subsidiarity principle may well result in communities, neighborhoods, and voluntary associations acting in a manner that divides or undermines the community, thwarts self-realization and fulfillment, and debases any sense of responsibility and cooperation. Such is the legacy of groups with ulterior motives that sometimes dominate communities or local jurisdictions.

This realization brings us to one of the key issues surrounding the underlying assumptions of our constitutional order. (These assumptions, in turn, point to the central role of families, communities, voluntary associations, and local governments—public and private entities at the lower levels—in providing for decent and orderly government at the highest levels.) To begin with, there are substantial reasons to believe that the Founding Fathers, although certainly not consciously thinking in terms of the subsidiary principle as such, subscribed nevertheless to the proposition that their pragmatic brand of federalism would provide ample room for the development of communities, private intermediate associations, and subsidiary groups of various kinds, along with wide authority for local and state governments. They undoubtedly believed that the level of morality and virtue of the people was sufficient to cultivate the potential virtues rendered possible by subsidiarity. In this connection, we should note, they certainly must have believed that the people, though far from perfect, at least possessed sufficient virtue for the new constitutional order—a new political order that provided for a degree of popular control unprecedented at that point in history. In this context a critical question that often arises is normally put as follows: How or by what means did the Framers believe the virtue necessary for the system would be cultivated and maintained? How, in other words, did they suppose the moral character and virtue of the people, so essential for republican regimes, could be maintained at sufficient levels so that the regime might endure for the ages? There is no easy answer to this question. We find no constitutional provision relating to, say, education that might bear upon this question.

The Constitution and the Problem of Virtue and Community

Over the years some scholars have suggested that the Framers anticipated that a national university would be established in order to educate future leaders who would provide for intelligent and moral leadership, thereby emphasizing for public consumption the values necessary to perpetuate and even improve the regime. Yet even if the Constitution is stretched to allow for the establishment of such a college, such a solution seems far from adequate given the magnitude of the problem of virtue and community.

The deliberations at the Philadelphia Convention proceeded as if this problem were really not a problem, certainly not one requiring a solution through any constitutional provisions, for example, granting appropriate powers to the national government in areas that would bear on this matter. Likewise, certain crucial positions and arguments in *The Federalist* are based on the presumption of a people sufficiently virtuous for self-government. At one point Madison even acknowledges that "Republican government" depends to a greater degree "than any other form" on those "qualities in human nature" that "justify a certain portion of esteem and confidence." He also recognizes that those backing the Constitution are assuming a "sufficient virtue among men for self-government,"[20] as he does in presenting his arguments for the proposed Constitution. For example, in explaining how the extensiveness of the new republic will serve to thwart the designs of majority "factions"—groups seeking ends "adverse to the rights of other citizens, or to the permanent and aggregate interests of the community"—he emphasizes the role of representation and representatives.[21] He maintains that "public views" when passed though "the medium of a chosen body of citizens" might well be "more consonant to the public, than if pronounced by the people themselves." Such a proposition, of course, depends on unarticulated assumptions, the most notable of these being that "fit characters," that is, those "whose wisdom may best discern the true interest of their country, and whose patriotism and love of justice, will be least likely to sacrifice it to temporary or partial considerations." Moreover, the voters will opt for these "fit characters."[22] Clearly, then, the presumption is that the voters know what virtues are necessary for representatives most likely to advance the national interest and resist the temptations of factions, both majority and minority.

Still another component of Madison's solution to the problem of factions simply assumes an electorate with sufficient character to foil the efforts of factions. The multiplicity and diversity of interests in the extended republic, he contends, render the existence of a "common motive" for the formation of unjust or repressive majorities less likely than in the small republic with fewer distinct interests. But even if, he continues, such a common motive were to exist, "a consciousness of unjust or dishonorable purposes" would severely restrict the communications necessary for the formation of a majority faction.[23] Such an argument again presumes that there exists among the people generally shared notions of what is "unjust" and "dishonorable" and that there is a moral consensus that can serve to thwart the formation of factious majorities, while not impeding the formation of well intentioned majorities.

Even supposing that factious majorities might overcome the impediments posed by the multiplicity and diversity of interest of the extended republic and get their way in the House of Representatives, Madison holds out prospects that the Senate and president might delay the passage of such factious measures, thereby providing the opportunity for "reason, justice and truth" to "regain their authority over the public mind."[24] For this delay to operate in the fashion Madison anticipates, however, rests on another unarticulated assumption relative to the character of the people, namely, that they possess a morality sensitive to the demands of the common good and the principles of justice. Stated otherwise, delay and deliberation will not deter those bent on committing wrongs; they will instead only provide the opportunity for more resourceful scheming. They will, however, make an enormous difference for those with the capacity and inclination to act virtuously.

In sum, while not spelled out explicitly in *The Federalist,* an underlying morality, not unlike that alluded to above, is clearly indispensable for the proper operations of the political system designed by the Framers. Moreover, it is a morality that must be perpetuated for the regime to endure. It embraces not only the virtues necessary to avoid divisive factionalism but also specific "constitutional" prescriptions that outline the proper roles, functions, and relationships of the institutions for the system to operate as designed.

To this, we hasten to add, *The Federalist* provides no answer to the question of how to maintain the virtue necessary for the regime. It offers no solutions, plans, or regime for inculcating or maintaining the requisite virtues. Nor should we expect it to, if our view of the evolutionary development of our political institutions is essentially correct. If, as seems clear, our political development up to the founding period is one in which communities and localities were successively linked into an ever expanding political universe, the most expansive of which is the national government created by the Constitution, this process necessarily had to proceed on the common values, beliefs, and morality that had already been nourished and refined within the constituent local units. And if, as we have endeavored to show, the Founders operated within a framework conformable with the subsidiary principle, perpetuating a level of morality appropriate for the regime was simply not considered to be a matter within the realm or control of the national government. This alone accounts for the fact that even *The Federalist* does not address this matter. Simply put, those of the founding era simply believed that the task of character formation through education in virtue was the responsibility of the "lower," or more basic institutions on the hierarchy, that is, church, family, community, and local governments. The responsibility of these institutions extended as well to sustaining and even enhancing the morality necessary for the regime.

Numerous statements from the writings of the Founding era and before could be cited to illustrate that a high degree of virtue was necessary for an orderly and decent republican government but that its cultivation primarily depended on institutions other than government. Typical are Jeremiah Atwater's views that address the problem of virtue in a republican regime by stressing the need for good citizenship through formative processes. This task, he writes, necessarily begins in the family where children "are taught habits of subordination and respect." It continues through schooling, where "the seeds of knowledge and virtue are sown in the youthful mind." In America, as Atwater puts it, "man, from the cradle to the grave, is constantly learning new lessons of moral instruction, and is trained to virtue and order by perpetual and salutary restraints," one of which he deems to be "public opinion." Echoing the observations of many commentators of this era, he notes that "in a country where christianity is believed, [public opinion] compels even profligates to be outwardly virtuous."[25]

One very plausible answer, then, to the question that the authors of *The Federalist* and the Founders left unanswered is, simply, that they took for granted what Atwater articulates: the family, church, and communities, the most basic human associations, would produce the morality needed for the constitutional system to operate as intended. This, in turn, meant that these institutions and associations possessed and would continue to possess the authority to assume that role in the moral and intellectual development of individuals associated with the principle of subsidiarity.

Centralization, Community, and the Erosion of Virtue

What is disturbing from the conservative perspective is that these primary institutions and associations have atrophied. The very sources of the virtue necessary for a moral regime are no longer functioning, at least not in the manner intended. This is alarming because the national government is itself only a synthetic institution lacking the wherewithal to operate as a substitute source of morality, a reality that becomes more apparent with each passing year. Thus the nation increasingly finds itself without a moral compass to guide it or by which to measure its behavior.

The reasons for our problems today are numerous and go well beyond politics as normally defined. But if we are essentially correct in our foregoing account of the organic development of the American system, one major problem would seem to revolve around the shrinking role played by the primary associations and institutions at the local or basic levels of human interaction in molding the character of individuals in the fashion anticipated by the subsidiary principle. To put this in terms that we used at the outset, the "room" or "space" originally provided for in the Constitution, which would at least allow for the "lower" institutions, both private and public, to cultivate individual character and morality, has notably diminished. The specific reasons for this are complex but they stem from the expansion of governmental powers and their centralization in the national government, a development prompted and sustained by a conviction that the national government can remedy any manner of social ills and problems and also produce a "national community" whose members share elevated moral principles.

Space does not permit an exhaustive examination of specific examples illustrating the degree to which this centralization, motivated by the best of intentions, has ignored the most fundamental elements of the subsidiary principle. Nevertheless, certain major developments are worthy of note because taken as a whole they show a shift of attitudes concerning the proper role of the government. First, the purposes and functions of our political system have changed drastically since the Founders' time. In *Federalist* 10, Madison could write that the "regulation of . . . various and interfering interests forms the principal task of modern legislation."[26] In these terms the government was to act as a referee or an arbiter among the conflicting, multiple, and diverse interests of the extended republic. As such, it was to be a relatively passive government, playing the rule of judge and jury. While the Congress now and then went beyond simply playing this role even in the early decades of the republic, it is safe to say that with the coming of the New Deal in the depression of the 1930s, the system permanently and unalterably shifted gears, so to speak, and assumed a positive role in providing for the security and well-being of its citizens. The "Great Society" programs initiated by President Johnson in the 1960s enormously expanded this welfare state, so that today—despite the failures and even counterproductive effects of these programs—American citizens look to the national government to provide services that in prior times fell to individuals, communities, and private charities.

The effects of this change in orientation are difficult overstate. Albert Jay Nock, an outspoken libertarian critic of the New Deal, saw in its implementation a transfer of what he called "social" power to the state. What once was considered within the realm of social control and responsibility was, with the advent of the New Deal, shifted to the central government. And he writes tellingly of our disposition for charitable giving after the transfer of this responsibility. "When a beggar asks us for a quarter," he observes, "our instinct is to say that the State has already confiscated our quarter for his benefit, and he should go to the State about it."[27] Because the national government possesses a near monopoly on the most bountiful and best source of revenues, the progressive income tax, communities, private charities, and local governments now find it impossible to meet demands. Thus, at the lower "tiers," the welfare state erodes voluntarism as well as the sense of responsibility—the task of providing charity, helping the less fortunate, now being assumed by a remote, faceless government. The orientation of the individual shifts from local to national.

Still another aspect of this shift from passive to active or positive government involves a new understanding of the scope and breadth of community. The New Deal, we must note in passing, is generally acknowledged to be the outgrowth of progressive thought and programs set forth in the earlier part of the twentieth century. The theory stressed the need for centralization in order, among other things, to make the nation more of a "community" than it had previously been. The drastic changes needed in the social and economic order for this purpose could only be accomplished through a strong central government. As this progressive thinking gained acceptance, our understanding of "general welfare" changed as well. Revealing in this regard is the debate in the House of Representatives over whether the national government should aid Savannah after it had been ravaged by the fire of 1796.[28] The arguments for extending aid were strong: Savannah was an important port city; it was a commercial center for the South; the aid would soon be recovered with increased revenues; and, among others, the citizens of Savannah desperately needed help. Yet the House rejected extending aid by a margin of over two to one, the major reason being that if aid were extended to Savannah, then it would have to be extended to all such cities and towns that had similar catastrophes, a responsibility Congress was not about to assume. The House clearly did not share our modern understanding of general welfare for it felt that the *general* welfare power could not be stretched to embrace aid to specific localities. Thus it left the restoration of Savannah in the hands of individuals, private charities, and the state and local governments.

In this connection, Nock's remarks concerning the Johnstown flood of 1889, which resulted in the deaths of over two thousand people, are pertinent. "When the . . . flood occurred," he writes, "social power was immediately mobilized and applied with intelligence and vigor. Its abundance, measured by money alone, was so great that when everything was finally put in order, something like a million dollars remained. If such a catastrophe happened now," he concludes, "not only is social power perhaps too depleted for the like exercise, but the general instinct would be to let the State see to it."[29] This provides another measure of how far our notions concerning general welfare have changed, no doubt in part due to the feeling that we compose a national community wherein there is an obligation to help localities in times of need. Whatever the reason, the change of disposition is significant, national aid flowing now as a matter of course for almost any misfortune that makes the national news.

There is scarcely any need to document how Congress's commerce power has been used to regulate matters traditionally regarded as well within the realm of the police powers reserved to the states—the direct result of the Supreme Court having to redefine commerce powers very broadly in order for the national government to meet the needs of the positive, welfare state. During the early decades of the twentieth century it was generally understood that, in recognition of the states' police powers, national enforcement of the prohibition on the manufacture, transportation, and sale of "intoxicating liquors" was thought to require an amendment to the Constitution. Today, however, it is widely acknowledged that the Congress could accomplish the same ends as the Eighteenth Amendment through simple legislation. In sum, constitutional federalism seems to have disappeared, and the Congress is now free to use the commerce powers to achieve what the states individually could not. The danger in this situation, of course, is that the Congress will feel free to assume functions best left in the hands of the people at the local levels, a practice that critics contend has already taken root.

Still other practices on the part of Congress could be cited that at least undermine the original understanding of national/state relationships. Often, for example, it uses the threat of withholding substantial sums of money from the states unless they comply with national standards. But the issues involved in this process go well beyond the use of the funds to extort state compliance. As most students of federalism are well aware, the state governments stand in need of federal monies, which in recent decades are dispensed through grant-in-aid programs that require some percentage of matching funds on the part of the states. The national government sets the terms for participation in these grant-in-aid programs, which serves to subordinate state and local governments to the control of the national government. Moreover, as governors, mayors, and other local officials point out, many grant-in-aid programs do not address the needs of the state or local communities. Political considerations, however, dictate that states and localities participate in these programs whether needed or not rather than forgo federal dollars. The net effect of these programs, consequently, goes well beyond the national government's setting priorities for localities by undermining the fiscal capacity of state and local governments to meet the felt needs of their communities.

It should be noted that the principle of subsidiarity does not always provide clear-cut answers to the kinds of problems that have arisen in American federalism concerning the proper domains of state and federal authority. Changing economic conditions, technological developments, altered patterns of life, threats to the national security, and the like often force the Congress to take action in areas that formerly were regarded to be well within the domain of the states. National speed limits, set at a time when there was genuine concern about our national defense due to dependency on foreign fuel, offer one such example. And the difficulties in drawing lines becomes even more difficult if we take into account another facet of the subsidiarity principle, namely, that the various levels should cooperate and help one another so that each can perform its functions. At one level, as we have seen, this means that the national government should forbear from needlessly assuming the functions of organizations, either public or private, in the lower reaches of the hierarchy. It also means that these organizations should willingly cooperate with the national government on matters central to its main purposes, even to the extent of ceding powers or responsibilities.

As intrusive as Congress has been on occasion, as damaging as its actions may have been to the ability of communities and local governments to deal their own problems, the Supreme Court has been far more persistent and destructive. Its decisions in recent decades have deprived localities of their authority to handle matters at the very core of their being. The Court has imposed its own notions of what constitutes due process in criminal cases upon the states, which, in the view of many, has severely weakened the criminal justice system at the local levels throughout the country. Its doctrinaire views of the religious clauses of the First Amendment have secularized the schools and the "public square," depriving communities and localities the benefits that would arise from the cooperation and involvement of religious groups and organizations whose efforts at ameliorating major social problems have proven more effective than those of government. It has authorized the lower courts to take control of entire public school systems, to order busing on the basis of race, and even to tax for the construction of new schools, taking away from neighborhoods their traditional controls over schools and education. It has allowed the federal courts to second-guess local school officials on matters of discipline in the schools, contributing in no small measure to their decline. It has overturned local laws designed to control obscenity, nudity, and pornography, in the process setting forth standards that permit the debasement of our culture. It has even eliminated state and local residency requirements for voting in local and state elections, decreeing new requirements that not only allow those with little knowledge of local conditions or candidates to vote but also those (such a college students temporarily residing in college towns) with no stake at all in the community.

Policies of the Court that have weakened the "lower" tiers in our federal system could be extended well beyond this. The morality, principles, and standards that it uses are, we are coming to recognize, of its own making; they did emerge over the course of time from the frustrations of the people with their communities and local governments. Nor do the Court's values and guiding principles constitute part of a tradition, developed over the years through the trials and tribulations of communities, local governments, or private associations in dealing with concerns closest to them. On the contrary, the creed to which the Court subscribes in dictating to communities and local governments is of its own making, originating in sources independent of society and the tradition. It bears a close affinity to the standards and morality that attach to the progressive vision of a national "community" marked by "enlightened" norms and principles whose inherent worth should be evident to all. As a consequence, one of the major difficulties in our present constitutional order can be put as follows: Whereas in the past the breeding ground for virtue and morality was the family, the church, voluntary associations, and the community, the source is now to be found at the national level, principally in the institution, the Supreme Court, that is most removed from an understanding of local concerns and problems.

Constitution and Community: A Final Word

As we noted at the outset, a constitution can only provide "room" or "space" for communities to flourish; it cannot create communities. The Framers may have felt they had provided for this space when they instituted a national government of delegated powers and limited authority, but our experience has been otherwise, increasingly so since the 1930s with Roosevelt's New Deal. A question that arises, then, is what additional safeguards might we add to the Constitution in order to ensure sufficient latitude for local communities, free from capricious and counterproductive control of the central authority. What additional constitutional provisions might serve to preserve the integrity of the subsidiary principle in light of our experience?

Two such provisions come to mind. First, some way of providing for a division of revenues might be devised, perhaps along the lines employed in the German Federal Republic, so that the states would not be fiscally dependent on the central government. Such a provision would remove the leverage the national government now enjoys over the states. Moreover, it would allow states and localities to set their own priorities, and thus spend their money as they see fit.

A second provision would be to establish a "neutral" arbiter to handle jurisdictional disputes between the national and state governments. In recent decades, the Supreme Court has abdicated its responsibility in this area, allowing Congress free rein. Moreover, the Court is itself an agency of the national government, which scarcely renders it an impartial umpire. Thus the object of this provision would be to constitute a body that would not be naturally disposed to favor one government over the other.

Something should be done to curtail the Supreme Court's needless and harmful intrusions into the affairs of states, localities, and communities. Whether this can be accomplished short of an amendment to the Constitution depends on Congress. If, that is, enforcement of the Fourteenth Amendment could be returned to Congress under the terms set forth in Section 5, there is every reason to believe that the states and localities would have a freer hand in dealing with certain of their most difficult problems.

Perhaps it is easier to point out what the safeguards should be than to effectuate them. But what seems apparent is that our system as presently constituted seems ill equipped to prevent even further centralization. Unless some structural changes are made, communities, in any genuine sense, face the prospect of extinction.

4

Mr. Emerson's Tombstone

Wilfred M. McClay

Few small American towns exude a more winning charm than Concord, Massachusetts. Much of that charm flows from the respectful but unpretentious way that Concord has preserved its many claims to historical importance—an uncommon achievement in today's America. On the northern edge of town stands an evocative reminder of Revolutionary Concord: a faithful reconstruction of the "rude bridge" where, in April of 1775, a ragtag band of American citizen-soldiers repulsed the British effort to seize their supply depot and fired "the shot heard 'round the world.' " And a visitor strolling the town's peaceful streets has little difficulty imagining the Concord of antebellum times, when that tiny town was a vibrant center of literary activity, during some of the best years of our nation's intellectual history. In those days, Concord could claim such distinguished residents as Ralph Waldo Emerson (who wrote the "Concord Hymn" quoted above), Henry David Thoreau, Bronson and Louisa May Alcott, and sometime resident Nathaniel Hawthorne, whose brooding Old Manse still stands silent watch, at a safe and skeptical distance, over the hallowed eighteenth-century battlefield.

As it housed them in life, so Concord also provided their final resting place. All of them lie within conversational range of one another on Authors Ridge in Sleepy Hollow Cemetery, a rambling old burial ground that winds through picturesque hills and woods just a few hundred feet from the town center. A place of more than passing interest, it draws a steady stream of pilgrims seeking to connect with the lives of these eminent writers. But there is also something to be learned from the manner of their burial. For one thing, all are buried with their families on ancestral family plots. Nothing remarkable about that, you will say. And yet it still comes as a bit of a surprise to be reminded that even writers who exalted the self-sufficiency and radical freedom of the individual, as Emerson did, were in the end—before and after all else—other people's sons, daughters, brothers, sisters, husbands, and wives. Which is to say that their self-made identities were deeply rooted in conditions and relationships they did not choose and could not change. Sleepy Hollow is rich with such ironies for students of individualism and community in American life.

A cemetery is a fitting place for sober reflection. Infirmity and death are the great levelers, the surest reminders of our dependency, the most painful thorns in the flesh of human pride. Just as we cannot escape our bodies, we cannot escape our origins. In death, the truth about us generally comes out. For example, it is only after the hero's death in F. Scott Fitzgerald's novel *The Great Gatsby* that we find the missing piece in the puzzle of who Jay Gatsby really is, by meeting his grotesque father. At Sleepy Hollow one can glean similar insights. Take the case of Thoreau. In his life, and in his writings, there was no more fiercely independent soul; and yet the visitor to Sleepy Hollow has to look hard even to find his name, in the middle of a long list of Thoreaus engraved on the collective family tombstone, and on his tiny individual stone. The manner of Thoreau's burial gives us a subtle clue to something important about him, about the ways in which his independence was entwined with forms of dependency—something that his writings denied or at least did not tell us directly.

Similarly with Emerson's grave, even though it seems, at first glance, to be making a different statement. Being a man of comfortable means, Emerson could afford a large, freestanding marker. But instead of using a conventional tombstone, Emerson chose to mark the spot with a giant boulder. (It is identified as Emerson's grave by a small bronze plaque affixed to the rock.) Needless to say, it is a very striking sight—and not an entirely harmonious one. Amid the tidy lots and meticulously carved Yankee tombstones all around it, Emerson's boulder looks a little out of place—as if a grizzly bear or a mountain lion had somehow stumbled into a Junior League luncheon and seated himself. The stone itself is rough and ragged, as if it had been hauled up from deep in the bowels of the earth.

These are, no doubt, just the impressions Emerson would have liked us to receive. His writings consistently linked the values of untrammeled individualism and unconstrained Nature, and they disparaged the conformism and artificiality of settled village life. Hence this craggy tombstone would stand as permanent testimony to his intimate connection with the wild energies of Nature, and his infinite contempt for a life lived within the safe margins of the conventional and the decorative. One might say, ringing a change on Michelangelo, that such a tombstone sought to free the stone from the sculpture. Perhaps our age, with its self-conscious penchant for parody and self-disparagement, is less sympathetic to such a romantic and self-dramatizing gesture (though I would be more inclined to blame postmodernism's self-protective unwillingness to have the courage of its neoromantic convictions). But whether one finds Emerson's tombstone beautiful, arrogant, self-indulgent, ridiculous, or merely strange, one cannot deny that it makes a striking statement.

But there is one significant complication in the statement, or rather one element in the picture, that, when we notice it, subtly complicates the overall effect. It is the fact that Emerson's grand and scruffy self-representation is flanked by two smaller tombstones marking the graves of Emerson's wife, Lidian, and his daughter, Ellen. The two stones are identical in size, symmetrically placed, absolutely conventional in their shapes and engravings. They stand beside and support their man, like reliable and devoted aides-de-camp marching beside their wild and brilliant general. But their subordinate status does not change the fact that they are an integral part of the picture. Their prominence in Emerson's death points to their importance in his life. Indeed, it is a question not of political correctness but of historical correctness to insist that these women were indispensable to Emerson's success. For without the domestic stability and satisfaction provided by them, Emerson's pathbreaking career as itinerant lecturer, essayist, and freelance secular intellectual would have been inconceivable.

Any good biographer would point this out. But there is also a much larger point to be made here, one encompassing not only Emerson's marital arrangements, or relations between men and women in his day, but the entire tidy world of Concord and of the American Protestantism within which Emerson was nourished and against which he rebelled. No man is an island, let alone a freestanding boulder; and Emerson's brand of heroic individualism silently presupposed—indeed, it took utterly for granted—a profound degree of social order and a wide range of social, institutional, cultural, and moral supports provided by the family and community life into which he was born. In short, the two smaller tombstones that flank Mr. Emerson's tombstone do more than commemorate his domestic life. They also symbolize the larger cultural supports that made it possible for Emerson to explore the limits of a certain style of radical selfhood. An awareness of them should alert us to the fact that such "radical selves" are not nearly so radical and unencumbered as they seem. One might even say that it takes a village to raise them.

Constrained Individuality

Perhaps we appreciate the solidity of those supports in Emerson's day even more than he did, precisely because of the tenuous status they enjoy in our own. Individualism looks very different played out in the mean streets, broken homes, and moral dissensus of today's urban America than it did in the gentle walkways of Victorian Concord. It is the burden of what follows to explore some of the reasons why that is so. But there are some important questions to be addressed along the way. When and how did the Emersonian ideal of the autonomous self become so prevalent in American society? Was it implicit in the foundational ideas and events informing the very beginnings of American society? Or did it arise out of some evolution, deviation, or detour from those foundations along the road to the present? If the latter, then when and where did the detour occur? If the former, then what are the implications for those of us who believe the ideal has now become pernicious and destructive?

To begin answering these questions, we must first address ourselves to a still prevalent misunderstanding of American history, one that has grossly overemphasized the nation's "liberal" political tradition, with its emphasis on individual liberty and individual rights, to the exclusion of other elements in the nation's initial cultural makeup, particularly its religious traditions. The hold of that view has admittedly been fading. But it was not so very long ago that most serious students of American politics and society were confident that the United States had been born "liberal" and "modern" and that little more need be said of the matter. And why not? Everyone knew that the "first new nation" was erected on a solid foundation of antiaristocratic, antimonarchical, anticolonial sentiment, and antipapist sentiments. Everyone knew that the political works of John Locke were widely read in the colonies and that the natural-rights language of the Declaration of Independence unmistakably echoed Lockean phraseology.

The most eminent authorities, from Alexis de Tocqueville on, seemed agreed that America's national development had been decisively shaped by the absence of any serious entanglement with feudal, premodern institutions. The handful of attempts to found such institutions, such as the pathetic case of the Hudson Valley's Dutch landed patroons, only reinforced the general rule: the conditions of American life ensured that feudal and aristocratic institutions could never succeed there. Even a conservative like John Adams had lavished his prodigious energies on a fiercely polemical book celebrating Americans' freedom from "canon" (ecclesiastical) and "feudal" (aristocratic) law. It seemed plausible to argue, as Hegel, Goethe, and many others did, that America had come into the world without historical baggage—a living fragment of pure modernity. Having been detached from its compromising antecedents, it could now manifest in pure, uncompromised form a regime founded on universalized individual rights that Europe could manifest only partially and fractiously.

But this "liberal" view of American history is clearly inadequate, as a whole generation of scholars in American history and political thought has repeatedly demonstrated. It ignores the distinct and powerful elements of civic humanist or "republican" thinking in colonial and revolutionary America, elements that stressed the individual's necessary involvement in, and dedication to, the polity. It downplays the wide influence of Scottish moral philosophy, with its emphasis on the inherent sociality of human nature, and of faculty psychology, which stressed the need to subject the human passions to rational and social control. It gives short shrift to the elements of English institutional and legal tradition that profoundly shaped North American colonial life. But most of all, it downplays the immense and pervasive influence of reformed Protestant Christianity, especially as embodied in Calvinistic covenant theology and congregational church polity. Of course, too, these diverse influences manifested themselves differently in different regions of North America, making large-scale generalizations difficult. But the point is this: The "liberal" elements in American political thought must always be understood as being propounded in tension with other, more constraining—and more communitarian—views of human nature and human society. Protestant Christianity must be regarded as the most important of these constraining forces. To the extent that Protestantism underwrote an emphasis on individuality, it was in the form of a *constrained* individuality.

It takes a rather willful eye to miss the moral and communitarian effects of the Protestant tradition on early America. True, if looked at exclusively from the standpoint of its revolt against the authority of Rome or its emphasis on the priesthood of all believers, Protestantism could be seen as an essentially individualistic, even antinomian, variant on Christian orthodoxy—one that, moreover, carried the seeds of political liberalism in its theological rucksack, awaiting the day when those principles could be planted in secular soil. But this sort of secular-liberal triumphalism does not do justice to historical reality. Concrete instances nearly always demonstrate the existence of a fruitful tension between the individual and the communal, the liberating and the constraining, in American Protestantism.

Few documents from that period are more famous, or familiar to scholars, than John Winthrop's 1630 speech, "A Modell of Christian Charity," delivered aboard the *Arbella* as she traversed the Atlantic bound for the New World. Although Winthrop describes a community formed by the mutual consent of its individual members, his vision could hardly be less "liberal." It begins by endorsing the principle of social hierarchy as divinely ordained and concludes with a vision of the colony as a community "knit together in [its] work as one man," committed to "make others' conditions our own, rejoice together, mourn together, labor and suffer together, always having before our eyes our commission and community in the work, our community as members of the same body."[1] Winthrop understood the strength of the community to be inseparable from its commission, meaning the religious mission of the colony. Its communitarianism did not arise out of a mere dedication to community for community's sake—and the body in question was that of Christ.

The existence of such strong communitarian sentiments in colonial New England does not alter the fact that from its earliest days reformed Protestant theology laid an extraordinary level of stress on the dignity, worth, and responsibility of the individual person. But it never envisioned that individual as a radically free and unaccountable actor. Instead, it always understood individual liberty as operating under the direction of highly prescriptive and binding moral constraints. This was the essential core of the reformed Protestant view, and freedom was inconceivable apart from such limits.

Protestants affirmed the primacy of the individual conscience in moral deliberation—but with the understanding that the individual conscience was unconditionally subject to God's will, a will that could be known definitively by every individual person through an unmediated encounter with the Holy Scriptures. It emphasized the individual's need for conversion, for an active and vibrant faith in the person of Christ, and for devotion to a life of holiness, all the while recognizing that these were the fruits not of one's human efforts but of God's free gift of saving grace. Indeed, reformed theology highlighted the role of grace by reemphasizing the doctrine of original sin and therefore insisting on the need for powerful restraints and checks on the naturally self-interested passions and uncontrolled behavior of a fallen and depraved humanity.

This is not to deny that there were any purely "liberal" notions of political freedom in competition with (or in tension with) the reformed Protestant understanding. Indeed, one could argue that some such idea of liberty is entailed logically in even the most severe Calvinism. Man is given a broad freedom to choose, as set forth in Deuteronomy 30:19 (the very passage with which Winthrop ended his "Modell"), between "life and death, blessings and curses." The decision to submit to God in Christ means nothing unless it is an utterly uncoerced choice. That such a choice may itself be dependent on the coercion of God's grace as administered through the Holy Spirit is surely a theological difficulty. But it was not a practical or political difficulty, at least not initially. The point was that no human institution should be permitted to interdict the individual's freedom to choose *wrongly* but permissibly—a view that would seem to entail, however shadily and minimally, the existence of a space for civil and political freedom independent of religiously based moral correction, a space for the infidels.

It makes a difference, however, whether such a space is regarded as instrumental and subordinate, or comprehensive and primary. Clearly, through most of the eighteenth century, for most Americans, the former was the case. The reformed Protestant ethos permeated the political culture of eighteenth-century America. That this austere and communitarian ethos was constantly being challenged by the growing commercial preoccupations of the colonists of British North America, whose Puritans were gradually becoming Yankees, is not to be doubted. Nor can it be doubted that the constant process of ecclesiastical conflict, upheaval, and division, particularly as revealed in such outbursts of revivalism as the Great Awakening, weakened the authority of established elites, undermined individual Christians' sense of attachment to their churches, and made the moral authority of those churches increasingly contingent on the approval of members. But these were not insuperable problems. Material success and denominational fractiousness and mobility were not at all incompatible with reformed notions of vocation and church polity. Reformed Protestantism could manage such developments without changing its nature.

It was not until the time of the American Revolution that the inherent tensions in the reformed Protestant social and cultural regime would begin to become more complicated. The crisis in colonial relations with England gave rise not to one revolutionary voice but to a complex web of political discussion and theory, in a variety of political languages, with a variety of political visions and ends. It would be an endlessly complex task to disentangle the many different strands and assess their relative importance; and in any event, that is not our present task. But two points need to be made. First, we do see the growing use of a secular language of strictly natural rights, expressed in some of the most famous texts of the period (e.g., Thomas Paine's *Common Sense* and Jefferson's Declaration of Independence). Second, the emergence of this language does *not* mean, as the "liberal" interpretation of the era had long implied, that it displaced all other ways of speaking and thinking about public life. The scholars of the past generation who have filled out the ideological picture have seen to it that our image of the Revolution can never again be rendered in strictly Lockean-liberal terms. Republicanism, Scottish commonsense philosophy and faculty psychology, English common law and history, reformed Protestant moral theology and social corporatism—all of these continue to play a meaningful and visible role in the final results.

It can be said, however, that the Constitution presumed, as George Washington, John Adams, and many others were wont to say, a moral and religious people, but that it did not do very much directly to perpetuate such a people. It established a stable and effective national government, expanded and institutionalized a sphere of political liberty, created ingenious systems of checks and balances, pitted vices against one another in order to absorb and channel the effects of human ambition and sinfulness, but it relied on other agencies of society to shape the kind of citizens who would be capable of exercising political liberty in a responsible manner. While the Framers hoped to make ambition counteract ambition, they clearly understood that thwarting vice is not the same as cultivating virtue, even if it is the more feasible of the two tasks.

Considered in this light, the First Amendment's guarantees of religious liberty take on a deeper meaning than the "liberal" ones usually attributed to them today. As Mary Ann Glendon has argued, the two religion clauses of the First Amendment, the "establishment" and "free exercise" clauses, were not meant to be read as entirely separate and competing concerns but as mutually reinforcing ones.[2] Taken together, the clauses expressed two things, first, an opposition to any coercion of conscience by the national government, either by compelling or proscribing religious exercise and, second, a recognition on the Framers' part that religion itself is an indispensable public good, whose exercise should be encouraged as much as possible. Such a view clearly represented an elaboration of the familiar Protestant idea of constrained individuality. Nevertheless, the Anti-Federalist fear that the Constitution itself was "godless" (it is striking to note that unlike the state constitutions the federal constitution pointedly did not invoke the name of the deity) and took no direct responsibility for the cultivation of a pious and virtuous citizenry was an abiding concern, and not an unfounded one.

Either way, though, the Protestant view of the freely choosing individual who is constrained (and thereby made genuinely free) by education and formative training, and especially by acquaintance with transcendent biblical principles, remained intact in the new constitutional order, even if that view had become more of a background assumption than a stated conviction. The need for such countervailing force would be intensified, too, by the growing tendency to define the individual as a "self," a free-standing entity ontologically distinct from the political and social order, endowed with imprescriptible rights, but still badly in need of discipline, education, and development so that those rights and powers might be exercised properly. That this sense of "selfhood" was not uniformly distributed across lines of class, race, sex, and religion is obvious. But that it was beginning to take shape is equally evident. Indeed, one sees it beginning to emerge in the 1780s in the text of *The Federalist*, with its emphasis on the Constitution as an engine of channeled self-interest—just the sort of talk that alarmed so many of the Anti-Federalists about the Constitution. How, they wondered, would the old order of virtue hold its own against the new order of self-interest, particularly if that order were deprived of the supports of officially sanctioned religion?

Even the irreligious were likely to share these concerns. Thomas Jefferson consistently stressed the critical importance of education as a way of impressing upon the people an awareness of their "duties" as well as their "rights." The United States would, in his view, be a laboratory for determining "what is the degree of freedom and self-government in which a society may venture to leave its individual members." Therefore, he thought, writing in 1818 to the commissioners of the University of Virginia, education would be of the highest importance in generating "habits of application, of order, and the love of virtue"; only education "controls, by force of habit, any innate obliquities in our moral organization."[3] So whether one was speaking of original sin or "innate obliquities" (whatever that meant) the practical result was the same: The newly liberated individual, whose freedom from "Romish" superstition Jefferson loved to celebrate, continued to need restraint and discipline if liberal and republican institutions were to survive and flourish. And it was not enough for those constraints to be applied externally, like so many fences and leashes. They needed to be completely internalized as well. The responsible democratic self would have to be (in David Riesman's famous term) inner-directed, or self-constrained.[4]

Self-Culture and Beyond

Once the new nation was firmly established in its new institutions, the problem of finding effective means of restraint soon became much more challenging. Beginning in the years after the War of 1812, and growing in the Jacksonian years, the nation experienced an explosion of economic energy and growth, the fruits of an industrial and market revolution, opening up fresh opportunities for social advancement and individual transformation. The combination of rising general prosperity, expanding economic opportunity, rapid technological change, the increasing democratization of politics, and the ubiquity of popular evangelical Protestantism all tended to accentuate awareness of the "self" as an independent agent, simply because of the weakness and transience of all other social determinants of identity. As Alexis de Tocqueville argued, a regime and society dedicated to social equality and social fluidity inevitably tended to emphasize the individual.

Tocqueville saw individualism as one of the principal dangers unleashed by American democracy. By individualism he meant not simply selfishness or egoism but something closer to what we would call privatism, the withdrawal of the individual from engagement with public life and the responsibilities of citizenship. In America this individualist disposition was not simply an emotion or passion, of the sort to which mankind had always been vulnerable, but a more or less settled and steady view of social life and, as such, something genuinely new under the sun, calling for new solutions. Tocqueville saw the real possibility of a debilitating social atomism in America, in which "the woof of time is every instant broken and the track of generations effaced," and individuals' interest is "confined to those in close propinquity" to themselves. With the passage of time, "the number of persons increases who . . . acquire the habit of always considering themselves as standing alone" and imagining that "their whole destiny is in their own hands." In the end, as Tocqueville observed in one of his greatest sentences, "not only does democracy make every man forget his ancestors, but it hides his descendants and separates his contemporaries from him; it throws him back forever upon himself alone and threatens in the end to confine him entirely within the solitude of his own heart."[5]

Thus might the worst fears of Anti-Federalists be realized. In such a self-oriented regime, how on earth could the virtues needed for self-governance be cultivated? Fortunately, Tocqueville believed, the Americans had devised various ways of counteracting this tendency, the most important for our purposes being the principle of "self-interest rightly understood." Such a principle forces one to concede much of the battle at the outset, by conceding that the reign of virtue was no longer feasible in an egalitarian, commercial, ambitious, and materialistic society. To ask Americans to do virtuous things for virtue's sake, he thought, was to waste one's breath; but to point out that virtuous behavior might be in one's self-interest—that, for example, honesty might be the best policy rather than merely its own reward—was another matter. Perhaps, he thought, the energy of self-interest could be harnessed to do the work of virtue. Such a strategy had, it seemed to him, been remarkably successful in the United States, where "hardly anyone talks of the beauty of virtue, but they maintain that virtue is useful and prove it every day." Hence the role of education was crucial to Tocqueville, since, he believed, "the time is fast approaching when freedom, public peace, and social order itself will not be able to exist without education." Such education should center on the *usefulness* of virtuous behavior and should be founded on the principle of "self-interest rightly understood" as "the best suited of all philosophical theories to the wants of the men of our time."[6]

In other words, Tocqueville capitulated entirely to the logic of the "separate self," merely seeking new ways to constrain it that would be both effective and acceptable. In that, he faithfully reflected the pattern of the age. As different as Whigs and Democrats were in their views of social policy, education, economics, and the scope of the national government, they were agreed that the "separate self" was the proper analytical beginning point in the determination of the public good. Jacksonian Democrats were fiercely laissez-faire and individualistic in their political, economic, moral, and intellectual stance. The American Whigs, on the other hand, were much more prescriptive and corporatist, with a strong admixture of evangelical piety and reformist zeal in their ranks. Yet the Whigs too started with the self and with the task of producing social order through *self*-control. The goal of Whig reformers, as Daniel Walker Howe has put it, was "to substitute for external constraint the inner discipline of responsible morality."[7] In other words, they sought to keep alive the Protestant idea of individuality constrained through a heightened emphasis on inculcating the tools of *self*-constraint, a task to be accomplished through education.

Small wonder that the single most influential figure in the early history of American public education, Massachusetts' Horace Mann, was a Whig. Recent American historians have often accused him (and other Whig leaders) of elitism and of advocating public education chiefly as a tool of "social control" in an increasingly diverse and polyglot industrial society. But in fact Mann consistently sought to instill mobility-enabling qualities of self-regulation and self-governance in the character of his charges. He and other reformers consistently linked the achievement of self-reliance with the power of self-improvement and self-control, which often focused on the cultivation of something called "character." An even more forceful and influential advocate of the gospel of self-improvement was the great Unitarian clergyman William Ellery Channing, whose 1838 lecture "Self-Culture" became a classic brief for the endless human capacity for self-improvement. Contrary to Calvinist teaching about human depravity and original sin, Channing insisted on the splendor and nobility of "the nature which is common to all men," pointedly including in his description all classes and stations of individuals. In Channing's view, God had marked the human race out for a destiny of perfection and had endowed us with the extraordinary power "of acting on, determining, and forming ourselves." The American ideal of the self-made man merely represented the most complete expression of this divine endowment.[8]

Indicative of the same self-oriented strain was the work of Horace Bushnell, whose child-rearing manual *Christian Nurture* (first published in 1847) made him the Dr. Spock of his era. Bushnell saw the role of education less as the transmission of ideas and moral principles than of an entire cultural and emotional set, imparted at such an early age as to be preconscious in nature. Bushnell anticipated modern depth psychology's emphasis on early childhood experiences, as well as the behavioristic understanding of operant conditioning—insights that led him to urge parents to surround the child with a comprehensive mental culture, administered largely prerationally, through which "the child is to grow up a Christian . . . by grow[ing] up in the life of the parent, and be a Christian, in principle, from his earliest years."[9]

No need, in his view, for the herky-jerky emotionalism of evangelicalism, with its roller-coaster ride of sin and conversion, conviction and repentance, fall and redemption. No need anymore, either, for the doctrinal rigor and austere intellectualism of Jonathan Edwards's Connecticut Valley Calvinism. Affects, not ideas, had consequences. Nurture was more important than instruction, feeling than thought, poetry than theology, character than intellect. Jefferson's original ideal had been transformed by Bushnell into a strictly psychological and sentimental education, a view of character formation that substituted affects and habits not only for external constraints but for internal beliefs. Like Channing, he saw the goal of education as the construction of the optimal self—the kind of self that would have the power to continue endlessly in its own self-making.

Lurking in the background of all these innovations, however, were certain ideas, particularly the growing liberalization of reformed Protestant theology. Mann, Channing, and Bushnell had in common a keen aversion, each in his own way, to the hard edges of Calvinism and in this they were characteristic of their era. Even those who rode the waves of the era's religious revivals, such as the great Charles Grandison Finney, the prototype of the modern itinerant American evangelistic preacher, veered in the direction of theological Arminianism, in practice if not entirely in theory. Conversions, Finney asserted, need not be left to the vagaries of the Holy Spirit but could be "worked up" by a skillful minister through the use of tried and true psychological techniques. Finney disdained the proposition that religion "has something peculiar in it, not to be judged of by the ordinary rules of cause and effect." On the contrary, the religious conversion and the revivalistic events in which it occurred were events falling within "the ordinary powers of nature."[10] Gone, it seemed, were the intense controversies over the sovereignty of grace that had roiled the Massachusetts Bay of John Winthrop, John Cotton, and Anne Hutchinson.

What grace had lost, human agency had won; but there was uneasiness and instability in the result. Tocqueville observed that the free democratic individual was subject to a strange feeling of being "at once independent and powerless," a paradoxical condition that extended well beyond the political sphere.[11] The "culture" of the self envisioned by Mann, Channing, and Bushnell involved one in seeing the self as both subject and object, as both actor and acted-upon, as both master of its own destiny and putty in the hands of others. Perhaps one could counter that such an outlook was no more intrinsically contradictory than a reformed theology that held humans responsible for things that only sovereign grace could accomplish. But however one copes with the paradox, it is not hard to see that the ideal of "self-culture" ran the risk of making the construction and refinement of the self into an end in itself, by transforming the cultivation of constrained individuality into the cultivation of affect and by rejecting the theology and morality of inherent human limitation.

That is precisely what happened in the thought of Ralph Waldo Emerson, who elevated the promptings of his inner nature to a status parallel to that of divine revelation in Nature, thereby breaking decisively from the older Protestant pattern of constrained individuality. Boundlessness, not constraint, was the Emersonian watchword: "The only sin is limitation." Like Channing, Emerson believed that human potential was endless: "Before the immense possibilities of man," he cried, "all mere experience, all past biography, however spotless and sainted, shrinks away." Such immensity meant disdaining the staleness of every thought or action that was inherited or derivative: custom, history, tradition, even society itself. The pieties of the past belong to the past; the free mind need not be detained by them, for "nothing is at last sacred but the integrity of your own mind." The older view of the free self as a tense equilibrium of countervailing forces had been replaced by the romantic and holistic injunction to "trust thyself"—the very advice a Jonathan Edwards would have strenuously cautioned us against. That our present-day sages would be more likely to warn us against Edwards than against Emerson speaks volumes about the place where we have now arrived.[12]

Salvaging the Protestant Principle?

There was a procession, then, from self-control to self-culture to self-worship. "All religion, all solid things, arts, governments," intoned Emerson's great admirer, the poet Walt Whitman, fall "into niches and corners before the procession of souls along the grand roads of the universe."[13] One might say that we have been following these grand roads ever since. Although we are not yet at the end of them, we are surely far enough along to see where they have been taking us, and the destination looks none too grand. We now live in an environment in which the Protestant idea has been nearly universalized (but at the expense of being truncated and diminished, à la Whitman) into little more than an unrestricted right of individual judgment, unbounded by any limiting principle or any source of authoritative moral rules or prescriptions. We are quite willing to accept a language of individual rights and entitlements. But all other constraints, even those of rationality, have fallen by the wayside, having lost their legitimacy and their power to bind.

This sobering consideration brings us back to some of the questions raised earlier. Is it possible that the Protestant principle itself was flawed from the beginning and was bound to lead us into something like the moral chaos of our own day, with its worship of the sovereign self and its sovereign appetites? Is there a straight line leading from "the shot heard 'round the world" to gangsta' rap and the North American Man-Boy

Love Association? One would like to respond that the question is silly and answers itself. But unfortunately it doesn't answer itself in today's world, where the mainline Protestant churches flounder in moral subjectivism and the language of the Declaration of Independence is routinely invoked to justify almost any affront to public order, no matter how puerile.

In an 1892 speech called "The Solitude of Self," Elizabeth Cady Stanton summarized "our Protestant idea" as "the right of individual conscience and judgment."[14] But that is only half the story, the sort of half-truth that is worse than a falsehood. The Protestant idea, to repeat, was always one of *constrained* individuality that entailed a freely accepted obedience to a thoroughly internalized authority, whose prescriptions were expressed in an accessible and authoritative text. American Protestantism liberated the individual believer from the authority of an ecclesiastical or social hierarchy—the canon and feudal law—but not without putting in their place other sources of authority. This move, of course, hinged a great deal on the trustworthiness of the Bible, which meant that if the assaults on scriptural authority by Darwinian science, "higher" criticism, and all the rest of modernity's acids were successful, there would be little left behind in mainline Protestantism other than the affirmation and cultivation of the "separate self."

One could argue that Protestantism is now paying the price for its textualist ways, its low view of ecclesiology, and its neglect of the communal and countercultural dimension of the Christian life. On the other hand, one does not need to be a fundamentalist to respond that whatever the sources of mainline Protestantism's current woes, an excessive attention to the Bible is not one of them. But the matter is too consequential for us to be content with scoring debating points. The fact remains that our civilization's most effective model for ordered liberty, whether in matters religious or matters civil and constitutional, rests on the constraining force of foundational texts, such as the Bible and the Constitution. To the extent that such foundational texts become problematized into impotence—to the extent that they are deemed to have no clear and fixed meaning available to all and are thereby removed from the common person's reach—to that extent will the church and the nation have yielded to new forms of canon and feudal law that are administered by the currently anointed "communities of interpretation," who are at liberty to make of a text what they will.

This is of course precisely what is at stake when judges and constitutional lawyers speak of a "living Constitution" or "the life of the law" as a way of disregarding the clear meaning of a text. The crisis of modern literary criticism and the crisis of modern judicial activism thus have some considerable connection with one another. Democratic liberty depends on our ability to invest a text with ordering authority and to allow the text to stand as a rock of stability and secure point of reference to which one can repair amid the confusing and disorienting currents of life. But when such texts become rendered endlessly fluid and problematic, they eventually become the property of a hermeneutical class, which then constitutes itself, rather than the text, as the real ordering authority—a government, so to speak, of men and not laws. To point this out is invariably dismissed as naive, and there may be something to the criticism. But surely it is more naive to think that a liberal and democratic order can continue to exist when its laws are utterly unintelligible to its citizens—or when the religious principles on which its "constraining" function depends are left without the support of intelligible and authoritative texts. Those who are disdainful of textual clarity ought at least to have the consistency to be equally disdainful of constitutional democracy, and of the rule of law itself.

This question of the fixity, transparency, and transcendent meaning of texts also points toward some of the objections to be made against the current movement of liberal or "progressive" communitarianism, which arose as a commendable attempt to answer the Emersonian hypertrophy of the self. The Protestant formula of constrained individuality is something very different from the idea of vesting authority in the community qua community. Both oppose the excesses of Emersonian individualism, but they do so in entirely different ways. Recall, in this connection, Winthrop's emphasis on the "commission" with which he and his followers were charged. They were asked to surrender their individual ambitions to the community and bear one another's burdens gladly.

But they did this for Christ's sake, not for the community's sake. Their copious diaries show that they sought, and found, the meaning of their own lives by passing them through an immense filter of biblical stories, parables, prayers, and admonitions. It is a very different matter to attempt to constitute community without a transcendent point of reference, and without reliance on the impersonal authority of a foundational text; and to imagine that the same effects could be produced without the same causes is folly. In failing to recognize this, our era's statist communitarians have, I fear, inverted Emerson's error instead of correcting it.

One of the most notable failings in much of the current communitarian movement has been its skittishness about specifying behaviors that are right or wrong and suggesting sanctions against the latter. Liberal communitarians are in love with the idea of limits, but they cannot agree on any particular limits to observe; they are in love with the idea of community, but they find all real existing communities to be fatally flawed (too narrow, too insular, too homogeneous, too intolerant, etc.). At its best, communitarianism tends to give short shrift to the virtues of individualism, particularly of what might be called "individualism rightly understood." As Reinhold Niebuhr argued, there is a profound moral need for the individual to be able, from time to time, to stand apart from all social groupings, since all groups are dangerously corruptible and all are subject to the interest-driven fallenness that governs human associations here below. But he never imagined that this individualism could or should exist without additional constraints and supports.

So the question remains: Is there a way to restore the older Protestant settlement of constrained individuality, which navigates between the hazards of radical individualism and suffocating New Communitarianism? The fate of the social policy of years to come, particularly policy directed at the strengthening of families, will hinge on that very task. It will be hard to get very far with that question without also coming to terms with specific conflicts over the sources of moral authority that have long separated Catholics and Protestants, particularly reformed Protestants. But one way to begin thinking about the matter is suggested by the scene in Sleepy Hollow with which we began. The flanking stones of Emerson's wife and daughter should remind us that, for all the ways that we worry ourselves about individualism, it is in some ultimate sense, an illusion, for there is really no such thing as an unencumbered self. There never has been and there never will be. The belief that the individual can live, as Emerson said, without constraint or hindrance means simply that one has forgotten about the sources of one's being, not that those sources have ceased to exist. In the fullness of time, a reminder of those sources comes to us all.

But another reflection, more charitable and perhaps more valuable, also arises out of the contemplation of Emerson's tombstone. It is the singular glory of the civilization we call "Western" that it places so high a value on the soul and conscience of the individual person. That this valuation has been allowed to grow beyond all bounds, like a Tower of Babel, should not finger it as flawed from the start, unless one is prepared to say that all the growth and constructive residue of history is vanity, and nothing more. (Partisans of *that* view may prefer to spend their Sleepy Hollow time at Mr. Hawthorne's tombstone.) Emerson's belief in the lavish creativity of the individual human spirit, and "the unsearched might of man," was, like most heresies, an intensification of something true, if not quite true enough.[15] Even the most grand and gloomy pessimists of our age are energized by a sense of Emersonian ambition when they sit down to tap out their dreary tomes (and fantasize about their sales figures). The expansive sense of individual possibility remains a part of who and what we are as a people, even in the most unexpected ways. To wish to extinguish that would be like wishing to extinguish life itself.

There are, however, far better ways to think about individual possibility. Addicted as we now are to the shallow and wasteful dynamic of unending generational rebellion—a dynamic that Emerson himself celebrated and helped to create—we often find it difficult to understand that one can both revere and criticize the actors of the past. But such a complex disposition is one of the chief achievements of a mature adulthood. It is capable of a love that pays homage to one's antecedents without worshiping them—a love that knows the steep price of repudiating one's ancestors, precisely because they are one's own. Emerson spoke for a noble spark in the human spirit, albeit one that has ignited a dangerous conflagration by its own excesses. It is important for us to acknowledge that spark and that error. For Emerson remains a part of our collective past that we should never repudiate entirely. He was a rebellious son but also a cultural father. And it is generally a good thing to pay one's respects to fallible fathers—even disturbers of the peace who fancied themselves boulders among stones, or lions among sheep. It is a good thing, because even the rowdiest of sons will come to lie down in the same earth as their fathers, and mothers, and wives. Thus is every individuality constrained, eventually.

5

Charles Taylor on Multiculturalism and the Politics of Recognition

Norman Barry

Charles Taylor is closely associated with the modern communitarian intellectual movement and the retreat from liberalism (of either the classical European individualist or the American egalitarian variety) that has become a dominant feature of post-Rawlsian political and moral thought (discussed below). Although he remains, broadly speaking, a *political* liberal, his philosophical stance differs radically from that assumed by most exponents of the doctrine. His recent venture into multiculturalism is not surprising, since the social theory associated with that style of politics seems to rest on similarly anti-individualistic foundations. The abstract agent of liberal economic and social theory, who is more or less identified by his immediate preferences (which are beyond rational evaluation), has been replaced in these doctrines by the concept of a person who is inextricably formed by social circumstances and whose tastes are not "given" but are explicable only in terms of the community he inhabits. The institutions by which he lives have a historical and social validity that is resistant to the universalistic prescriptions of liberal theory. Since philosophical liberalism has always laid claims to a morality that transcends the claims of the particular and the local it seems to be at odds with doctrines that specifically locate individual morality in the language of identifiable and known cultures.

Thus the familiar liberal postulate that individuals have rights without correlative social obligations can have only a negative impact on social theories that understand morality exclusively in the context of particular historical communities—entities which promote collective goals that are not reducible to the wants of essentially private persons. In this context the arguments of the multiculturalists have a particular resonance since they are specifically addressed to liberalism's claim of having offered a compelling ethic appropriate for all human circumstances. From this critical perspective liberalism itself is no more than a culturally determined moral code, and it would be imperialistic to impose it on other communities. And worse, from a broadened moral perspective, it prescribes merely a set of instrumental arrangements that egoistic individuals require for their security.

It would be a mistake, however, to place Taylor in the antiliberal camp. As we shall see, his substantive political position is not opposed to its main tenets. He is an egalitarian in economic and social terms and a firm believer in the traditional liberal civil liberties. His objection to liberalism is addressed to its ontological foundation in atomistic individualism, not to its actual prescriptions, although there is some subtle, if not mysterious, connection between philosophy and policy. What is a little more difficult to appreciate is Taylor's attempt to make his somewhat convoluted liberalism consistent with communitarianism. Perhaps in trying to make this connection he has weakened the decisive features of both.

To understand Taylor's views, for example, on the Quebec problem in Canada, or on any other political issue involving rivalry between potentially incompatible traditions, we have to understand his underlying philosophical position. It is an approach that tries to hold a precarious balance between that pluralism (and doubt about ultimate values) associated with most versions of liberalism and the quasi-objectivism of a moral structure that can be nested in the security of received and *unchosen* social arrangements. It is the latter, communalistic theory, that is specifically opposed to the overriding claims of individual choice traditionally associated with liberalism. Throughout his work there is the theme that a notion of the good exists that is independent of preferences. It is a philosophical predisposition that encourages serious doubts about the power of the market and the mechanism of individual choice (even though the exchange system is undervalued by most post-Rawlsian liberals) to resolve many of our social and economic problems.

Philosophical Presuppositions

Taylor's attempts to integrate an account of the social and communal varieties of political experience (cultural differentiation) into a doctrine that maintains the broad features of political liberalism can only be properly understood through an appreciation of his underlying complex philosophy. In his *Multiculturalism and the Politics of Recognition* only an abbreviated version of this is presented. What it amounts to is a rejection of philosophical liberalism: a theory that presupposes that the major elements of liberalism can be reconstructed out of a notion of the self abstracted from any preexisting social arrangements. Rawls's *Theory of Justice*, though not his later work, is perhaps the paradigm of this approach, for in it the author presupposes that appropriate rules, institutions, and distributive criteria can be derived from the choices of rational individuals under conditions of uncertainty. These abstract agents are deprived of knowledge of those social and personal facts that might generate discord.

In an earlier anti-individualistic work (not specifically addressed to Rawls but rather to those who derive a theory of rights from the same methodology) Taylor condemned this approach as "atomistic" because, in a philosophical sense, it dissolved society into individuals who are identified only by their choices, either as the rights possessors of liberal moral theory or the utility-maximizers of economic theory, and not as members of preexisting political communities. This membership not only gives meaning to individual lives but also establishes the foundations of morality. As he says, "Primacy-of-rights theories . . . accept a principle ascribing rights to men as binding unconditionally . . . But they do not accept as similarly unconditional a principle of belonging or obligation."[1] This, he says, is an error, for a person can be understood only if he can be located in a complex of social relationships. These relationships determine the form and limits of morality. There is a similarity between Taylor's notion of socially situated individuals and traditional communitarian Alasdair MacIntyre's theory of the "narrative self." There is a notion of individualism in Taylor's work, but it is a "holistic individualism," one that identifies the person by reference to his involvement in shared values and is resistant to the economic (or classical) liberal's conception of the individual as an *anonymous* choosing agent.

This rejection of the notion of "antecedentally individuated" persons is further elaborated in *Multiculturalism* in Taylor's distinction between *monological* and *dialogical* descriptions of human relationships.[2] In the monological vision a person finds his true identity and authenticity in isolation from social relationships. When unleavened by any preexisting moral constraints, it leads to a peculiar asocial "narcissism" and has the direct political implication that such an individualism cannot sustain the liberal order, which is supposed to be its political reflection. All our social arrangements become provisional, dependent on an unstable agreement or some calculation of immediate utility. In contrast, Taylor argues that, "my own identity crucially depends on my dialogical relationships with others."[3] What this means is that only by communication with others can the person know who he is, what his values are and how he can understand the social world. These meanings cannot be constructed from purely individualistic premises.

Most importantly, there is no antecedent notion of the right that could allow us individually to determine a notion of the good apart from the meanings given to it by our relationships with others. The monological ideal presupposes that private worlds of value, bounded only by the requirement of a morality (determined by a supposed agreement) that we respect other people's individualistic conceptions of the good, constitute the ideal form of a liberal society. However, this ideal "forgets how our understanding of the good things in life can be transformed by our enjoying them in common with people we love; how some goods become accessible to us only through such common enjoyment."[4] In contrast to liberal economists, who see "public goods" as, in effect, private goods that cannot, for technical reasons, be supplied by the market, Taylor understands them to represent those values that we *share* as members of a community. Their existence is not merely a response to private desires and their rationale is not to be explained by reference to coordination problems that occasionally occur in decentralized markets. The state is therefore not a conduit for the expression of private desires for public goods but the depository of shared values.

The good life is ineluctably defined in terms of the public sphere. Although Taylor cannot (now) deny the significance of market relationships, they do not meet with the criteria of morality because they necessarily involve the satisfaction of private desires. There is a collective dimension to the good, which is not to be confused or identified with some proposed form of economic organization. It is derived explicitly from Taylor's conception of what it means to be a human being. Persons are not understood as preference-maximizers, as orthodox classical liberal theory often implies but as "strong evaluators,"[5] whose decisions are a result of reflection on their preferences. It is a form of reflection that can only take place in a language that is already replete with moral concepts.

Thus language is the ultimate and paradigmatic form of community. The existence of a communal "good," irreducible to desires or preferences, enables us to make moral judgments, as distinct from mere expressions of emotion. Similarly, freedom is a form of self-determination in which the ephemera of our desires are transcended by a kind of collective endeavor in which nonatomized individuals participate in the realization of the good. Even those liberal theorists who assert the priority of the right over the good require a notion of the right that is itself socially embedded. This embeddedness determines the "moral accent"[6] or emphasis on obligations to others that transcend private desire, which he thinks has been lost in modern, narcissistic notions of authenticity.

Whatever form Taylor's liberalism takes, it cannot be neutral about ends, for even the types of procedural liberalism to which we are accustomed depend for their viability on a social commitment to the rules that undergird them. The mistake that he claims to see in neutral liberalism derives from its purely instrumental conception of reason—a conception that limits reason to the achievement of immediate goals. The criterion of efficiency replaces objective standards of morality, which he thinks led to a "flattening" of society and its fragmentation into private, and potentially warring, groups and alienated individuals who are held together, precariously, by the price mechanism and abstract rules.

Multiculturalism and Recognition

It is within this philosophical framework that we can understand Taylor's analysis of multiculturalism and the politics of recognition. For as he shows, the communitarian impulse that lies behind all this is a response to a dissatisfaction with liberalism. The advocate of multiculturalism does not require merely the neutral laws of the procedural republic but the positive affirmation of the distinctive features of particular cultural groups. The voice of a cultural entity cannot be expressed satisfactorily through abstract rules and political arrangements that treat everybody formally the same; indeed, the integrity of unchosen social affiliations may require exemptions from a mechanical application of them. The politics of multiculturalism represents in a special form the dialogical relationship that for Taylor is the key to self-understanding. In the contemporary world it would appear that individuals need some form of affirmation of who they are. And this can only be discovered through their membership in a form of association that is not reducible to individualistic, monological goal seeking. Membership in such associations, indeed, serves to differentiate them from others. Individuals require for their self-realization not merely the protection provided by instrumental rules but also the recognition by others of their distinctiveness. In contrast to the narcissistic exemplifications of self-fulfillment, that might be products of atomized individualism, Taylor's conception is only meaningful in a world that has been collectivized in a curious moral sense—if not in economic terms.

The reason for this desire for recognition would appear to derive from the absence in the contemporary world of the traditional outward signs of differentiation, notably honor. In the past, one person could be distinguished from another, and rewarded by high social status, when his actions met with accepted, and unchosen, standards of excellence. However, the achievement of this necessarily implied that others had somehow failed. A world that honors everyone honors no one. Some ideal of equality, however inchoate, has permeated most modern social doctrines and has made any version of honor impermissible.

The contemporary doctrinal surrogates for honor, the politics of *dignity*, and the politics of *difference* seem, superficially at least, to point in radically contrasting directions. The former posits a universalistic notion of equality that obliterates the differences between people and subjects them to the equal application of law. We are all equal in dignity as persons and are entitled to the same protection and opportunities for self-fulfillment, irrespective of differences of race, sex, religion, and nationality. This does not, of course, exclude the possibility of the retention of certain defining characteristics through spontaneously emerging social arrangements. What it does preclude is any modification of legal egalitarianism and liberal constitutionalism that would privilege one group over another.

Differences can remain but only if their survival is spontaneous and compatible with the rigorous and impartial application of nondiscriminatory law. This has become significant in a world in which economic and social developments, governed by universal law, have threatened the integrity and permanence of particular cultural groups. Taylor is convinced that in the modern liberal world these differences can survive only by a relaxation of the rigor of universal, liberal law.

The alternative doctrine (the politics of difference), however, specifically identifies persons by those cultural features, for example, language and religion, that do differentiate groups, and it does insist that the equal application of law should be suspended if its unintended outcome is one in which one group emerges as dominant and others are repressed, or at least their permanence and integrity are threatened. If their distinctiveness is not recognized, they may even be said to be "harmed." This can occur despite the formal preservation of equality and the conventional liberal panoply of affirmative action and other measures to correct past discriminatory actions against deprived groups. Indeed, the spokespersons for this form of multiculturalism deny that the politics of equal dignity (which is really liberalism) lives up to its claims of equality but practices a subtle form of repression by imposing its standards of excellence (in art and literature as well as in law and politics) on others in the guise of their being the best (as revealed by the results of some impartial process of evaluation). In their most virulent denunciation of Western values these critics assert that liberal equality and neutrality are themselves culturally determined and can have no justifiable claim to a universal validity.

Taylor remains a liberal pluralist, in a somewhat convoluted sense, but recognizes the power that "cultural relativism" has on the modern mind. He wishes, in effect, to redefine it so that it is compatible with the more (morally) feasible expressions of cultural variation. Importantly, he wants to distinguish his position from any form of relativism. Indeed, he has to because his philosophical framework, especially his affirmation of the crucial significance of dialogical relationships for individual self-understanding, requires a more expansive form of communitarianism than the familiar versions. Most of these are suffused with a certain kind of relativism. It is this search for objective moral standards that probably drives Taylor to speak of "community" rather than communities. However, is it not the case that his community is simply the liberal community?

Taylor's consideration, and ultimate rejection, of a main element in Rousseau's doctrine illustrates the difficulty he is in. For Rousseau tries to find a way in which recognition can be achieved without the invocation of cultural difference, or any other feature that would differentiate persons. Vanity, normally produced by economic striving, is a feature of a form of individualism that generates the kind of differentiation that Rousseau's "communitarianism" is designed to overcome. The order of economic liberalism produces, for him, an abject form of dependency (that is, subservience to others) that can only be overcome by an absolute and unqualified commitment to the community, of which we are all equal members. Taylor rightly objects that the crucial elements in Rousseau, "freedom [nondomination], the absence of differentiated roles and a very tight common purpose," are all features that have highly illiberal implications.[7] They would certainly eliminate the pluralism for which he often speaks, which is a characteristic of multiculturalism.

The real problem with accepting Rousseau is perhaps not just the fear that oppression lurks behind the General Will but the fact that his notion of dignity through equal participation does not allow for the urge to express cultural differences that inspires most communitarian, antiliberal theories. Rousseau's doctrine is the harbinger, in a somewhat perverse form, of modern liberalism rather than an incipient expression of cultural and linguistic autonomy. Multicultural theorists may yearn for a kind of Rousseauistic practice in the internal arrangements of their particular communities but the doctrine has nothing to offer them in the context of a discussion of the relationships between culturally defined communities. The concept of an extended General Will would go a long way toward eliminating the very differences that give various communities their identities, and it seriously attenuates the political impact of pluralism. Although Rousseau's anti-individualism (in its economic aspect) is acceptable to Taylor, his unreceptiveness to cultural differentiation is not. Later I shall suggest that in his skepticism with regard to the market and his elevation of the public over the private, Taylor has not completely liberated himself from the spell of Rousseau.

Taylor is seeking a version of liberalism that can satisfy a number of potentially competing demands. It must meet with a moral code that embodies more or less universal human values. It would include rights to life, liberty (of expression, association, etc.), and their judicial protection, although the claims to property and to economic freedom seem to merit scarcely a mention. It is his commitment to the potentially universal social values of liberalism that entitles Taylor to membership of that ideological community.

However, he seems not to want this Weltanschauung to override all collective demands. His doubts here derive from his objections to liberal neutrality or to the ideal of the pure procedural republic. These concepts treat all persons as abstract agents, detached from any communal affiliations and subject to perfectly general laws (which is actually a strong implication of Rousseau's jurisprudence). Not only is this an inadequate foundation for liberalism itself but its severely monological pretenses lead theoretically to atomism and social fragmentation. In the practical realm its excessive legalism destroys the world of shared values and meanings on which even the liberal order depends. That corrosive individualistic legalism precludes the deliberate privileging of collective values—the defining feature of the politics of recognition. Thus if Taylor is a liberal then his version of that protean doctrine is much "thinner" than that associated with Rawls.

Defenders of liberalism often argue that it is the only political and legal order that allows for the expression of various cultural forms precisely because it has no overall conception of the good; its self-proclaimed pluralism requires that the good be a product of private desire or the outcomes of spontaneously forming voluntary groups surviving in a structure of perfectly general rules. Its multicultural critics deny that it is neutral, since its so-called nondiscriminatory and universal laws permit the imposition of a culturally determined (Western) social form in the guise of freedom. The rigid and impartial application of liberal jurisprudence simply preserves the liberal order and, indeed, contributes to the potential destruction of its rivals. In other words, liberalism cannot be genuinely pluralistic (a position with which, ironically, the metaphysicians of the doctrine might well agree).

Taylor is aware of this and proposes alternative forms of liberalism that "call for the invariant defence of *certain* rights. . . . But they do distinguish these fundamental rights from the broad range of immunities and presumptions of uniform treatment that have sprung up in modern cultures of judicial review. They [the alternative forms of liberalism] are willing to weigh the importance of certain forms of uniform treatment against the importance of cultural survival, and sometimes favor the latter."[8] He is clearly worried that if liberal political rules were uniformly applied, certain groups would be, in effect, discriminated against even though no formal liberal rights were breached. Yet he is equally concerned that a total commitment to the politics of recognition would obliterate cherished freedoms. It might also reduce morality to a form of relativism and thus eliminate those ethical appraisals that are a part of what it is to be human.

Taylor's Liberalism and the Problem of Quebec

Taylor takes the example of Canada's current problems to illustrate the distinction he proposes. Once the Canadian constitution was repatriated in 1982, the country became a fully autochthonous legal order and adopted a purely liberal constitutional code based on American principles of human rights and judicial review. But this, of course, poses serious problems for a country like Canada with its crucially important French-speaking minority in Quebec (although that province is itself multicultural, French speakers are merely the majority).

The problem is that the liberal judicial procedures in principle protect individual rights and it is the enforcement of these rights that could undermine the collective values of the community. Hence the serious doubt as to whether the province's language laws, which require commercial signs to be in French, and its educational policy, which forbids Francophiles and immigrants from sending their children to English-speaking schools, are constitutional. But irrespective of the question of positive law, the morality that lies behind all this is clearly not consistent with the prevailing vision of liberalism. The demand for recognition clearly competes with claims of liberal individualism. Further, the law should not merely protect the interests of living French Canadians; it should also preserve the French community for future unknown generations. Its vigor might be attenuated quite spontaneously by social evolution. It is unlikely that this culture would wither away, but Taylor is prepared to tolerate what might be thought illiberal measures to prevent that from happening.

The point here is that Taylor cannot really combine the features of liberalism, as he understands them, with the politics of recognition. For the former unavoidably includes moral elements that are potentially in conflict with collective goals, as the Canadian example clearly shows. What is required in a diverse society is an attitude of mind that respects diversity itself, and it is not at all clear that Canada has this. Successive political endeavors have, in fact, revealed there to be a majority that is not prepared to grant Quebec its unique status. Nor is there any evidence that the French-speaking majority in Quebec is prepared to recognize the autonomy of cultural minorities within the province, at least not in the way that English-speaking Canada is expected to acknowledge the claims of the French.

In circumstances in which liberalism clearly cannot be a solvent, an obvious solution would be to take secession as a serious option. Taylor does not take this way out, largely because he hopes for some nice compromise between the rigorous demands of liberalism and the claims of recognition. Despite his recognition of diversity he is to some extent not a genuine pluralist but a believer in the doctrine that most of our social differences can, in the long run, be overcome by dialogic relationships.

Secession may very well pose a threat to traditional liberal values, since the seceding cultural group is unlikely to be overzealous in its protection of minority rights. This fear could to some extent be mitigated by the fact that a *generalized* right to secession (which the Quebeckers have not demanded even though the province contains a number of minorities) would produce political units within which minorities would pose no threat to social order. Indeed, if perfectly implemented there would be no such minorities. In this presently hypothetical world cultural particularities would spontaneously maintain themselves precisely because there would be no need for a coercive imposition of one set of cultural norms on other people.

In the Canadian example, what would be required would be a more consistent application of the principle of diversity. More decentralized forms of government would encourage variety within Quebec, which is itself multicultural, so that subsections of the province could adopt whatever language laws they liked and natural competition would determine outcomes. At present the deliberate propagation of Frenchness by coercive law is logically no different from the imposition of Englishness through an allegedly universal set of liberal constitutional principles.

Exit and Voice

What is being suggested here is that the only right that a liberal order needs is the right of exit. There is a very important distinction between exit and voice. There are two ways in which individuals may influence events. By the use of exit they withdraw their support, as when in a market they simply refuse to buy the unsatisfactory good and leave to shop elsewhere. By exercising their voice, they try to change things by engaging in the familiar political activities (voting, lobbying representatives, etc.).

The economic arena is the prime example of exit, and politics illustrates voice perfectly (although voice can be effective in markets as when shareholders exercise power over managements without actually selling their stock). Of course, the advantage of exit in markets is that it is not very costly, whereas the exercise of voice in political activity involves the expenditure of time and resources. However, the application of exit to politics could be prohibitive, since it necessitates uprooting one's life and possibly the sacrifice of assets. Shopping around for a new country is not like searching for a new consumer good. However, whole communities, united by certain cultural characteristics, could exit from some comprehensive political arrangement, so reducing the costs for individuals. Still, in some cases the right of exit requires that countries or local communities reciprocate, that is, allow the right of entry, if it is to be effective. There are political arrangements in which it is feasible; indeed, the threat of exit from minorities may very well act as a restraint on potentially oppressive actions by the dominant cultural group.

The potential costliness of exit should not therefore preclude it from consideration as a viable mechanism for the solution of multicultural problems. It certainly seems just as feasible as Taylor's case for what he calls "asymmetrical federalism,"[9] a form of government that apparently permits special privileges for a cultural group, for example, the Quebeckers, to promote and sustain their collective values within an otherwise liberal constitutional framework. The trouble with this is that, as I have already stressed, in the Canadian case minorities in Quebec would be at the mercy of an alien collectivism.

At the moment, exit (which the English speakers in Quebec are already doing) is only possible under unpropitious circumstances—they have to leave the province—whereas under a genuine decentralization they could express their cultural differences, through seriously devolved government, within a broad but not compulsory Francophile system. One suspects that Quebec is similar to most of the conventional candidates for secession throughout the world. They themselves are not normally good examples of cultural homogeneity. One also suspects that Taylor does not consider the exit option, despite his many appeals for more decentralization, because his general social philosophy presupposes the possibility of agreement, however limited that might be. For him, a constitutionalized exit option would be a somewhat exotic version of a purely instrumental rule, that is, a device by which individuals try to realize their subjective desires rather than strive for a genuine fulfillment through dialogic relationships.

What is required, then, is *confederalism*, a political arrangement that allows real diversity. Purely local considerations and cultural traditions would be reflected in highly decentralized institutions: Whatever collective values are pursued would have wide support precisely because the sources of dissent could find their own outlets. As long as people are free to move and communities are free to secede, liberties would be protected, or at least a home could be found for them. It is the kind of political order the Anti-Federalists had in mind in their opposition to the original U.S. Constitution and may indeed have been implicit in the ideas of the Founders themselves (though the constitutional arrangements, if they were designed for this project, proved to be inadequate).

In fact, modern liberalism developed in a quite different way. It became accepted that liberal principles and individual rights could only be protected by the whole panoply of judicial arrangements—Bills of Rights, judicial review, etc. The result has been divisive litigation and the decline of communal intimacy and trust. Not only does this liberalism have the appearance of cultural domination but in practice it has proved impossible to prevent the expansion of liberal rights (look at the behavior of the U.S. Supreme Court since the ratification of the Fourteenth Amendment). It is these that turn out to be offensive to cultural minorities. The rights become a prey to the most powerful group and not the guarantors of diversity.

Taylor is reluctant to embrace even a modified doctrine of exit because it is too redolent of that atomism to which he is so resolutely opposed. It looks, superficially, like a case of *individuals* tearing up cultural traditions and planning anew, in a classically monological way, their social arrangements. To put it more cynically, perhaps he fears that people would exit into arrangements that did not meet the liberalism, albeit convoluted, that he still espouses.

The fact that it is a logical derivation from the principle of the market (a system whose necessity he reluctantly accepts but the influence of which he wants to reduce) is sufficient to deter him. But the persons who would take advantage of the possibility of exit are not antecedently individuated agents, abstract people lost in a sea of relativity, but members of given communities who seek more appropriate institutional forms by which to express their undoubted sociability. The fact that the exit model has often been used by economists to demonstrate how the problems of big government and excessive taxation could be resolved by the existence of competitive jurisdictions (people fleeing highly taxed and heavily regulated areas and thus producing by political rivalry an overall decline in both phenomena) should not be used as a reason to reject its applicability elsewhere. The fact that the exercise of the exit option involves choice should not be taken to mean that it is an example of what Taylor calls "subjectivist, half-baked neo-Nietzschean theories."[10] Those who choose to exit are still deciding in a social context and their decisions are a result of reflection. They are not mere preferences determined by the exigencies of the moment. Indeed, the very possibility of exit could restrain the dominant group from acting illiberally (in Taylor's sense); loyalty might then be generated by instrumental rules. This is important because Taylor has insisted that procedural rules can only be effective if they are buttressed by a sense of patriotism. What he doesn't seem to realize is that the rules themselves, if they are respectful of choice, could promote just that fealty.

The Allure of Participation

Although he doesn't label it as such, Taylor's approach is a an example of voice. In his comments on democracy, in *Multiculturalism* and elsewhere, he constantly emphasizes the importance of participation in the political process to bring about certain collective ends and to overcome the fragmentation that the "soft despotism" of contemporary society produces. This is the Rousseauistic liberalism that lingers on in Taylor's thought. There are a number of problems with this superficially anodyne and currently fashionable recommendation. The main one is that it is self-defeating for his aim of preserving pluralism. The success of such political activity is likely to lead to the imposition of the values of the politically successful. Because his mechanism is implicitly collectivist, individual liberties would still be precarious (although that fragility would be mitigated the smaller the size of the political unit over which the collective is supreme). Furthermore, since the mechanism depends on purely political action, the likely outcomes of it will depend on the differing propensities that people have for politics. Those for whom the opportunity costs of political participation are relatively low will come to dominate the process, leading to a new form of elitism. Indeed, in such circumstances the naturally politically apathetic might find it less costly to exit (if they were allowed).

There are, in fact, serious limits to Taylor's pluralism because he does seem to believe that a form of liberalism is morally desirable, even if its implementation may occasionally attenuate certain cultural values. It is not, of course, pure procedural liberalism, of which exit might be seen as a variant. He does propose a kind of liberal end-state embodying the traditional civil liberties (though not the specifically economic ones) that is representative of the "good." This liberal end-state is a kind of "hypergood" that exists as a solvent for the conflicts between goods that will flourish in a pluralist society. The achievement of hypergoods seems to depend entirely on action in the public realm, where a kind of "conversation" predominates over choice. The possibility of private solutions to the unending disputes that are conducted between people via the state (in which each rival aims at total victory) never seems to occur to him. From this it follows that liberalism is simply another publicly oriented good (quite unlike the conventional public goods of orthodox economics) that ultimately seeks domination over other goods.

Culture, Equality, and Politics

As Taylor correctly notes, the demand for the recognition of cultural autonomy, and the extension of the liberal doctrine of "difference blindness" via universal and impartial law to the protection of certain collective goods, has had a further, perhaps unanticipated, consequence. This is the more radical claim for an equality between the various cultures—that none has any claim to superiority. The Western liberal tradition is particularly condemnable because it has, apparently, appropriated to itself the artistic and intellectual standards that are necessary for cultural achievement. Other traditions are to be valued only to the extent that they have satisfied them (hence Saul Bellow's notorious comment, referred to by Taylor, that he will value Zulu culture only when the Zulus have produced a Tolstoy). Apparently Western educational systems impose their standards on alien cultures. Against this cultural hegemony it is now demanded "that we all *recognize* the equal value of different cultures; that we acknowledge their *worth*."[11]

Taylor is in something of a difficulty here. He does not want to surrender to relativism; indeed, his collectivist version of liberalism presupposes that public discourse will produce some kind of agreement about the good. His repeated attacks on subjectivism suggest that he does adhere at least to the possibility of there being more or less universal standards of value. In politics, for example, cultural diversity is permissible only in the framework of (some) indefeasible rights. I take it that the kind of institutional competition referred to above, which would have the cultural analogue of allowing parts of the population to opt out educational arrangements that produced what could be regarded as oppressive and alien curricula, would not be welcomed enthusiastically by him. The latter claim would require, ultimately, the privatization of schools, a position that I suspect would be precluded by his commitment to the role of the public in the determination of value. This radical solution would, presumably, be dismissed as another version of subjectivism.

Yet despite his scarcely concealed yearning for some objective standards he is inhibited in the search for them by his own commitments to communal understandings of the good and his insistence on the crucial importance of dialogical relationships; he rejects the idea that we can seek any value outside the social arrangements that alone give value to our lives and provide us with the context for our self-understanding.

It is a problem that Taylor cannot resolve, but his struggles with it are instructive. He gets to the heart of the matter with his argument that the a priori assumption of the equal value of divergent cultures is fundamentally flawed. As he points out, it is in fact demeaning, for without the possibility of making critical judgments (which necessarily discriminate between rival cultures in the realms of art and science) all cultures are, in fact, homogenized. Without a proper enquiry into the practices of divergent cultures we are, in effect, disabled from making any evaluations at all. "It can't make sense to demand as a matter of right that we come up with a final concluding judgment that their value is great, or equal to others."[12] It is, indeed, the most blatant form of Western imperialism since the standards that undergird the assumption of equal worth are necessarily Western standards. The transformation of the demand for recognition into the assertion of equal value can only lead to a stultifying form of leveling.

In Taylor's view the debate about multiculturalism has disintegrated into an irresolvable argument between those (including the subjectivists) who would eliminate all differences under the banner of cultural equality and those who retreat into a kind of aesthetic laager and resist all attempts at genuine cross-cultural comparisons. He somewhat plaintively asks for a midway position between an "inauthentic and homogenizing demand for recognition of equal worth . . . and the self-immurement within ethnocentric standards."[13]

He will, enthusiastically, concede a presumption of cultural equality and says that it would be quite wrong to evaluate alien ways of life in accordance with how far they reach Western standards.[14] These are not arbitrary, but it would be an example of cultural hegemony to insist that they should determine the criteria of judgment. All cultures have a claim not only to equal consideration but also to evaluation by reference to criteria that are not derived exclusively from one culture. It would appear that not only do differing cultures have a claim to consideration but the criteria for judgment ought not to be drawn from the insular horizons of one particular perspective.

But if there are no ultimately decisive cross-cultural criteria (or perhaps there are?), how can meaningful judgments be made? Does not the admission of multiculturalism, however much diluted by a cryptic and sotto voce commitment to some objective standards, throw us once again into a sea of relativity? To this obvious objection Taylor invokes some platitudinous arguments about the need to explore divergent cultures, to internalize their rules and practices and to acquaint ourselves with the intricacies of differing ways of life. The nearest that Taylor gets to invoking a tangible criterion is to suggest that "[as] a presumption, the claim is that all human cultures that have animated whole societies over some considerable stretch of time have something important to say to all human beings."[15] But even here he is prepared to admit that this feature is itself inadequate to justify a claim to equal worth and that cultures can go through phases of decadence. Furthermore, one can doubt that all this is fully consistent with his other references to liberal values. After all, quite illiberal cultures have maintained themselves through time, have guaranteed a certain kind of predictability in their legal arrangements, and have generated certain standards of civility.

What Taylor is searching for is a kind of nonrelativist combination of values that are derived from an extensive study of the variety of cultures. It is an approach that he hopes will deter us from ethnocentrism and encourage a resistance to the temptation to judge others by our own standards. What he wants of us is a "willingness to be open to comparative study of the kind that must displace our horizons in the resulting fusions."[16] But the determined antiliberal multiculturalist would claim that the assessments that are made of the contributions that differing groups make to the march of civilization are inevitably biased. Are we not implicitly invoking allegedly universal liberal standards when we make the necessary discriminations?

It should be noted here that these anodyne comments sit rather uneasily with pluralism, an orientation that seems to animate much of Taylor's thought. The pluralist does not pretend that concentrated study of rival cultures will produce some modus vivendi, some convenient confluence of the various cultural, social and political streams that flow (apparently) haphazardly in the world. With Isaiah Berlin he explicitly asserts that there is no way that such diversity can be resolved and no Archimedean point by which rival claims can be assessed. Instead, for the genuine pluralist, we inhabit a world characterized by incompatible ways of life. The most that can be said for liberal pluralism is that it implicitly recognizes this disharmony and that liberal societies do at least provide institutional arrangements through which competing value systems can peacefully coexist (though ultimately they cannot be reconciled). Still, the determined multiculturalist will maintain that even this tolerance is a subtle form of hegemony. Perhaps pluralism reduces to the claim that there is some kind of generic moral code that at least aims at the security that must be guaranteed if individuals who claim allegiance to widely different cultures are to coexist. This might consign public rules to the status of coordinating mechanisms. But in a genuinely pluralistic world that is all they can be.

Taylor clearly wants more than this. Although he admits that we are "very far away from that ultimate horizon from which the relative worth of different cultures might be evident,"[17] that is his ultimate telos. It is indeed consistent with all that he says about the public realm and the importance in a democratic society of fostering it, of engaging all in a public debate out of which might emerge common standards. There is little recognition of the argument that the most promising way of preserving some kind of peace between potentially warring cultural factions is simply to allow competition between them. This is not a competition from which one conception of the good will ultimately win, or one in which some common horizon might be reached, but a social arrangement that allows all to survive, though some will do better than others. This does require that social institutions should be founded on the recognition of, at least, a generic morality—a morality that provides security for the participants in cultural competition.

There is an obvious parallel here with the above argument that political diversity can be best coped with by decentralized government, one with wide opportunities for exit from undesirable regimes (either cultural or political). This would clearly require considerable scope for privacy and the necessity of arrangements that allow, for example, opting out of state-controlled schooling. But in Taylor's scheme of things this would be a surrender to subjectivism (or atomism)—an admission of the impossibility of finding common cultural ground (though in his case, one supposes, this must now be a cross-cultural common ground). But it does not follow from a denial of an ultimate point of harmony that we are thrown back on purely personal judgments about cultural standards. We are not committed to that narcissistic notion of authenticity, the destructive nature of which he correctly diagnoses, merely because we are skeptical of the possibilities of decisive cultural comparisons. The exercise of the exit option (and the retreat into privacy) is not to abandon the very notion of nonsubjective judgment, to make all morality merely a matter of taste and to confuse ethical appraisal with purely emotive responses. We can still concede that our self-understanding will be largely a function of our relationships with others and reject the notion that self-understandings have to be rooted in some one incontrovertible public domain. There can be little worlds of self-chosen privacy that may logically be incompatible with each other but still mutually tolerant of their differences. This approach does not so much represent the hegemony of Western values as much as a Hobbesian recognition that there is a fundamental human desire for security.

Taylor and Contemporary Conservatism

In some ways Taylor's philosophical anti-individualism, and his rejection of that moral subjectivism which is such a feature of the modern world, can be interpreted sympathetically by contemporary conservatives. His exposure of the rootlessness of the modern individual and his critique of modern liberal society as consisting of little more than anonymous utility-maximizers held together by abstract laws strikes a common chord with those traditionalists who despair at the damage to communities that an unrestrained market system has produced (though these conservatives seem to be unaware of the inhibitions that actually constrain market traders). A more economically minded conservative would also stress that the fraying of the moral fabric of society is not so much the outcome of an anonymous market as the inevitable consequence of a welfare state that provides benefits without reciprocal obligations. The society of "dutiless egoists," at which Taylor is disturbed, is more the product of unencumbered welfare payments than the price system, which necessarily instils in people a certain sense of responsibility.

Still, conservatives would share with him a great disquiet at the extent to which America especially has succumbed to a soulless legalism and has created a culture in which everyone knows their "rights" but no one has any (social) duties. When once intractable problems, like abortion, religion in schools, and so on were coped with (I do not say solved, especially with regard to abortion) by local opinion, they have now become "constitutionalized" and made the subjects of definitive and incontrovertible legal judgments. One of the specific constitutional errors of *Roe v. Wade* (1973) was its elimination of that communal input into crucially important decisions that federalism theoretically permits. This, of course, has increased social tensions and has badly corroded those communal bonds that are the essential features of civil society. As Taylor says proper liberalism "must offer some view of how the individual should live with others." He is surely right in his claim that "we may still need to see ourselves as part of a larger whole which can make claims on us."[18]

What seems unlikely to appeal to a conservative (least of all a *classical* liberal) is the grounding of many of his critical observations on modern crises, and his prescriptions for their resolution. He still seems to be the prisoner of a teleological belief that there is an overall purpose to social life and that this can be perceived philosophically. More controversial is his claim that public policy can be restructured on the basis of a potential agreement about such a purpose. Even in the context of multiculturalism, which one would have thought most inhospitable to this way of thinking, Taylor persists in his search for an ultimate harmony in human affairs. The pluralism that he tentatively espouses is not, apparently, a reason for despair, for even in diversity there is some hope that superficially irreconcilable groups can reach some common purpose. That is why he has invoked the concept of hypergoods. But here it is ironic to notice that cultural diversity is permissible only in the context of judicially protected rights.

This is most apparent in his analysis of Canada. He seems not to be aware of the fact that, historically, rights claims have functioned as boundary lines within which different cultures have survived (though not always flourished). No one culture could claim a decisive victory (either ethical or political) in such protective arrangements but each could acknowledge the integrity of the others. My other comments on the possibility of exit should be interpreted in this deliberately nonteleological manner. It is simply not the case that the whole of morality is derived from rights premises, although it is factually the case that a kind of expansive rights-based mutation has occurred in the twentieth-century development of liberalism. One suspects that a Taylor type of collective telos would function in practice rather like the intrusive, rights-based liberalism he is anxious to discourage.

What is important here is the stress that Taylor has always placed on the public as the primary resource for individuals to use for the achievement of freedom, morality, and community. I have already alluded to his rejection of Rousseau's invocation of a potentially oppressive General Will that would destroy the differences between people. But his other works, which insistently call for the emergence of collective movements that can, apparently, deal with the problems of alienation and the citizens' detachment from democracy and politics, reveal distinctly Rousseauistic overtones. The public is a kind of arena in which common decisions can be reached over an unspecified range of issues: "People who never meet understand themselves to be engaged in discussion, and capable of reaching a common mind." And in an explicit critique of single-issue politics he argues for the "formation of democratic majorities around meaningful programs that can then be carried to completion."[19]

He may well be right about fragmentation and retreats into either legalism or single issues and sectional interests that feature so strongly in modern society, but the mobilization of public opinion that he seems to demand is unlikely to solve these problems. We know too much from public choice theory to be at all sanguine about the prospects for individual self-realization and meaningful freedom in regimes characterized by a large degree of political action. Indeed, the vast politicization of private life that has occurred in the twentieth century is partly to blame for those ills of society that he has, not inexpertly, diagnosed.

The problem of fragmentation could be explained more cogently by the public choice school's exposure of the inadequacy of conventional democratic rules to transmit the genuine public good. Under simple majority rule the wealth of a nation becomes a resource that can be exploited by coalitions of interest groups that almost always act contrary to the interests of citizens taken as members of the anonymous public. Constitutional restraints are no longer effective. What is required here is not a Taylor-style public "conversation" but a redesigned set of constitutional rules that more expeditiously unites private and public interest.

Again, Taylor's understanding of "reason" is not conducive to the kind of harmony he desires. In an attack on "instrumental" reason, by which he means the limited, calculative role attributed to it by people such as Hume, Taylor seems to think that a more expansive, Aristotelian aspect of our cognitive faculties would produce a kind of agreement about values that transcends a commitment to procedural rules, even in a pluralist society. But in the multicultural world that now interests him, the fact that people define themselves in terms of *difference* is a death blow to the ultimate unity for which he yearns. What he is not prepared to concede is that a refined notion of political choice, as defined above, could be an acceptable surrogate for this. People in a multicultural society may not be able to live together in pursuit of a collective goal, but they can surely live side by side under limited common rules.

I suspect that his refusal to consider this radical political pluralism derives from his distrust of the market, which is undeniably the model for the jurisdictional competition I have outlined. Both the political and the economic market are predicated on the notion of *choice,* and that, for Taylor, would be a descent into atomism. With regard to the market he simply asserts that "stability, and hence efficiency, couldn't survive (the) massive withdrawal of government from the economy, and it is doubtful either could long survive the competitive jungle that a really wild capitalism would breed, with its uncompensated inequalities and exploitation."[20] And in an implicit rejection of the claim that the market is the only coherent ordering mechanism in a world of diversity and potential conflict (leaving aside its contribution to peace that writers since Montesquieu have noted) he argues for some highly politicized vector that encompasses "market allocations, state planning, collective provision for need, the defence of individual rights and effective democratic initiative and control."[21]

It is difficult to think of a vaguer political program to present to a multicultural society. And when it is not vacuous it is likely to be a much bigger cause of social division than the market has been. What is noticeable here is that Taylor's brand of communitarianism operates primarily at the national level. His support for the conventional welfare state and public action needed to alleviate deprivation (as revealed in the above quotation) shows no awareness of those more adventurous communitarians who seek the solutions to many of our problems in the recreation of those vibrant communities that once attended to needs at the local level. Nathan Glazer points out that "every piece of social policy substitutes for some traditional arrangement . . . in which public authorities take over, at least in part, the role of the family, of the ethnic and neighbourhood group, of voluntary associations."[22] What Taylor seems not to be aware of is that those liberal rules of equality, fairness, nondiscrimination, and so on (which Taylor supports, despite the asymmetries he tolerates elsewhere in the liberal creed) make this sort of communal action virtually impossible. Communities will discriminate against nonmembers, and this is alien to Taylor's liberalism. It would, however, be permitted in the world of competitive jurisdictions I have tentatively outlined.

Conclusion

The task that Taylor set himself in *Multiculturalism* (and related works) was to reconcile two apparently conflicting doctrines: liberalism, with its stress on formal (or substantive) equality, universal and nondiscriminatory law, and communitarianism, which emphasizes the distinctive properties of identifiable groups and demands that the law recognize them and, indeed, privilege them if the remorseless progress of a free and open society threatens their integrity. He hopes that a properly articulated transcendence of these two warring categories will make their invocation in political debate redundant.

However, far from achieving any kind of modus vivendi, he has only managed to confuse their intellectual identities so that they would scarcely be recognized by their apologists. Taylor's deliberate downgrading of personal choice in the liberal credo succeeds only in eliminating all those mechanisms that a properly articulated set of liberal institutions had developed for dealing with problems of potential communal tension. And the effective "nationalizing" of the concept of community has similarly drained it of its traditional vitality in the creation of decentralized arrangements for coping with not only the problem cultural difference but also the isolated cases of deprivation that occur even in advanced and prosperous societies. Because Taylor accepts only the contemporary American notion of liberalism, with its acceptance of statism, excessive tolerance (i.e., of potentially socially disruptive groups), and antimarket prejudice, he leaves the liberal order defenseless against a virulent multiculturalism that would impose a new form of intolerance on a nominally free society. We see this in the dominant relativist doctrine that any cultural tradition is as good as any other and that there are no real standards of critical appraisal that can have a more or less universal appeal. Taylor is himself aware of the latter danger in his somewhat desperate (and reluctant) rejection of the idea that each cultural tradition is of equal value.

If he had looked to an older tradition of liberalism, he would have noticed that freedom, properly understood, is remarkably fecund at creating institutions and practices for coping with difference. The theory of competitive jurisdictions, in which decentralized polities offer their own sets of laws and cultural practices in a marketplace of laws, ideas, and values, suggests invaluable mechanisms for resisting the encroachment of one group on the affairs of another and for preventing the imposition of one code of conduct on society as a whole. Of course, Taylor is frightened of the illiberalism that might predominate in smaller groups in such a system. It is true that the right of exit is less than satisfactory as a solution to such a problem, since the costs it involves harm those people who are compelled to take this option. But the imposition of a liberal code, with all the paraphernalia of legalism and the judicial protection of rights involves just that imposition of values to which the multiculturalists object. But this dissent from liberalism has come about largely because the contemporary liberal political order has enshrined into law certain moral values that have offended the sensibilities of religious and other culturally differentiated groups. The enforcement of liberal welfarism has seriously weakened voluntary action based on "little communities" (which might well be based on race or religion) and has generated seemingly insoluble problems of dependency and fractured communities.

The market may indeed be the only form of social arrangement that can unite otherwise disparate peoples (or members of multicultural quasi-communities) as the globalization of trade suggests. People of different cultures seem to transact economically with some security without any of the philosophical attributes deemed by Taylor to be essential for stability. We may look forward to an age when cultural differences really do not matter or at least can be confined to those aspects of life that do not need the constant supervision of the state. The cultural flourishing of communal groups does not have to be a matter of political concern. When it does become part of the agenda of government, the tensions between groups, each determined to secure recognition through political action, become serious.

6

On the Extent of Community: Civil Society, Civil Religion, and the State

Brad Lowell Stone

The main forms of communitarianism differ in their conception of the extent of community. Some communitarians believe that human nature restricts salutary fellow feeling to a particular and limited sphere. Others believe that community of an extended, even universal, scope is possible. In its most concrete and divisive form, however, the communitarian controversy relates to the proper role of government. Those who conceive natural limits on community see state action as potentially destructive of communities, whereas proponents of the extensive view of community consider the state the only viable organ for achieving their aims. Robert Bellah and his associates express the latter view in *The Good Society* when they say they

> feel that the word "communitarian" runs the risk of being misunderstood if one imagines that only face-to-face groups—family, congregations, neighborhood—are communities and that communitarians are opposed to the state, the economy and all the large structures that so dominate our lives today. Indeed, it is our sense that *only* greater citizen participation in the large structures of the economy and the state will enable us to surmount the deepening problems of contemporary life.[1]

By "greater citizen participation in the large structures of the economy and state," Bellah and his coauthors are expressing their hope that citizens will see the wisdom of state intervention in the economy, a hope shared by other communitarians, including Ronald Beiner, Amitai Etzioni, Roberto Unger, and Michael Walzer.[2] On the other side are communitarians such as Robert Nisbet, Peter Berger, John Neuhaus, Charles Murray, and Michael Novak who believe that natural communities are face-to-face groups opposed to and by the state.[3] Nonetheless, when advancing their perspective, statist communitarians typically ignore contemporary thinkers who speak of natural community, and they ignore or misrepresent the intellectual tradition of which these thinkers are a part.[4] A common strategy involves contrasting "liberalism and communitarianism," where liberalism is represented by thinkers such as Robert Nozick and John Rawls, and communitarianism in its statist variety is presented as the alternative.[5]

This state of affairs, is unfortunate because of both who is participating and who is not participating in these debates, a condition I cannot completely address within the scope of this essay. I will not focus directly on the contemporary communitarians who conceptualize community as having natural limits. Nonetheless, very prominent among my purposes is identifying and recommending the principal intellectual tradition from which these thinkers draw, in addition to describing and criticizing Robert Bellah's statist communitarianism and the intellectual tradition inspiring Bellah. No matter what language is used, it is important to recognize that questions about the extent of community are as old as the modern era itself. What is at stake in the current debates over the nature of community is the relationship between "civil society"—the associations of family, locale, conscience, and commerce—and the state. This relationship preoccupied the likes of Alexis de Tocqueville and Karl Marx, but it was in the eighteenth century that the distinction between civil society and the state was drawn. The original postures on the relationship of the two were struck by the Baron de Montesquieu, the Scottish moralists (David Hume, Adam Ferguson, Adam Smith), and Edmund Burke on the side of natural community, and by Rousseau on the side of extended political community.

Bellah's writings on "civil religion" demonstrate Rousseau's distinct influence. But even when Rousseau's direct influence is not apparent, Bellah is typically inspired by famed French sociologist Emile Durkheim who is himself best viewed as a Rousseauean.[6] Bellah shares his intellectual forebears' disdain for civil society, and he echoes their belief in the redemptive powers of the state. For their part, Robert Nisbet, Peter Berger, Michael Novak, and other contemporary conservative communitarians take their bearings from eighteenth-century conservative or classical liberal sources. For Montesquieu, the Scottish moralists, and Burke, the distinction between civil society and the state was essential to their conception of the liberal or commercial republic. These men asserted the ontological priority of communities or society over the polity. They saw civil society as containing natural ends regarding which the state must be a neutral umpire or servant, never master, in order to maintain ordered liberty and avoid political tyranny. For these men, humans are by nature social or communal. In their view, the reach of communal affection and obligation is necessarily limited, and because of the size of nation-states, these thinkers distinguished between two realms within civil society—a communal, private realm and a public, primarily commercial realm. These two realms are arranged on very different principles. Within the private realm of family, faith, and friendship, character is formed, benevolence toward intimates is shown, and common aims are undertaken. Within the public realm of commerce, on the other hand, laws of justice regulate encounters among strangers, and self-interest is pursued. According to these theorists, neither the commercial realm nor the state itself can be organized as a community, given the natural limits on human sociability, or, to say the same thing differently, given the presence of human partiality. However fine statist communitarian sentiments or rhetoric may seem, a state actually founded on the "general will," "collective conscience," or a supposed common good (beyond common defense, the creation of public works, and the administration of internal justice) is a state that lacks the institutional means for checking the ill effects of human partiality and the concentration of power.

I will proceed by discussing Bellah's statist communitarianism and the sources of Bellah's inspiration. I do this chiefly through an analysis of civil religion as conceived by Bellah, Rousseau, and Durkheim. I will then suggest that the empirical evidence does not support Bellah's worldview and that conservative or classical liberal communitarian views better illuminate contemporary American problems, while providing clear directions as to how these problems might be addressed.

Civil Religion and Statist Communitarianism

Robert Bellah has been nothing if not consistent over the last thirty years. In the introduction to the 1996 "updated" edition of *Habits of the Heart,* he and his coauthors state that "if communitarianism means opposition to the neocapitalist agenda and to a theoretical liberalism for which autonomy is almost the only virtue then we are communitarians. But if it means a primary emphasis on small scale and face-to-face relations . . . we are not communitarians." Our present difficulties, Bellah and his coauthors assert, are "deep structural problems" that cannot be addressed by "an increase in devotion to community in this narrow sense." Instead, solutions to American problems such as poverty, the shrinking middle class, and waning trust in public institutions require "collective responsibility," a form of "republicanism or even nationalism" at the center of which is "national consensus and national action." The authors call us "to wider and wider circles of loyalty, ultimately embracing that universal community of all beings. . . ." They state, "Any community short of the universal community is not the beloved community."[7]

These same views of community and the state are contained in Bellah's writings on civil religion, the first of which was written in 1967. In that original essay Bellah uses the term "civil religion" to refer to "certain common elements of religious orientation that the great majority of Americans share . . . a set of beliefs, symbols and rituals." At its best, he states, American civil religion "is a genuine apprehension of transcendent religious reality as seen in or, one could almost say, as revealed through the experience of the American people." Such a civil religion, Bellah says, guided this nation through the crises of the Revolutionary period and the civil war and is essential to addressing what he deems a third great crisis. "This is the problem of responsible action in a revolutionary world, a world seeking to attain many of the things, material and spiritual, that we have already attained." Thus Bellah's civil religion not only transcends the particularism or exclusivity of church or sect, it potentially transcends national boundaries. His "eschotological hope" lies with a new international order. "So far," he acknowledges, "the flickering flame of the United Nations burns too low to be the focus of a cult, but the emergence of a transnational sovereignty would certainly change this. It would necessitate the incorporation of vital international symbolism into our civil religion or, perhaps a better way of putting it, it would result in American civil religion becoming simply one part of a new civil religion of the world."[8]

Bellah's utopian vision of a future transnational sovereignty is one that he shares with Rousseau and Durkheim. For Bellah (like his forerunners), this vision follows from a belief in something of an arcadian past. Bellah conjures images of a time when individuals overcame their particularistic attachments in the pursuit of a common good—a circumstance that stands in stark contrast to our egoistic and individualistic age. For these men, the individual and the community are at odds. The good is located in the moral consensus of the community, and although we exist in a fallen state, community could be made pure once again, while growing ever larger, if individuals were to embrace their common humanity.

The state, in this view, is essential to maintaining moral consensus. In a comment on Durkheim's conception of "common conscience," Bellah says that "since the state is the organ of consciousness of society, it must have a relation to common conscience which is at the same time moral and religious. The state must be intimately related to the deepest level of value consensus in the society, what I have called in another connection, following Rousseau, the civil religion."[9] In this view, state sponsored value consensus is both a means to an end and an end itself. Civil religion, for Bellah, is public reverence for the public. It requires and encourages "zeal for the public good," the source of virtue, the antithesis to which is "concern for one's own good," the source of corruption.[10] Civil religion, for Bellah, is conveyed through whatever sponsors self-abasement and love for the social aggregate or collective, the broader the collective the better. In his view, zeal for the public good sustains a pious respect for the state. The state is deemed the only means for achieving the public good, and material equality is considered essential to the common interest. Thus, according to Bellah, within a properly conceived civil religion, "equality is a condition for the fulfillment of humanity," freedom requires submission of individual desires to the common good "and is almost identical with virtue," and the pursuit of happiness is "the realization of our true humanity in love of Being and of all beings."[11]

For Bellah, religion and politics are fused within civil religion. Politics is sacralized, creating a unity in which religious sentiments have political ends. (As Rousseau puts it, civil religion represents the "unification of the two heads of the eagle and the complete restoration of political unity, without which no state or government will ever be well constituted."[12]) For Bellah, the ideal is a republican order within which virtue is identical with political virtue. Within this republican vision, political life although instrumental to other, especially material ends, is also an end in itself. Liberty is liberty of the public, and the voice of the demos knows no limits. (All law is willful and conventional.) Because the extent of community is unlimited, there are no natural limits on the capacity humans have for fashioning and refashioning society according to the lights of metaphysical reason. And because material life and luxury can divide humanity and destroy the equality necessary for a commitment to the public good, material conditions must be brought under the supervising authority of the state.

According to Bellah, selfishness and a lack of humanity are not natural; they are attributable to our social circumstances. We inhabit a civil condition in which social pluralism, luxury, and commerce breed egoism or individualism, the alternative to which is a republican order supported by civil religion. Such views clearly and consciously derive from the French humanist tradition of Rousseau and Durkheim, brief attention to which further highlights Bellah's fundamental assumptions and orientation. Each of these three men displays an abhorrence for separation and a profound, almost narcissistic desire for unity; for each, the religion of humanity combines with a "spirit of system" (as Adam Smith called it) or a preoccupation with "general ideas" (as Tocqueville described it) that makes each man indifferent to or even hostile toward individual liberties and genuinely natural attachments. Each sees civil society as engendering evils for which a unifying civil religion is the proper antidote.

Rousseau originated the term "civil religion." He believed that humans naturally possess a form of self-love (*amore de soi*), "which is always good and always in conformity with order."[13] In the state of nature humans enjoyed simple and undivided *amore de soi* and "the natural sentiment of pity took the place of laws, mores and virtues."[14] Civil society, however, replaces this form of self-love with *amore-propre,* a form of self-love that relies on social comparison and is never content. Civil society unleashes reason, imagination, "and man's sentiment of his connections with others," creating perversities in the naturally good heart of man—jealousy, envy, imperiousness, and deceit. For Rousseau, civil society is the cause of an inauthentic dependency on "opinion" and is the source of invidious distinction. Rousseau sees the history of civil society as largely a history of the enlargement of *amore-propre* within the human heart, for civil society sponsors luxury and inequality. "Luxury, impossible to prevent among men who are greedy for their own conveniences and for the esteem of others, soon completes the evil that societies have begun. . . . From society and the luxury it engenders, arise the liberal and mechanical arts, commerce, letters and all those useless things that make industry flourish, enriching and ruining states." Luxury is "the worst of all evils in any state," and, for Rousseau, the supposed progress of civil society represents "the decay of the species."[15]

This decay, however, did not unfold uninterruptedly, according to Rousseau. Rousseau perceived in ancient Sparta the closest real approximation to his ideal society: a true republican society where personal affections ran to the homeland rather than the land and where *amour-propre* was shaped into expressions of patriotic and marital virtue.[16] In Sparta, men were true *citizens* and patriots. But in modern civil society men are mere *bourgeois.* "The bourgeois," in the words of one commentator, is Rousseau's "great invention." It "is unpoetic, unerotic, unheroic, neither aristocrat nor of the people; he is not a citizen, and his religion is pallid and this-worldly."[17] Nonetheless, there is no literal going back to our natural condition or to the age of tribes and city-states in order to remedy the problems of bourgeois society. Consequently, "he who dares to undertake the establishment of a people should feel that he is, so to speak, in a position to change human nature, to transform each individual (who by himself is a perfect and solitary whole) into a part of a larger whole from which this individual receives, in a sense, his life and being."[18] According to *The Social Contract,* the solution to the problem of modern civil society is a state guided by a legislator capable of fusing particular wills into a "general will."

Although the extreme individualism of *The Discourses* and the collectivism of *The Social Contract* have sometimes perplexed readers, these works form a whole that exhibits a thoroughgoing disdain for the pluralism, luxury, spontaneity, interdependency, and independence of modern civil society. For Rousseau, civil society splinters and fragments the elementary and unified soul of natural man, the modern remedy for which is a unifying state. Accordingly, in the final chapter of *The Social Contract*, "On Civil Religion," Rousseau proposes a unified and authoritarian state religion as an essential alternative to divisive Roman Catholicism and to the weakness of what he calls "True Christianity." Roman Catholicism, for Rousseau, is "bizarre," hardly worth the effort required to prove its faults. Because it exists independent of the state, Rousseau says, it "gives men two sets of legislation, two leaders, and two homelands," thereby subjecting them "to contradictory duties" and preventing them "from being simultaneously devout men and citizens." True Christianity, meanwhile, is a religion of the heart without rites or a homeland. It "preaches servitude and dependence. . . . True Christians are made to be slaves." What is needed, therefore, "is a purely civil profession of faith, the articles of which it belongs to the sovereign to establish, not exactly as dogmas of religion, but as sentiments of sociability, without which it is impossible to be a good citizen or a faithful subject." These articles should be simple—the existence of God and an afterlife, "the happiness of the just; the punishment of the wicked, the sanctity of the social contract and the laws." It is the sovereign's duty "to banish anyone who does not believe" these articles.[19] Cults and intolerance cannot be tolerated, Rousseau says. Nothing should compete with the sovereignty of the state.

Rousseau's influence on Bellah is great, and Bellah readily acknowledges his debt in his writings on civil religion. For Bellah, as for Rousseau before him, egoism is a socially constructed disposition. The individual in commercial society is at odds with the greater good. Because of its inequality and attenuated public spiritedness, the decadence of the bourgeois order is revealed when it is compared with certain previous conditions or an imagined ideal republican order. The ideal is a civil circumstance in which individuals overcome their local and parochial attachments, committing to the public good whose vehicle is the state and whose maintenance requires self-abnegation. Beyond Rousseau's influence, though, the significance of Durkheim to Bellah's views must be acknowledged. Durkheimianism is Bellah's main bridge to Rousseau. Bellah calls Durkheim "a high priest and theologian of the civil religion."[20] The two elements of the term "civil religion" are almost redundant for Durkheim, since he believed that the origins of religious sentiment lie with the awe individuals inevitably feel for the overweening power and authority of the social aggregate. Society is God, for Durkheim, and in worshiping God, we are worshiping society.[21] He believed this phenomenon is most clear in the original religion, totemism, in which sacred symbols represented the clan/society, but it is no less true of other religions. Religion, he says, "is nothing other than a body of collective beliefs and practices endowed with a certain authority." Thus for Durkheim, Rousseau's "religion of humanity has everything it needs to speak to its faithful in a no less imperative tone than the religions it replaces." Durkheim saw an unfortunate individualism in Rousseau's ideas, but he observed that "doctrines are judged above all by what they produce—that is by the spirit of the doctrines to which they give birth." In Durkheim's eyes, according to this criterion, Rousseau must be very highly esteemed. "As for Rousseau, we know his individualism is complemented by his authoritarian conception of society. Following him, the men of the Revolution, even while promulgating the famous Declaration of Rights, made of France an indivisible and centralized entity. Perhaps, we should see in the work of the Revolution above all a great movement of national concentration."[22] For Durkheim, "national concentration" represents moral advancement because moral advancement depends in every instance on what he calls "common conscience" or "collective representations."

Durkheim supported the Third Republic, but he shared Rousseau's disdain for the egoism of the bourgeois order. He lamented the paucity of unifying sentiments in modern society. Like Rousseau before him and Bellah after, Durkheim considered the state the only viable organ for unifying the general will out of particular wills. He described but did not lament the decline of traditional intermediate or secondary groups such as the family, the church, and local and regional territorial affiliations. He saw national unity as an ideal to be realized through a state-directed priesthood of secular educators capable of instilling a "spirit of discipline," and an "attachment to the group" through the creation of "corporations."[23] For Durkheim, corporations are "public institutions" whose membership would be mandatory for everyone in different professions or industries. Since "the market, formally municipal, has become national and international, the corporations must assume the same extension." Such corporations, for Durkheim, would have economic functions (they would set wages and prices and arbitrate labor disputes), political functions (they would be the very basis of representation), and especially moral functions: "What we especially see in the occupational group is a moral power capable of containing individual egos, of maintaining a spirited sentiment of common solidarity in the consciousness of all the workers, of preventing the law of the strongest from being brutally applied to industrial and commercial relations."[24]

Bellah speaks of "cancerous individualism" instead of *amore-propre* and *egoisme* and refers to "national consensus," "collective responsibility," and the "common good" instead of the "general will" and "collective conscience." But his conception of civil religion simply reiterates the basic themes of French humanism. Also, despite a few changes in language, there is perfect continuity between Bellah's work on civil religion and his more recent coauthored works *Habits of the Heart* and *The Good Society.* I will turn immediately to these recent works and to alternatives to Bellah's work as a whole after making two additional observations on civil religion. First, although Bellah claims that his view of civil religion is "consonant with classical natural law," at no point in his writings does he make any effort to ground such law in God's law or nature. After referring to the famous *Time* magazine article announcing God's death, Bellah says that today "the meaning of 'God' is by no means . . . clear or obvious." Indeed, he likens Christianity to a Stalinist variant of Marxism and criticizes it for making "idolatrous commitments to particular structures and people." The good society is not composed of individuals serving others according to God-given, immutable, standards; nor can nature serve as a reliable guide, for it yields no prescriptions. The good society, for Bellah, is "a society dedicated to its own transcendence, to the realization of human values."[25] As a good Rousseauean/Durkheimian, Bellah has a thoroughly socialized conception of the law. What remains of religion in Bellah's "civil religion" is social, temporal, and instrumental; it is simply yoked to political ends.[26]

Second, regarding Bellah's vision of a future international order, an appeal to the good sense and authority of James Madison is in order. The Founders made few references to Rousseau. But Madison, in a 1792 article in *The National Gazette* entitled "Is Universal Peace Possible?" discussed his view of a transnational sovereignty. Madison commences the essay by observing, "Among the various reforms which have been offered to the world, the projects of universal peace have done the greatest honor to the hearts, though they seem to have done very little to the heads of their authors. Rousseau, the most distinguished of these philanthropists, has recommended a confederation of sovereigns, under a council of deputies, for the dual purpose of arbitrating external controversies among nations, and of guaranteeing their respective governments against internal revolutions." Madison continues by saying that Rousseau was unaware of the impossibility of executing his pacific plans because he failed to comprehend the allurements of governments to war and "what is more extraordinary, of the tendency of his plan to perpetuate arbitrary power wherever it existed." Of Bellah's hopes and projects concerning a transnational sovereignty sustained by an international civil religion we may conclude as Madison concluded concerning Rousseau's projects: "They will never exist but in the imaginations of visionary philosophers, or in the hearts of benevolent enthusiasts. . . . The project of Rousseau, was, consequently as preposterous as it was impotent."[27]

For various reasons, Bellah's writings on civil religion generated a great deal of controversy and he consequently quit using the term. Nonetheless, he acknowledges the continuity between his position on civil religion and his recent writings most associated with communitarianism. He observed in 1989 that the argument in his original essay on civil religion "seemed obvious to me. It is the sort of thing any Durkheimian would have said. I have never recanted my position on civil religion. . . . *Habits of the Heart* is very much concerned with the same substantive issues as my writings on civil religion."[28]

Some of Bellah's ideas are sensible. For example, certain of his writings recognize the significance of religious pluralism and the importance of local and parochial attachments, described as the "soft structures" of society.[29] Indeed, much (but far from all) of what he and his younger associates say regarding "communities of memory" in *Habits of the Heart* is lyrical and profound. Moreover, this book displays a fine sense for the problems of contemporary American life, which it identifies as a "cancerous individualism" and, following Michael Sandel, the problem of the "unencumbered self." For all this, however, Bellah and his coauthors completely lose sight of the natural communal institutions of civil society when they conclude *Habits of the Heart* with substantive recommendations for "reconstituting our social world."

They envision a social movement that "would lead to changes in the relationship between our government and our economy." Specifically, they quote Christopher Jencks in saying that government needs "to reduce the punishments of failure and rewards of success." They continue, "Reducing the inordinate rewards of ambition, and our inordinate fears of ending up losers, would offer the possibility of a great change in the meaning of work in our society and all that would go with such a change. To make a real difference, such a shift would have to be a part of a reappropriation of the idea of vocation or calling, a return in a new way to the idea of work as a contribution to the good of all and not merely as a means to one's own advancement." Additionally, they maintain, older notions of the corporation need to be rehabilitated so that the corporation is recognized as involving a "concession of public authority to a group *in return for* service to the public good." Doing so, they say, entails a form of "effective public accountability" that "would change what is now called 'the social responsibility' of the corporation from its present status . . . to a constitutive structural element in the corporation itself."[30]

Bellah and his associates conclude *Habits of the Heart* with a view of work and vocation that bears the clear imprint of Marx, and their conception of the corporation is fashioned along lines set out in Durkheim's discussion of corporatism.[31] These conclusions are unfortunate for a number of reasons, particularly their distortion of Tocqueville. Bellah and his coauthors claim Tocqueville as their chief source of inspiration in *Habits of the Heart.* Such a claim is odd at best and is possibly disingenuous. The wielding of state power in order to constrain liberty in the name of greater equality is what Tocqueville feared most about the democratic age. According to Tocqueville, equality fosters individualism—the tendency based on calm judgments to isolate oneself with one's family and friends with no civic concern beyond this small circle. Individualism in turn creates a void that is filled by a centralized authority that enervates and stifles initiative. Free and local "civil associations," on the other hand, for Tocqueville, combat individualism, encumber the self, instill "habits of the heart" and weaken the tendency toward democratic despotism.[32] *Habits of the Heart* is animated by the spirit of Rousseau and Durkheim, not Tocqueville.

To their credit (in a sense) Bellah and his coauthors drop the references to Tocqueville in *The Good Society,* the sequel to *Habits of the Heart. The Good Society* simply reproduces the statist recommendations of *Habits of the Heart.* Indeed, the most appreciable difference between these works is that *The Good Society* displays an even more extreme animus toward the public order of limited government and unregulated economies.

Civil Society and Conservative Communitarian Solutions

Bellah and his coauthors express indignation over the enduring economic inequality in America, which they believe is caused by the unhappy and discriminatory arrangement of the "large structures" of the economy and state. The facts of the matter, however, are much more mundane. American economic inequality exists because of familial, educational, religious, and ethnic differences among groups. Those groups that have low divorce and illegitimacy rates, for example, are at the top of the income heap, whereas those with high rates are at the bottom. Thus Jews have household incomes 50 percent greater than white gentiles; American-born Asians make 50 percent more than whites; Irish-American Catholics earn 25 percent more than Irish-American Protestants; on a per capita basis, African immigrants make 45 percent more than the American average; black Americans from the West Indies have income parity with whites. Overall, white household incomes are 50 percent greater than black household incomes, but college-educated black couples have virtual income parity with white couples of the same description.[33]

These facts are easily comprehended from the perspective supplied by Montesquieu, the Scottish moralists, and Burke, the original conservative communitarians and advocates of commercial republicanism. In a free market economy guided by impartial civil law, economic differences among groups reflect differences in acquired habits, skills, and capacities associated with the familial, religious, and ethnic variety of the American private realm. Bellah and many others see little but evil in the commercial order, but the original conservative communitarians believed that commerce can have beneficial effects. They believed that commercial activity, stimulated by luxury, innocently occupies people who might otherwise be prone to dangerous passions. They also believed it would reduce prejudices among nations and among groups within nations. They saw economic self-interest as the supreme means for leveling barriers that separate people. When sufficiently potent and when guided by reason within a free market, self-interest renders people insensible to someone else's method of baptism, foreskin status, taste for pork, and skin pigmentation. Calculating interest prohibits such concerns. Money is of no particular color, and unregulated markets render accurate judgments of talents and capacities.[34]

Bellah cannot image a spontaneous public order that relies on different interests rather than value consensus, and he has a difficult time imaging the existence of any group differences that are not at root class differences. In Bellah's egalitarian materialist view, group differences are, and must be, a function of material conditions and/or discrimination, all evidence to the contrary notwithstanding. In the new introduction to *Habits of the Heart,* Bellah and his coauthors claim that "poverty breeds drugs, violence and unstable families. . . ."[35] Unfortunately, for those who hold such a view, the evidence today for a materialist/Marxist sociology is about as strong as the evidence for a materialist/Marxist political economy—virtually nonexistent. The evidence does not show that poverty or any other structural factor produces unstable families. Rather, it is unstable, fatherless families that produce poverty, in addition to producing drug use, violence, and other forms of social pathology. Families headed by females are five times more likely to be poor than are male-headed families.[36] Similarly, children in fatherless households are at least twice as likely as children in two-parent homes to use drugs.[37] And the relationship between fatherlessness and violence is so strong that if the effect of fatherlessness is controlled, the relationship between poverty and crime and between race and crime disappears.[38] Seventy percent of all juveniles in state reform institutions, 70 percent of long-term prison inmates, 60 percent of rapists, and 72 percent of adolescent murderers come from fatherless homes.[39]

Regarding violence, it is also worth noting, given the media misrepresentations of the issue, that the decline in marriage is the root cause of increased violence against women and children. Generally, unmarried and divorced women are four times more likely to be victims of violent crime than are married women. Regarding domestic violence against women specifically, the National Crime Victimization Survey reveals that unmarried and divorced women suffer much more abuse than married women. As David Blankenhorn observes, "For example from 1979 through 1987, about 57,000 women per year were violently assaulted by their husbands. But 200,000 women per year were assaulted by boyfriends and 216,000 by ex-husbands."[40] And children are at greater risk of physical and sexual abuse when they live in single-parent households, live-in-boyfriend households, and stepfamilies. Abuse is extremely rare in households headed by both biological parents when compared to single-parent and stepparent households. For example, one Canadian study of preschoolers found that preschool children in stepfamily households are forty times more likely to suffer physical and sexual abuse than children in intact households.[41]

Consistent with their materialist conception, Bellah and his coauthors maintain that differences in material resources account for differences in educational achievement. They assert that "the money that would have been required to provide an infrastructure of education and economic opportunity for those in chronic poverty was never spent."[42] Again, there is absolutely no evidence to sustain these beliefs. Since the mid-sixties at least two hundred studies of the relationship between educational expenditures and achievement have been undertaken, not one of which has demonstrated a causal relationship between the two.[43] Meanwhile, numerous studies of family composition and achievement have found that when single-parent children are compared to two-parent children they are at least twice as likely to drop out of school and only half as likely to be educational high achievers.[44] Moreover, although the amount of evidence available at this point concerning the role of ethnicity is relatively slim, the evidence suggests that ethnicity may be even more important in accounting for the variation in educational achievement than family composition. Laurence Steinberg has found, for example, that family income, family composition, and maternal employment are all associated with school achievement. But when these factors are controlled for, none of them is as important as ethnicity. "In terms of school achievement . . . it is more advantageous to be Asian than to be wealthy, to have non-divorced parents, or to have a mother who is able to stay at home full-time." Steinberg is quick to point out that ethnicity is clearly a cultural, not a racial, phenomenon. "Asian students perform better in school because they work harder, try harder and are more invested in achievement—the very factors that contribute to school success among all ethnic groups." Furthermore, immigrant children outperform second or third generation schoolchildren from the same ethnic group. The "longer a student's family has lived in this country, the worse the youngster's school performance and mental health."[45]

All in all, the available evidence suggests that it is not material circumstances that shape culture. It is culture that determines material circumstances. (One is tempted to put Hegel right once again and say that it is the "superstructure" that determines the "understructure," not the reverse.) Our problems are chiefly problems of the heart. They arise from a freely chosen culture. Although subcultural differences exist and are important, the drift of our culture is uniform and destructive of human well-being. Ours is a culture in which the natural purpose of marriage, the rearing of children to maturity, has been replaced by the emotional and sexual gratification of adults; in which a natural division of labor has been replaced by an androgynous ideal buoyed by avarice; in which we have somehow convinced ourselves of women's exclusive right to choose but in which we are perplexed to find that men often refuse to shoulder responsibility for women's choices. Ours is a culture in which we hope for paternal investment but allow paternal confidence to erode. It is a culture in which marriage is deemed a mere contract and in which volitional fatherlessness has become routine. Our manners and morals have led to laws by which shucking one's spouse and children is easier than firing an employee, and violators of the marital covenant suffer fewer consequences than someone who breaches a business contract. Most generally, ours is a culture in which individuals are estranged from natural sentiments, natural attachments, natural duties, and natural institutions.

On more theoretical grounds, I believe the evidence suggests the validity of many conservative or classical liberal communitarian views. Traditional communitarians, of course, recognized the existence of nations but did not regard them as communities. They recognized that love of nation arises only from love of family, friends, neighbors, and other intimates—Burke's "little platoons." Loyalty to nation cannot exist without local and parochial attachments. Moreover, according to these thinkers, without local grounding the sort of universal loyalty or benevolence recommended by Bellah is at best impotent and at worst potentially dangerous. Benevolence, these men believed, is a natural sentiment; we are naturally inclined toward generosity and selflessness directed at our intimates. By its nature, however, salutary benevolence is particularistic.[46] For Adam Smith, universal benevolence is the source of "no solid happiness." He states that the "administration of the great system of the universe . . . the core of the happiness of all rational and sensible beings, is the business of God and not of man." Our lot is a humble one. Our duties lie close to home. As Smith observes, "The most sublime speculation of the contemplative philosopher can scarce compensate the neglect of the smallest active duty." And as Burke observed concerning Rousseau, who deposited his bastard children in foundling homes, Rousseau exhibited constantly "the stores of his powerful rhetoric in the expression of universal benevolence, whilst his heart was incapable of harboring one spark of common parental affection. . . . He melts with tenderness for those only who touch him by the remotest relation, and then, without one natural pang, casts away, as a sort of offal and excrement, the spawn of his disgustful amours and sends his children to the hospital of foundlings."[47] The danger of universal benevolence is that it can mask smug, indolent self-love and lead to the neglect of natural and tangible duties.

Views such as these are at the center of eighteenth-century classical liberal or conservative communitarian thought. According to Montesquieu, the Scottish moralists, and Burke, we are by nature social; our natural condition is conjugal, tribal, or communal. Within this condition humans were devoted to each other but hateful toward strangers. Political society, in this view, is not natural; it is the human solution to the problem of innate partiality and to the related problem of conflicts over property. Conservative communitarians distinguished between a private intimate realm and the public realm of commerce and government because of the extent of nation-states and because of the presence of human partiality. Regarding the public realm, these thinkers believed that selfish tendencies should be neutralized and exploited by free markets and by the separation and balancing of governmental powers. These things had to be in place in large modern nations because unlike citizens in ancient republics who could attain a large measure of fellow feeling based on similitude and intimacy, citizens in large republics typically encounter strangers for whom any sense of genuine fellow feeling is greatly attenuated. Thus public institutions in modern nations should be concerned chiefly with justice and just dessert, not with communal aims. These institutions must be arranged so that order is actually sustained by the intercourse of nonintimates who will tend to seek their respective interests and advantages.

In recognizing this, however, these thinkers were hardly of the opinion that the public side of human nature is human nature's only side or that public institutions are the only human institutions. Nor does this recognition imply that humans are either incapable of, or without need of, virtue. These men were convinced that both the public order and the individual pursuit of happiness require a citizenry who are enlightened about the good, whose characters are tempered and restrained. At a minimum, in their view, the public order requires occasional leaders capable of greatness, a sensible and civil electorate, certainly one that does not plunder the public till, and citizen workers who are capable of delaying immediate gratification and are diligent, frugal, and straightforward in their dealings. The liberal public order is designed to accommodate our most knavish qualities, but it could not persist if we were all knaves. These thinkers are one with the ancients in acknowledging the dependence of public life on virtue, although the virtues they recommended to sustain public life were moderate, mundane, and appropriate to popular governance.

The eighteenth-century conservative communitarians departed most dramatically from the ancients over the institutional sources of virtue and more particularly over the role of public institutions in their formation.

Although public institutions rest on virtue, these institutions tend to erode virtue. Consequently, these men believed that the inculcation of salutary qualities must occur chiefly outside the public realm within the natural, communal realm of intimates. In this view, goods are chiefly private goods; character formation is the responsibility of familiar institutions, especially the family and religious organizations; and the primary beneficiaries of noble and benevolent actions are our families, friends, neighbors, and fellow parishioners. Humans are neither angels nor hedonistic beasts. Instead, we are touched by both the angelic and the beastly, the individual mixture in each depending in large measure on the solidity and direction of the prepublic familiar or communal institutions in which we are reared, the tendencies of which are determined by the institutional settings in which we subsequently find ourselves.

According to the original conservative communitarians, certain differences between these types of institutions are essential to their identity and purposes. Whereas public institutions rely on benign tolerance and contain ideally blind, universalistic laws and procedures, communal institutions require a sense of exclusivity and are necessarily particularistic. The public institutions of government and commerce require a cool calculation of interests, the sophistication and harshness of which lead them to bar children from the institutions. Communal institutions, however, are home to natural benevolent sentiments and to children. Historically, liberal public institutions replaced traditional hierarchical ones, but communal institutions rely on traditional forms of authority and are the principal means by which individuals are linked to the past.

According to the original advocates of natural community, when these two types of institutions are properly distinguished and well framed, public institutions liberate, whereas familiar, communal institutions conserve. In this resides complementarity, not contradiction. Whereas impersonal public institutions cannot respect individual identity, genuine communal institutions provide identity by linking individuals to themselves and to the traditions they contain. Identity is primarily a function of natural, local, and parochial attachments, even if we outgrow them. The ability to stride forth into the public realm and undertake the risks that bring great rewards is provided by a sure and stable identity formed by genuine communal institutions.

To acknowledge that Rousseau was wrong to speak of the state transforming human nature is not to conclude that some form of transformation is not needed. The manners and morals of a people are conceivably just as essential to the modern order as the original conservative communitarian maintained. Without a culture that engenders approbativeness and promotes the natural communal institutions of civil society, a Hobbesian/Rousseauean solution—"a custodial state" for at least the few, if not the many—begins to appear to more and more people as the only solution to the extreme problems of "cancerous individualism" and the "unencumbered self," problems such as poverty, teen suicide, violent crime, drug abuse, and illegitimacy. We must recognize that our problems are problems of the heart; our culture and character require rehabilitation. Much more may in fact be at stake than we typically wish to admit. As Nathan Tarcov reminds us, "If the character of a people changes, then liberal institutions may no longer suit them; and since liberal institutions are not primarily character-forming, they seem to provide no guarantee against this eventuality or remedy for it if it does occur."[48]

7

Is William Galston Really a Liberal?

Peter Augustine Lawler

William Galston aims with *Liberal Purposes* to convince us that liberalism is a regime, a whole, a coherent understanding of the purposes of human life: "Liberalism contains *within itself* the resources it needs to declare and to defend a conception of the good and virtuous life that is in no way truncated or contemptible." He opposes the view of those "from Irving Kristol to Jurgen Habermas," those on the critical but sympathetic right and left, who say that liberalism depends on "the accumulated moral capital of revealed religion and premodern moral philosophy" and that the skepticism of liberalism more or less inevitably erodes those moral resources over time.[1]

Galston correctly observes that both Marxists and conservatives argue that liberalism has within itself the seeds of its own destruction. Galston argues that liberalism can free itself from illiberalism, or what he loosely calls moral traditionalism. But Galston's argument is unconvincing and rather obviously rhetorical. Galston wants contemporary liberals to accept him as one of their own and not reject him as a conservative critic. Tocqueville advised showing oneself to be equality's friend in order to moderate egalitarian extremism. Following Tocqueville's advice, Galston proclaims that his friendly criticisms of some contemporary liberals are made within the perspective of liberalism. As a liberal partisan, he corrects his fellow liberals only to secure better liberalism's perpetuation and progress. But what he actually shows is that any stable society is not wholly liberal and that a regime devoted primarily to securing human liberty does so by maintaining a host of tensions and contradictions.

Galston has written more candidly in other works about liberalism's self-destructive character. Allan Bloom, his teacher, wrote a best-seller that seemed to blame American relativism and apathetic "niceness" on the alien infusion of Nietzscheanism into a healthy liberal context. Galston corrected that impression by pointing out that relativism is a late moment in American liberalism's own development, the product of the spreading of the Lockean spirit of individual choice or contract into every area of human life.

Lockeanism is salutary only if properly limited, but it contains no limits within itself. So, Galston argues, "Bloom's own account suggests that modern liberal democracy is not stably well-ordered unless it is somehow mitigated by external forces (religion, traditional moral restraints, aristocracy) with which it is at war and which it tends to corrode."[2] Galston's own account of the excesses of contemporary liberal theorists makes the same suggestion. But what most liberals call "illiberal" Galston says we should now accept as functional from a liberal perspective. According to Galston, we should incorporate religion, moral traditionalism, and aristocracy into liberalism because it cannot survive without them. Galston humors liberal pretensions by declaring compromise victory.

My purpose is to show some of the ways Galston presents the forms of theoretical and practical incoherence that sustain human liberty. I address a question that Galston acknowledges remains a question, "whether the tensions I explore are wholly within liberalism, or between liberalism and other sources of moral authority as well."[3] The question is especially difficult because human liberty itself is not one thing but many. Galston's liberalism at its best is actually a "moral pluralism" that sees some intrinsic good in a variety of human qualities, some of them illiberal.

Liberalism as a Regime

In his view following Aristotle, Galston argues that modern liberalism is a regime, which means that liberal political decisions infuse every area of human endeavor. This view of the "primacy of the political" means that some liberals misconstrue "conscientious objection" as a right. No one can exempt himself from the duties of a citizen by some claim of personal or conscientious freedom. Liberal regimes may allow more space for personal freedom and diversity of ways of life than others do. But even they must put the preservation of political order first. A certain kind of political order is required for the effective exercise of liberty. Thus, in Galston's view, liberalism is far from morally neutral. Asserting definite or political claims about the human good, it favors some ways of life and tends to disrupt and even suppress others.

One liberal claim about the human good is that the deepest human longings and the highest human goals transcend the realm of politics. Religion, art, and philosophy are distorted by attempts at their political determination, but the liberal regime cannot help but shape them to some great extent. The amount of space to be allowed for the pursuits connected with transcendent freedom is a political or prudential decision and that space can never be infinite. So liberalism's comprehensive political claim over citizens is contradicted by its claim about personal transcendence. The liberal citizen is free enough to know that he is not fundamentally a citizen and the fact that he has that knowledge is in large part the result of a liberal political decision. Nonetheless, the liberal regime can, if it judges it necessary, treat citizens fundamentally as citizens or as instruments for securing its political perpetuation. Citizens, of course, can be compelled to fight and die in battle. They also must be subjected to civic education, persuasion, and habituation with the purpose of attaching and devoting them uncritically to their political community.

Galston states the liberal dilemma with ironic simplicity: "To be a citizen of a liberal polity is to be required to surrender as much of your own private conscience as is necessary for the secure enjoyment of what remains."[4] Surrender, security, and enjoyment are not words usually associated with conscientious thought and action, let alone citizenship. Liberalism distorts both the conscience and the citizen. Galston concludes his book by acknowledging that liberalism is only very imperfectly a regime; he distinguishes it by its consciousness of its imperfection. Liberalism leaves the relationship between public citizen and private individual very ill defined, giving itself "an endless task of imperfect adjustment."[5]

Ancient Liberalism

Galston regards Aristotle as a liberal. Aristotle held that human beings transcend political life through thought and that perhaps the only genuine human freedom is that of the philosopher. But Aristotle's philosophic way of life is possible, at best, for only a few, and the many are chained to the way of life, the laws, traditions, and so forth, of a particular political order. Political life cannot be transformed but only influenced indirectly by philosophers. Even philosophers depend on the existence of a stable political community that is endangered by the corrupting influence of the excessive politicization of philosophic skepticism. Aristotle viewed the primacy of the political as an ineradicable necessity rooted in human nature. Ancient liberalism did not intend to be the animating principle of any particular regime. All political orders are fundamentally illiberal.

For an Aristotelian, or ancient, liberal the claim of modern liberalism that all human beings transcend their regime through their personal liberty is problematic in many ways. The personal quality that is the cause of the transcendence is usually left vague or undetermined. No one with any astuteness at all says that all human beings can become philosophers. For liberals who are also Christians, the transcendence occurs through

God's grace and one's relationship with the personal God. But other liberals say, quite rightly, that Christian belief makes liberal consistency impossible. Galston himself calmly but persistently insists that Christianity and liberalism are in tension, if not necessarily at war. He also says that liberalism depends not at all on Christianity's claim for truth, agreeing with ancient and almost all modern and contemporary liberals.

It seems clear that ancient, Aristotelian liberalism, for Galston, is at core Socratic. All liberalism depends finally on Socratic views of the truth and human liberation. Liberalism is really the protection of liberated reason, the way of life of the philosopher, from popular prejudice or traditionalism. Liberalism is good because it reflects and allows human beings to know the truth about their nature or condition, which is always being repressed by wisdom-hating fundamentalism. Liberalism is a good regime because, better than any other, it allows a few human beings to fulfill their natural potential to become rationally liberated. For Socratic liberals, political and moral community and tradition are not good in themselves. The liberal support for them is always functional or conditional. The unfortunate fact is that rational liberty cannot come into its own without their support.

Ancient liberalism affirms the contradictions of elitism, acknowledging that its abolition in the name of consistency would be at the expense of philosophy. Galston finds the elitism of ancient liberalism still present to some extent in the early modern liberalism of the American Founders. He sometimes presents that elitism as a true reflection of an ineradicable human problem, and he attempts to remind contemporary liberals of the consequences of the fact that liberalism is always intellectual elitism. Galston contends that "few individuals will come to embrace the core commitments of liberal society through a process of rational inquiry" and so "on the basis of purely philosophic considerations."[6]

According to Galston, American liberalism in practice depends less on philosophical liberation than on a "civic pedagogy," primarily a rhetoric that attaches Americans to liberal principles and virtues as their own, not as what is true. It also depends on religiously based arguments and incentives that inquiring, rational liberals cannot accept as true. One indispensable liberal contradiction, part of its self-conscious elitism, is that religion provides nothing "essential to the validity of liberal arguments." But religious belief supports liberal theory and practice in the minds and hearts of most citizens of a liberal regime. As George Washington said in his farewell address, the fundamental distinction is between the rational and the religious, and the former do not really regard the latter as liberals at all.[7]

Liberalism is always, in practice, a liberal democracy, a mixed regime of the many democrats committed to equality and the few liberals committed to liberty. The liberals cannot free themselves from the necessity of acquiring the consent to rule from the democrats. So the liberals must deceive the democrats in order to rule. The many necessarily understand the foundation of liberal democracy differently from the few. Can Galston really convince contemporary liberals to accept self-consciously the necessity of prudent deception, the contradiction or paradox that the pursuit of the truth depends on lies? As Tocqueville says, are not our times too dogmatically egalitarian, too opposed, as our intellectuals say, to privileging anyone or anything, for liberal intellectuals to acknowledge even to themselves that their partisanship is antiegalitarian?

Enlightenment Liberalism

The Enlightenment, for Galston, is the attempt to eradicate the contradictions present in ancient liberalism by transforming political order in accordance with reason. It is the most naive educational theory that philosophic or critical education is *the* form of education for liberal community. The aim is to make every human being a Socrates, *the* liberal hero or model.

But Galston recognizes that naive liberals are not naive enough to state their aim so directly. They define human excellence and so education as relentless self-examination, the radical questioning of all one has been given by society and even nature. That questioning is defended in terms of what is required for personal choice of one's own way of life and so social diversity. But Socrates was no partisan of diversity. He thought there was a way of life best for human beings, and naive liberals really believe so too. Thus liberal education seeks to prevent us from choosing to act in accordance with tradition and authority because this would restrict "true, natural" choice. The only choice that finally passes the process of self-examination is a life devoted to critical self-examination, or the choice constantly to prepare for choice. Naive liberals are so far opposed to favoring a genuine diversity of choices that they tend to view the closure that comes with moral choice as an arbitrary self-deprivation of liberty.

Contemporary liberals say they aim to expand the achievement of public religious neutrality to complete moral neutrality. They claim to relativize moral claims in the name of diversity. They oppose all hierarchy and repressive conformism. Everyone is free to do his or her own thing: Gays are free to be gay, women not to be wives and mothers, men to leave their wives and not support their children, citizens not to be patriotic, and conscientious objectors to follow their conscience without fear of the law. There are no public limits to choice.

But Galston recognizes that modern Socratic liberals are not consistent in their promotion of public moral relativism. They do not question the goodness of freedom of thought, and they do not apply their relativistic method to Socrates' moralizing about the unexamined life. Their relativism seems mainly to be a strategy to liberate the mind and an intellectual elite from moral or popular control. The real offense of those who would closet gays or restrict divorce is that they would do so from a perspective that ranks moral order or duty above intellectual liberation. Modern Socratic liberals, in a way, are quite traditional in their view of the possibility of such liberation. They are partisans of the Socratic tradition.

Modern Socratic liberalism's model regime or utopia is, in the precise sense, an aristocracy of everyone. Its Enlightenment tendency is to correct ancient liberalism by universalizing or democratizing it. But this apparent correction of ancient elitism can also be viewed as its intensification. The aim is to impose intellectual liberation on everyone, although all human experience suggests that most human beings will never really want it. The error of modern liberalism is always, Galston says, that "the motives and satisfactions of a tiny elite somehow constitutes the (hidden) essence and desire of all human beings."[8] As Galston shows in his criticism of the libertarianism of Roberto Unger, the democratic aspiration of modern liberalism inevitably tends toward coercive utopianism. Galston's view is that the rise of the fundamentalist right in America is democratic opposition to the liberal propensity to tyrannize, and he even indicates his agreement with the view that the "secular humanism" of bureaucratic experts in American public education is a mild form of coercive utopianism.[9]

Liberal Self-Destruction

Elite efforts to impose popular liberation inevitably inspire popular resistance. Galston disagrees with Bloom's portrayal of the victory of the moral relativism of the intellectuals in contemporary America. The fundamental political fact in America is the culture war, with the popular forces supporting moral traditionalism more than a match for the liberal elitists. Liberals have to take the religious or moral criticism of liberalism seriously. If they simply show contempt for it, they are sure to be defeated politically.

Galston takes this traditionalist criticism seriously in a number of ways. Sometimes he flatters contemporary liberals by saying that their liberated wisdom must be moderated by the requirements of consent to be effective politically. Certainly one of Galston's main purposes is to teach his fellow liberal Democrats what they must do to win democratic elections. By taking the moral majority seriously as a force to be defeated, he appears less elitist or more pragmatic than other liberals.

If liberals cannot "recognize their partial dependence on" and forthrightly "accommodate" within their political theory "the moral restraints espoused by ordinary citizens," they "cannot regain in practice the general acceptance needed to guide public life in a constitutional democracy." Galston invites liberals to reflect on "the tenor and outcome of the 1988 U.S. presidential election," when Dukakis was branded demagogically and successfully as a liberal, a partisan of unbridled libertarian permissiveness. Liberals should rule, Galston says, on behalf of "the resumption of progressive politics," but they cannot present the abolition of moral restraints as their vision of progress and win elections. Unlike Dukakis, they must spiritedly defend themselves against those who claim they have no spirit.[10]

In a way Galston is more elitist than other liberals because he is less deluded about the possibility of popular liberation through persuasion. One reason Galston is not a conservative Republican is that he is more confident that popular, moralistic resistance will be an effective curb on liberal excesses than that liberals will succeed in curbing popular antiliberalism. Historical evidence mainly points to the fragility of liberty and the resilience of morality.

Galston's own liberal elitism seems most extreme in the very unflattering view he sometimes gives of popular opposition to liberalism. It is an "escape from freedom." Liberal openness is liberating and exhilarating for some, but others become confused and afraid. The latter "flee from the burdens of self-determination to the comforts of submission to authority." Liberals have to acknowledge that most human beings cannot live well with much freedom, and their psychological limitations are the cause of antiliberal politics.[11]

But Galston sometimes complains that the modernist ideal of personal liberation is not Socratic at all. Modern liberals aim to liberate the self from all stable contexts, from all dogma and convention, but for nothing in particular. This radical, wholly negative form of liberation is, as Socrates says, pure democracy or anarchy. Modern liberals have become too democratic to privilege even philosophy, to remember the purpose of human liberation.

Galston actually sees that the dominant tendency of modern liberalism is to free itself from the constraint of Socratic rationalism over time. The more liberalism frees itself from reason, the less conscious it becomes of the true ground of its elitism. Hence liberals become more able to flatter democratic audiences without the pain of deception. Universal liberation is more plausible on the vague premise "that everyone could become creative, autonomous, a source of new values." Liberal freedom becomes relativistic self-assertion. Once it does, liberals no longer have, even among themselves, an argument for their elitism.[12]

The dominant form of contemporary liberalism, Galston reports, is easygoing Kantianism. What makes Kant's thought attractive to intellectual elites today is its radical view of human freedom as freedom from both "divine authority" and "any form of naturalism." That radically negative freedom is what distinguishes human beings. Liberals radicalize Kant by placing "freedom . . . prior to rather than as a manifestation of moral law." Freedom must be wholly "unbounded," and so autonomy must be free from "rational constraint." Kant's thought must be freed from what makes it most attractive to Socratic liberals, "its broad agreement with Aristotle about what is highest in man." Libertarian or anarchist Kantianism is at the foundation of today's "secular humanism," the identification of morality or autonomy with unconstrained choice.[13]

Galston's criticism of easygoing Kantianism seems to be of its liberal coherence or consistency. He knows, of course, that early modern liberalism was only inconsistently in agreement with Aristotle or Socrates about human purpose. The American founders, whom Galston praises for their philosophic self-awareness and their prudence, he views as Lockeans more than anything else. Locke, to whom Galston often returns for his relative sobriety, based his teaching about liberty on the state of nature. In that state, human beings are both radically free from political and social ties and rational enough to invent solutions for their natural penury and fear. Locke, when he discusses human beings living in civil society, is perfectly aware that the functioning of human reason and the exercise of human liberty depend on proper socialization. But by nature human individuals remain unsocialized, and so they could not possibly be rational. Locke's teaching about nature, and so about the contractual basis of human political and social ties, is obviously inconsistent.

The American Founders inconsistently accepted the state of nature teaching and tended to think of themselves as Socratic rationalists. The Lockean teaching is that there is no support in nature for the human desire to know. So the Founders said both that the purpose of human reason is to free human beings from nature and that the rational life is man's natural perfection. They may have been, compared to thinkers and statesmen today, practically reasonable, but they were theoretically confused. Galston criticizes Bloom insofar as he suggests a return to the Founders might be a cure for the intellectual malady of our time.[14]

The most consistent form of modern thinking, Galston says, is Rousseau's. If human beings are by nature free from all social ties, then they are by nature wholly irrational. They could not reason their way to property or government or even beyond the end of the day. What distinguishes human beings, their human liberty, emerges accidentally and unfortunately over time. What they had by nature, stupid contentment and an asocial self-sufficiency or inhuman liberty, was good. So human liberty is accidental because it is not chosen. It is not even choiceworthy because human beings become progressively more discontent or miserable as they become more self-conscious or aware of time. The most consistent version of modern liberalism denies the goodness of human liberty and human reason.

Kant attempted to restore the perception of the goodness of rational, human liberty on a Rousseauean foundation by allowing human beings to take proper pride in the dignity of their freedom from nature. They have become unhappy, but their acquisition of reason has given them the dignity of moral choice. But Kant's separation of nature from morality produced a new inconsistency. We are divided, in effect, into animals and gods. We are both beings who seek happiness and beings who seek rational, moral consistency. For Kant, no animal can be moral or rational. The Kantian aims at a self-denying coherence by saying he is moral and rational and so no animal. Kant denies the obvious, the connection between what is highest in man and the rest of his being. He rationally denies natural evidence.

Easygoing Kantians free themselves from this impossible fanaticism. They return to the candor of Rousseau. They say that human existence, insofar as it is free from nature, is accidental and disordered. Human liberty is unlimited by nature. Dignity is not rooted in moral consistency but in the misery of our freedom, for which we deserve compassion. Our freedom divides our existence and makes us unhappy, but there is no reason not to use our freedom to pursue what happiness we can. We are mysteriously compelled to choose how best to live with our misery. The doctrine of autonomy or free choice means we cannot criticize those who choose narcotics or diversions over rational or moral consistency. They actually follow the philosopher Rousseau's choice of the negation of self-consciousness of the reverie, a perfectly anti-Socratic or antirational choice in the name of reason.

If there is no natural support for reason, and if opposing reason to nature mainly makes us miserable, then how can an antirational choice in the name of happiness be criticized by reason? Such a choice, in fact, might be called the most rational one, because it favors the rational, impersonal order of nature and opposes the disorder of human liberty. But the total negation of one's human liberty is impossible; no narcotic, diversion, or reverie works perfectly all the time. So easygoing Kantianism is based on the principle that human liberty is not good but inevitable. We are condemned to be deserving of compassion, but no one can blame us for whatever we might have to do to make it through our lives.

Liberalism, finally, seems to want to destroy itself. Its basis is Socratic, but its logic shows the examined life to be undeserving of privilege and functionally impossible; such a life is a particularly miserable, even irrational choice as a human pursuit. Galston seems to reject the logic of this argument, however, suggesting on occasion that the fatal undermining of the Socratic view of liberty came not with Locke or some other modern thinker but with Christianity.[15]

Rousseaueanism, Galston suggests, is secularized Christianity. Both the Christians and the modern liberals say that man is mysteriously free from nature and the requirements of political life. The Lockeans do not seem to reflect much on that freedom. The Christians attribute it to their creation in the image of a personal God. The Rousseaueans, not believing in that God, say it is purely accidental, bringing forth the foundation of Lockeanism. For the Rousseaueans the accident of human liberty is an unfortunate evil from which human beings should be liberated, whereas the Christians view their liberty as that of creatures who can know and rely upon their Creator, and so as good.

Galston's own contempt for liberalism's self-destruction can be called partly Socratic and partly Aristotelian. He holds that liberation through reason of the philosophic life may be the only genuine form of human liberty. But he also has the Aristotelian view that an indispensable premise of moral virtue and political life, whether they are good for their own sake or are preconditions for philosophy, is personal responsibility for one's own conduct. That "necessary presumption of human freedom must not be replaced with the debasing psychology of victimization." That psychology has its foundation in the Rousseauean view that human liberty is a miserable accident and nothing more. All human beings are essentially victims, and they all deserve compassion. On the other hand, both the unsecular Christians and the Aristotelians hold that human beings are free and responsible. They have a moral and so somewhat illiberal view of liberty.

The Reasonableness of Traditionalism

From both an Aristotelian and a Christian perspective, contemporary secular humanism is not a humanism at all because it rejects both Christian and Socratic views of the goodness of human liberty. American Christians today, Galston observes, perceive that "our system of public education . . . embodies a bias against authority and faith." They do not perceive that bias as Socratic, but simply permissive and so opposed to the truth about human liberty. Sociologically speaking, the Socratic Galston admits they are correct. The great threat to human liberty today is not that children "believe in something too deeply" but that they tend to have no deep beliefs at all.[16]

Following Bloom, Galston makes the Socratic observation that one must begin with beliefs, opinions, and authorities in order to experience the exhilaration of rational liberation from them. Relativism acquired too easily and early is a dogma particularly closed to the truth. Americans, Bloom argues, may have become incapable of rebelling against and otherwise responding to their mortality because they are no longer touched by it. Liberated from their awareness of death, they seem almost to have returned to their natural condition as Rousseau describes it.

The dependence of philosophy on the cultivation of opinion by traditionalist parents and other authorities means that intellectual liberalism is endangered by excessive political liberalism. Philosophic liberation is from passionate, illiberal conviction, and political liberals, in their tendency to reduce all human relationships to calculation, contract, and consent, aim to undermine fatally such conviction. Philosophy or Socratic liberalism is parasitic. Its liberal political influence undermines the conditions of its existence.

From Galston's perspective, the relativistic, permissive liberalism of today's intellectual elite is too democratic. For him, popular, religiously based conservatism or traditionalism is permissive liberalism's salutary and truthful corrective. The popular, salutary view is that elite libertarianism is impractical; it ignores the requirements of everyday life. It is also willfully detached from the pleasurable, satisfying experiences that come with the performance of ordinary social duties. The forms of happiness associated with marriage, the family, friendship, love of God, and political life are distinctively human yet rooted in nature. Their enjoyment requires personal commitment and social stability and so moral resistance to change.

The popular view is that the libertarianism of easygoing Kantianism is ugly. It willfully ignores the fact that human liberty is necessarily limited, and so cannot be detached from moral seriousness. Human beings cannot live or even think well without acknowledging some dependence on tradition and nature. Radical liberation, in truth, is dizzying and terrifying, and nothing more. The insistent denial of intrinsic order and necessity to human life is really a denial of death. That fantasy of total liberation is actually, in Galston's words, "more of a narcotic than the stable patterns of daily life could ever be."[17] According to Socrates, philosophy is first of all accepting one's mortality without flinching. So no conception of the self is less philosophical than the radically modernist one.

The popular view Galston recommends is that human beings have a finite existence in this world but infinite desires. So their deepest desires will forever elude satisfaction by any form of social transformation. Religiously grounded traditionalists place little faith in modern, Lockean-Rousseauean projects for such transformation. If the infinite desires of human beings are to be satisfied, it must be by an infinite Being. If such satisfaction is certainly impossible, then perhaps the relativists or antimoralists are correct about life's futility and the need for narcotic fantasies. The Christian traditionalist often believes *the* human choice is between Christianity and moral relativism. The Socratic liberal would not agree but is put in a difficult situation. If the only genuine form of human liberation comes through philosophy, then the Rousseauean conclusion about human liberty retains great force in most cases.

Contrary to contemporary liberals, traditionalists agree with Aristotle that no regime can "remain indifferent to the moral character of its citizenry."[18] The development of character usually depends on a stable family with two heterosexual parents, political stability, an educational system that does not oppose but reinforces parental concern with virtue and patriotism, and a vital religious life. Such socialization is indispensable for exercising liberty and for personal responsibility. So Galston seems most in agreement with popular traditionalism when he says that his "guiding intuition is that the United States is in trouble because it has failed to attend to the dependence of sound politics on sound culture."[19] Culture, for Galston, means tradition, civic education, and religion. He is aware of Bloom's view that the heart of culture is religion. He is also aware of Bloom's Socratic distaste for the term.

Galston does not disagree with Alasdair MacIntyre's view that contemporary liberal theory is anti-Aristotelian or antirational and antimoral or "emotivist." He makes the observation instead that there is "a gulf between the moral doctrines of many elites and the moral sensibilities of most ordinary citizens." He puts forward the interpretation of "American politics of the 1970s and 1980s as a kind of moral conflict—a swelling revolt of antiemotivist citizens against those who appear to abet, if not espouse, the prejudices and practices of emotivism." The people still prize reason and virtue, but most of the members of the intellectual elite do not. That the people are more Christian than Aristotelian does not alter the fact that they view humanly worthy liberty as good. The imprudence of contemporary liberals is rooted in a theoretical error that makes them less humanly wise than their traditionalist or seemingly less rational critics. Galston's antiemotivism seems to ally him more with traditionalists than with liberals today, but he explains that this alliance is limited by his continued devotion to liberalism rightly understood.

Liberal Justice

One reason Galston remains a liberal is that he views the practical rationalism of Enlightenment liberalism as having produced undeniable moral progress. He sees its goal as the creation of a universal and homogeneous society, eradicating arbitrary and so unjust distinctions based on economic class, race, gender, and so forth. That society minimizes cruelty, the oppression of one group by another on behalf of some arbitrary or controversial view of the soul. Galston, for the most part, affirms in the name of justice the victories of universalistic liberal principles over moral traditionalism in America.

Liberal universalism is a form of egalitarianism: "The full development of each individual is equal in moral weight to every other. . . . Thus a policy that neglects the educable retarded . . . is considered in itself, as bad as one that reduces extraordinary gifts to mere normality."[20] Galston's interest in justice here is not really Socratic, and it produces inconsistencies in his liberal thought. What might be good for the retarded, the marginalized, and the unfortunate is not necessarily good for thought, unless one takes the un-Socratic view that liberal political progress both reflects and is a cause of thought's progress. Is not the view that the retarded are equal in moral weight to the philosophers really Christian, even if it expresses itself in the form of the Rousseauean compassion of secularized Christianity? One indication that Galston inconsistently shies away from this conclusion is he never seriously considers extending this concern in his own name to the unborn, and he believes that those who do so are essentially religious traditionalists. He shares the confusion of contemporary liberal Democrats, who want to embrace simultaneously libertarian permissiveness and compassionate duty.

It is unclear that liberal political thought has progressed in America since the time of the Founders, as Galston is aware. The Founders, as Lockean individualists, did not prefer one religion to another and were in principle antiracist and antisexist. So Galston presents the civil rights movement of the sixties as in one respect conservative, a call to eradicate the contradiction between the founding principles and the racism and sexism that had become part of our moral/religious tradition. Raising blacks and women to full citizenship was "long overdue." Galston even paraphrases Walter Mondale, a candidate he advised, as having said that "the changes that have swept through U.S. society are on balance not only consistent with but actually supportive of Americans' basic principles."[21] He goes on to qualify Mondale's enthusiasm in light of evidence of social disintegration, but never does he reject it.

But Galston's analysis of culture or moral traditionalism in America seems actually to be subtle criticism of even the Founders' liberalism as excessively abstract. They understood that liberalism needed moral and religious support, but they were vague about how it would come into being and perpetuate itself. What Tocqueville called "distinctively American political culture" had to develop into a mixture of secular liberalism,

Christian morality, and white Anglo-Saxon Protestant mores. This "moral traditionalism" was decidedly illiberal. It marginalized Catholics and Jews, subordinated blacks and women, and promoted "unquestioning patriotism" and respect for authority. It also included the more liberal virtues of self-reliance, self-restraint, and personal responsibility.[22]

Galston is rather vague about what allowed this vigorous moral particularism to develop. Tocqueville points to the limited authority of the national government and to "administrative decentralization" even within the states. The Constitution, against the intention of the leading Founders, created a mixed regime, the universal and homogeneous but limited national government and relatively particularistic and illiberal states and localities. Because the Bill of Rights applied only to the national government, the states were relatively free from national supervision or correction.

Galston makes more than Tocqueville does of the white, male, and Protestant character of traditional American morality and mores. Tocqueville's description of American virtue is mostly that of the middle class, of beings who are free politically but compelled by their situation to work; his description of American Christianity includes Catholicism, and his emphasis is on the unprecedented freedom, equality, and responsibility women have in America. In overstating the WASPishness of the past, Galston discredits it in the manner of a contemporary liberal. One reason Galston remains a liberal Democrat is that he believes that the nerve of the Republican Party remains traditionalist—racist and sexist. But there is no particular reason why Catholics, Jews, women, and blacks could not be incorporated (in fact they were) into traditional American culture. Personal responsibility, self-sufficiency, self-restraint, the family, religion, and patriotism are not sources of virtue that necessarily exclude particular American groups (except perhaps liberal intellectuals).

Galston's nuanced presentation of the civil rights movement of the sixties moves from a conservative beginning aiming to purge racism and sexism from the tradition to the more consistently liberal view that all moral traditionalism is repressive. The conservative antitraditionalism that liberated blacks and women became "an inspirational metaphor for other aggrieved groups," the young, gays, atheists, and so on. It became an assault against all hierarchy on behalf of freedom and democracy. The radical democracy of liberal theory became the social or political movement of "expressive" individualism. Rather limply, Galston says that this movement embraced uncritically the "controversial premise that traditionalism *as a whole* was opposed to the actualization of liberal principles."[23]

The destruction of all hierarchy, all moral ranking, left only pure difference. So liberalism became the celebration of difference for its own sake.

That celebration, Galston says, began with blacks, who came to demand not only equal citizenship but equal recognition of all features of their distinctive way of life. Celebration of the difference of groups is a marked departure from the Founders' liberal individualism. What we now call multiculturalism is really a series of claims for exemptions from the requirements of common citizenship and personal responsibility.

The idea that blacks can be legitimately exempted from the American practice of moral virtue has not been good for blacks. Galston allows us to wonder whether that exemption was really a black demand or one largely made on their behalf by white liberals. The black precedent was the key for gay liberation. Gays use the rhetoric of difference more radically and understandably. It is unclear, finally, what really separates white and black. Much of what we call black culture originated in the white South, and most middle-class blacks have contempt for public celebrations of the differences that are black English or underclass indolence. But if gays choose to define themselves primarily with reference to their sexual activity, then what separates them from heterosexual Americans is clear. Galston acknowledges, if only in a limited way, that defining gay and straight relativistically as just different choices or orientations undermines the family and so the proper inculcation of moral virtue.

Galston means to leave us with the impression that the legacy of the sixties is ambiguous. The destruction of racism and sexism was progress. The assault on tradition as a whole and the celebration of pure difference were not. What broke down with amazing rapidity was the American mixture of liberalism and traditionalism. That breakdown is the cause of liberalism's immediate crisis and the repugnance that the relatively moral majority has toward it today. Galston cannot argue against the traditionalist critics who say it is largely responsible for the "fearful toll" exacted by "epidemics of crime, drugs, and teenage pregnancy." Was not that breakdown caused in part by excessive, imprudent zeal in the pursuit of liberalism's universal and homogeneous view of justice? But Galston affirms the liberal "tendency to employ constitutional law to extend the sway of liberal public values throughout the society."[24] He agrees with the Court's meddlesome extremism in banning religious observances, creating new "rights" leaving the unborn without protection, and extending federal and judicial powers to all aspects of our lives. But he remains aware that "pushed to their limit, the juridical principles and practices of a liberal society tend inevitably to corrode moralities that rest either on traditional forms of social organization or on the stern requirements of revealed religion"[25] and that liberalism's functioning depends on the vitality of such morality. So Galston attempts to establish rather expansive limits to the application of those principles.

Functional Traditionalism versus Religious Belief

Galston seems to hold that the traditional morality undermined by liberal principle and practice deserved to be undermined. But he also holds that liberalism cannot perpetuate itself if that morality is destroyed altogether. So he distinguishes between "intrinsic traditionalism," which understands traditional morality as good in itself (as part of divine law) and "functional traditionalism," which affirms certain parts of traditional morality not as good in itself but as necessary support for liberalism in practice. Intrinsic morality understands marriage as a sacred duty and divorce as intrinsically evil or sinful. Functional traditionalism opposes divorce in view of the "economic and psychological damage" it does to children, reducing "their capacity to become independent and contributing members of the community." A functional traditionalist approves of public policy that supports a particular tradition if a "plausible" connection can be made between that tradition and the exercise of personal freedom. But a functional traditionalist is also "wary" of hierarchies of race, gender, and ethnicity inherent in intrinsic traditionalism. His assumption is that traditions can be liberalized consciously to some extent while remaining effective.[26]

For example, public policy can discourage divorce in view of its effects on children and can encourage heterosexual two-parent families over others in view of their better record in raising children. That means there is no "rational basis" for restricting divorce among those who are married without children. It may also mean there is no such basis for not legalizing gay marriage, although public policy might discourage adoption by gay couples.

Galston does not mention that his alleged traditionalism here is Lockean. Locke transforms with impious humor the biblical teaching about marriage's indissolubility by saying that the stern divine injunction is that a couple must remain together until the children can fend for themselves. Marriage is for procreation, Locke says, and the marriage contract must include the acceptance of the responsibility that having children brings. But Locke cannot consistently root the duty of parents to children in calculation and contract. The question Locke cannot answer through consent is the one Americans today apparently so often cannot answer: Why should one prefer the liberty of one's children to one's own liberty? Locke cannot explain why one would stay married just for the kids' sake, and so our Lockean law does not compel that unreasonable choice. Locke's inconsistency, which is a time bomb at the core of his doctrine, is that liberalism in practice depends on the family, but family ties limit one's liberty in a way that cannot really be justified by liberal individualism.

Can "functional traditionalism," not at all an affirmation of sacred duty, really reverse or even retard the social disintegration caused by liberalism's nearly total victories over traditionalism? Galston says that "liberal notions of free choice and contractual relations . . . have permeated the previously sacramental understandings of marriage and the family. The notion of an irreversible, constitutive commitment has been undermined by the notions of liberalism and autonomy."[27] He has not shown the way to free the sacrament from its capture by the individualistic spirit of contract. The reforms he recommends are sensible but far too minor to be of much consequence. He has not shown how religious duty, surely an indispensable foundation for "irreversible, constitutive commitment" in most cases, can be incorporated into liberalism. Galston has not even explained how today's liberals might be induced to push for small pro-child restrictions in the divorce law. They may have some unease about the effects of easy divorce, but can they really be attracted to legislation that would actually restrict their choice? Galston points toward the conclusion that liberalism depends on "intrinsic traditionalism" that resists liberal assimilation or comprehension.

Galston's praise of functional traditionalism is in tension with his affirmation of the "informal gravitational influence liberalism has on individuals and institutions." He explains how that influence transforms American religion. American Catholic bishops have opposed Rome because their "liberal political culture encourages rational criticism of all forms of authority."[28] Because biblical religion depends on an authority beyond human reason, "political culture" opposes itself to religious culture, making the latter more liberal and less religious. Liberalism undermines the traditionalism that makes religion functional. As Tocqueville said, it was the Americans' decision to exempt religion from such rational criticism that allowed them to exercise their political religion so well. Galston notes that the stability of the Americans' political institutions still depends on the comparative strength of their religious commitment. Thus American liberty is not well served by American bishops' applying their liberalism to ecclesiastical and theological questions, but it is the gravitational pull of political liberty that inclines them to do so.

Galston describes liberalism's propensity to derange or disorder American religion. He sees two extremist sects growing today as a result of liberalism's excesses: the secular humanists and the fundamentalists. Neither of them could be described as functional. The secular humanists are really easygoing Kantians or morally destructive relativists. The fundamentalists are spearheading a radical "traditionalist counteraction to liberalism," which now "threatens the centuries-old doctrine of religious toleration itself."[29] Another reason Galston is a liberal Democrat is that he genuinely fears that threat. He thinks the neoconservatives, such as

Irving Kristol, who ally themselves with the religious right are playing with fire.

Galston seeks to placate the fundamentalists by being clear that political liberalism is compatible in principle with fundamentalism and that a liberal view of political life can be combined with devotion to the discipline, traditionalism, and piety of a transpolitical religious community. But Galston admits that it is becoming increasingly more difficult to do so because "any liberal commitment to key elements of both Socratic and Enlightenment rationalism has important corrosive effects on a wide range of psychological and social structures."[30] Genuine Christianity is becoming progressively more countercultural, and those who practice its way of life must have a "spirit of vigilant resistance" to maintain its integrity. As the need for resistance becomes more extreme, their opposition to liberalism should become stronger. Does vigilance inevitably approach fanaticism? The question is not as new as Galston believes. Tocqueville, writing in an allegedly more stable time, found religious madness, a reaction against liberal secularism, quite common in America.

Not only fundamentalists but all traditionalists and all Christians are justified in believing that today's liberalism threatens the integrity of their way of life. Galston calls that one of liberalism's virtues. But the threat is not strong enough. Liberalism can distort but not destroy the spirit of religion in America. Functional traditionalists are finally not traditionalists at all, and they cannot really explain how to bring into being and perpetuate only the functional aspects of tradition.

Galston usually writes as if his liberal doctrine of functional traditionalism is Tocquevillian. But in his article on Tocqueville's view of religion he admits that Tocqueville actually regarded Christianity in several senses as true. For Tocqueville, it might be possible to harmonize the spirit of liberty with that of religion because human beings have religious longings that liberalism cannot eradicate. Galston elsewhere acknowledges that human beings do have an "infinite longing" that can be satisfied only by "an infinite object that also is a subject"—a personal God. He agrees with Sartre that "in the absence of such an object, man truly is a useless passion."[31] Man's need to pursue that infinite longing that transcends political satisfaction is one justification for the limitation on government that is part of liberalism. And if that longing is useless, then so are man's liberty and his self. Liberalism would seem to depend on the truth of both Christianity's psychological account of the transcendence of human individuality and the possibility, at least, that the God of revelation truly exists.

But Galston does not usually reach this conclusion about the truth of Christianity or biblical belief. He says that the main change since Tocqueville's time is that America is now too diverse to be called a Christian nation; "Tocqueville's linkage between Christianity and the moral basis of liberalism—however historically accurate—can no longer serve as our point of departure." Americans still need the moral guidance that religion provides, but gone is the Christian consensus Tocqueville described. So Galston's view is that we must return, in our post-Christian time, to the Founders' view that liberalism does not or cannot depend on Christian morality in particular, but only on religion in general.[32] Is this need for post-Christian morality sociological, or is it connected with Galston's un-Tocquevillian silence about religious longing as an intrinsic part of the human condition? Surely Galston exaggerates the degree to which America actually has become post-Christian, and that exaggeration is a characteristic feature of contemporary liberal partisanship.

The Divided Self and Moral Pluralism

Galston sometimes admits that the actual liberal self properly understood is "the *divided* self." A description of that self is somewhere between "hyperindividualism," which abstracts from "social bonds or natural duties," and "hyperoganicism," which abstracts from the fact that to be human is to be "a demarcated being" with "an independent consciousness." Galston agrees that the "unencumbered self" criticized by fellow liberal communitarian Michael Sandel is neither realistic nor desirable. All human beings are shaped to some extent by their social attachments and commitments to family, friends, community, and so forth. But to be human is also to have the capacity to reflect on and even rebel against those commitments. The doctrine of rights, which all liberals, Galston says, affirm, depends on the possibility of many or most human beings using their "critical faculties" to obtain "critical distance" from authority and tradition. But Galston adds that rights doctrine is not and cannot become a complete account of human morality or motivation. We need rights because the divided self makes love or affectionate attachment unreliable.[33]

Galston's most complete presentation of the liberal self rightly understood is at variance with ancient liberalism, as well as the liberalism of the Founders. It is not based on the distinction between the very few who are deracinated philosophers and the many who are citizens. No human being achieves complete liberation from "social bonds," but many or most human beings achieve some liberation or rational distance from their society. "The liberal conception of the self," Galston observes, "requires the kind of reflective distance demonstrated by the ability to become aware of the contingency of one's own social position and the latent contradictions of one's society."[34] The liberal self may not become a philosopher, but he has many Socratic qualities, including the experience of social or political deracination and relativism. The liberal self is relatively open to the truth that he is not simply a social or political being.

It seems clear that the liberal must say more than that the divided self is a human possibility. He must defend the goodness of that experience of self. The Socratic philosopher or radical individualist would say he must strive to overcome his dependence through more rigorous and critical reasoning. The communitarian would say that the cure for his alienation or division is greater social or political devotion.

But Galston seems to say that the divided self is the true self. Human existence really is mixed or contradictory. We are partly social or political beings and partly individuals. Liberal societies, Galston says, reflect the truth both of human diversity and of "the inherent incapacity of the public sphere to encompass more than a portion of human activity or to fulfill more than a part of human aspiration." Can we say that the disorder of liberal society mirrors the disorder of the human soul or self? As Tocqueville says, man is the beast with the angel in him, and that mixture is the source of both his misery and his greatness. But is it really accurate to call a society that mirrors the self or soul liberal? Only if we mean human liberty, which is always quite limited. The society he calls liberal, Galston admits, is really characterized by a "hard-to-describe 'inbetweenness.' "[35]

The self's division or alienation makes our existence miserably incoherent. We are inclined by nature to try to overcome it, to move toward communitarian (including socialist, republican, and traditionalist) or libertarian consistency. It seems to me that, once again, liberalism depends on biblical religion to some extent. Our alienation must point to a greatness beyond or imperfectly reflected in human experience. Otherwise, we return to the misanthropic conclusion that to be human is to have our natural unity or coherence ruined by useless passion that truly points in no direction.

Galston elsewhere achieves greater precision by saying that the divided self is actually only partly liberal, and so the universal and homogeneous society aimed at by liberalism is not simply good for human beings. Modern movement toward that society cannot definitively be called human or moral progress. It brings moral gains, but also losses, and so liberalism can be called both better and worse than the more traditional regimes that preceded it. With this analysis, Galston approaches his genuine theoretical goal of articulating the "moral pluralism" intrinsic to the human condition. No regime, society, or self embodies perfectly the whole human good, and even the best imaginable human self or soul would be a mixture of human qualities in tension or contradiction.

Galston criticizes Richard Rorty's narrative of human progress toward the moral universality of "cosmopolitan altruism." That progress is "the widening of moral sympathy to encompass endangered strangers." Galston does not deny that moral action based on such sensitivity is admirable. But the cultivation of such sympathy "entails significant moral costs," and particular devotion to and action based on preference for one's family, friends, and community is no less morally worthy. Aristotle's account of friendship is "rooted in the finitude of our consciousness." The truth is that the human powers of knowing and loving are limited, and so one can have only a very few genuine friends. The fact that one has some as friends rather than others includes an element of irreducible arbitrariness: "That we effectively identify with one virtuous individual rather than another may be an accident of personal history, but once the sphere of available psychological space has been filled, it is impossible to broaden the sphere of deep connection." The liberal or universal, homogeneous, and abstract view of justice opposes itself to the conditions that make virtuous friendship possible.[36]

Rorty describes liberal development as a road that ends in "a world in which our capacity for solidarity overrides boundaries of family, class, ethnicity, politics, and religion." It "seems to require the negation of particularistic obligations and the attenuation of special emotional ties." But that negation could hardly be called progress because "those forms of human connection can hardly be set aside without moral loss."[37] Even today, despite liberalism's progress, Americans still say that friendship and the family, or love of a few particular human beings, are what makes life most worth living. Is that perception the deepest explanation of the popular rebellion against liberal theory? It is not mainly a negative escape from freedom, but a positive affirmation of human love. Galston says that the "liberal-contractarian view of the family" aims to negate our "natural relatedness" and so our natural duties to each other, an illiberal truth about human nature.[38]

We cannot help but recall here Bloom's Socratic objection to liberalism's excesses on behalf of love. Galston corrects Bloom on American relativism by noticing that most Americans are still capable of love and hate, and so they are capable of hating unfettered liberalism, liberal theory, for threatening what they love most. He also opposes Bloom's inclination to accept too much of what Rousseau says about nature. Galston finds natural support for familial love even in men, and so he is more hopeful concerning the family's future in the wake of women's liberation. The political activist and devoted father Galston cannot help but have diverse experiences of the human good. To the extent that Galston really disagrees with Marxists and traditionalists on the inevitability of liberalism's self-destruction, it is because he has greater confidence that human nature, the nature of social beings who love and hate, can resist liberalism's historical progress.

Galston's criticism of Rorty is really a criticism of Christianity. The Christian God loves all human beings in their particularity equally and intensely, and He calls on us to imitate him in that love. But the powers of human knowing and loving are finite, and so any attempt to widen their scope dilutes them. One aspect of the project of liberal universalism is to weaken the unjust particularism and cruelty of human love by agreeing with God that justice requires that each individual extend his concern equally to every other. The combination of Christianity and liberal justice erodes friendship, family, political community, and virtue.

But Galston's criticism of Christianity is partial. He does not deny that its moral universalism is partly true. He agrees with Tocqueville that the coming of Christianity made manifest a truth that the pagan thinkers obscured. All human beings have souls and so are in some ways morally equal. But the danger of that view is that it denies the need for human beings to perceive and affirm human differences and to love particular human beings to the exclusion of the rest. Tocqueville might add that Galston's criticism of Christian universalism is actually Christian. The Christian God does not love human beings as abstractions or in general; He favors the perpetuation of the conditions that secure human particularity or liberty. Only human beings capable of loving one another are capable of needing and so loving a personal God.

Moral pluralism, for Galston, is the recognition that liberal partisanship, like all human partisanship, is in pursuit of only part of the human good. To the extent that it is secularized Christianity, it pursues the impossible goal of having all human beings love each other equally and intensely. That pursuit in some respects is good for the intellectual liberation associated with philosophy and for justice, but it is bad for human love, including even love of God and love of wisdom. The deepest practical aim of liberal theory is the replacement of love in all human relationships with the libertarian spirit of calculation and consent. But a life full of calculation and without the orientation or direction of love would be full of misery, and it would, as Rousseau said, quickly self-destruct. For liberty to be lovable, it must be constrained by love.

Liberalism is only partially good, and it is only good when mixed with illiberal elements. Liberalism is only good as part of a mixed regime, one with elements that elude its comprehension and control. So we can wonder why Galston does not conclude that genuine partisans of moral pluralism today are conservatives. They are the ones aiming to protect the local community, religion, and the family from liberal intellectualism, the courts, and the bureaucracy.

8

Commitment and Obligation

Bruce Frohnen

> *I can define my identity only against the background of things that matter. . . . Only if I exist in a world in which history, or the demands of nature, or the needs of my fellow human beings, or the duties of citizenship, or the call of God, or something else of this order* matters *crucially, can I define an identity for myself that is not trivial.*
>
> —*Charles Taylor,* The Ethics of Authenticity

Whatever one's criticisms of the new communitarians, one must recognize that they have grasped an important fact overlooked by most modern liberals: Man is no mere disembodied choice maker. If he does not feel that his choices are important, he will lose rational control over those choices. His appetite of the moment will reduce his life to meaningless disorder.

Taylor is wedded to the notion that the individual's personal flourishing, his development of his own capacities and achievement of his own self-defined goals, is of paramount importance. But he, like other new communitarians, recognizes that even this individual flourishing requires some context. It requires that we be committed to something so that we may define ourselves in relation to it—whether as a man of God, a soldier, or a friend of the earth.

But commitment is not enough. Here I will argue that many contemporary thinkers, including but not limited to new communitarians, are incapable of resuscitating community. Why? Because, despite their espousal of commitment, they refuse to recognize the necessary, fundamental role of the sacred in binding individuals to those around them. Only if we see family, local association, and other institutions as more important than our own self-defined self-development can we give ourselves to these institutions; only then can we maintain the relations on which any decent community must rely.

Liberal communitarians are willing to recognize the need for commitment, or the feeling that one is working toward an important goal such as world peace or the equal distribution of wealth. But they are unwilling to accept the need for obligations, for debts that must be paid even if not voluntarily incurred and not subject to being "trumped" by individual rights or goals. Nor are the new communitarians willing to recognize the ultimate source of obligation in transcendent, God-centered principles.

We are accustomed to recognizing that laws obligate; we obey them or suffer punishment, even if it is only the expense of a lawyer who manipulates the legal system to spare us further sanctions. But fewer and fewer of us recognize that laws are obligating because derived from an authority higher than the state. Progressive communitarians in particular eschew any substantive vision of the transcendent and its role in ordering society.

One need not be a religious zealot to recognize that in their laws and customs societies necessarily reflect a common vision of God's dictates if they are to survive. Yet, recognized or not, it remains the case that common moral precepts, derived from a common vision of the sacred, are the only means short of force that can bind the vast majority of mankind the vast majority of the time. And no society that must literally enforce obedience on most of its members most of the time can survive, let alone flourish.

Like most contemporary intellectuals, new communitarians seek to secure stability by convincing the people that democratic politics itself is sacred. Such attempts are doomed to failure because they put politics in the place of God. As such they make political conduct in this life all-important, demanding that it provide us with all we need. Thus they breed foolish attempts to build heaven on earth and/or simple cynicism.

Here I begin with a discussion of the differences between commitment and obligation, and the importance of these differences. I then discuss the sense in which all communities depend on a shared vision of the sacred for their survival. Next I apply this observation to the crucial area of law. I then discuss contemporary attempts to rebuild virtue without recourse to the sacred—attempts doomed by their intellectual origins and motivations. Finally, I present some thoughts on the need for a rebirth of a true religious understanding if we are to have any hope of restoring fellowship to our lives.

Commitment versus Obligation

According to liberal communitarians, our choice of commitments shapes our identity. But it is the independent development of this identity, in pursuit of self-defined goals, that is of paramount importance for them.

And if individual flourishing is our highest goal, then our commitments are valuable only instrumentally. In a sense it does not matter whether we worship God through prayer in church or Mother Earth through pagan sacrifice or equality through socialist revolution. What matters is our self-directed development of our individual ideals and capacities. We must always remain free to make new and different choices. We must be able at any time to abandon God, family, or earth in favor of a new "thing that matters."

Taylor and other new communitarians approve of individual commitment but not lasting moral obligation. Taylor's "backgrounds," his "things that matter" may vary and even change over time for particular individuals. *Self*-fulfillment requires social commitment. As Taylor puts it, "If the intense relations of self-exploration are going to be identity-forming, then they can't be in principle tentative—though they can, alas, in fact break up."[1] The same goes for our "background understandings" or "things that matter." If we see God or the earth as merely tentative goods—useful only so long as we find enjoyment in serving them—we will not be able to use them to develop ourselves. Yet it remains true that we may, and often should, cast off marriage, religion, or friendship in the name of individual development toward self-defined ends.

This raises a problem for progressive communitarians and for community in general. Unless the marriage tie, for example, is recognized as sacred, it will fall prey to the demands of either party's career, extramarital lusts, or other potential sources of self-development. When either party determines that there is not enough in the relationship to continue his or her "growth," he or she will simply leave, frequently abandoning financial and other obligations as too onerous.

If it is to survive, a relationship (be it marriage, citizenship, or any other) must not merely "matter" to the individual. The individual must recognize that the relationship and/or the other party to it matters more than he does. He must be willing to sacrifice not only passing fancies but also definite goods. For example, an important job promotion, if it would move one's wife far away from a sick mother who is wholly dependent on her, is incompatible with marriage. At this point one must choose either to pursue one's career or to live up to one's marriage vows. And if one sees individual development as primary, if one does not see one's marriage as a sacred obligation, the marriage will be left behind.

In the Western tradition, the marriage bond has until recently been recognized as superior to the wishes of those it binds. The Church, from before the Middle Ages, sought to protect the interests of the parties to marriage by insisting that they enter into it voluntarily. But the resulting tie was no mere contract. Rather, the parties contracted, voluntarily, to enter into a permanent status as a married couple. With this status came a whole plethora of rights and duties dependent on that status. The wife had not just the right to support from her husband but a right not to be physically abused. What is more, both parties had a right to one another's bodies for purposes of sex, a right that could trump even the demands of one's lord and the dangers of disease. If a husband or wife contracted leprosy, he or she might still demand payment of the marital debt from his or her spouse. All was to be shared, to bind together the spouses, whether in health or in dreadful sickness.[2]

Entrance into marriage also brought fundamental change to property arrangements. A family was treated as a unit in terms of its financial holdings and obligations. Of course, this went for the couple's children as well. Though not entering into their family in any sense voluntarily, children were bestowed at birth with rights and responsibilities derived from their existence and place within that family. From regal title to legal servitude, from riches to debt, parental status was visited upon the children.

Today, of course, enlightened observers condemn the limitations and burdens placed on individuals by sacred, often involuntary attachments. Yet the alternative that our society has experimented with hardly seems more kind. We have condemned 30 percent of our own children to illegitimacy and life in single-parent households, knowing as we now do that they will be at significantly greater risk for crime, delinquency, drug use, poverty, and even suicide, all in the name of the individual choice of the mother and long-absent father.[3]

For inherited status we have substituted a dangerous, demoralizing anarchy. The principal means of this substitution has been declining respect for the sanctity—the sacred status—of marriage. Sex having become merely another sport, marriage has become even less than a contract for delivery of goods; the marriage contract can be broken by either party at will, the interests of the other party be damned. If individual flourishing is the goal, permanent, life-shaping encumbrances cannot be allowed. Encumbrances must be discarded when they no longer serve our self-chosen ends—our "self-interest." The individual is left with no permanent bonds of family or community, and society crumbles.

Despite abundant evidence that self-centered pursuits do not produce stable, nurturing societies, we continue to replace sacred obligations with at best halfhearted explanations of self-interest as the force binding our societies together. Even the obligation of citizens to die for their country when defense of the nation so requires has been reduced to a kind of self-interest. John Locke, the seventeenth-century founder of modern liberalism, attempted to show that each of us has consented to service in the military, along with its unfortunate consequences, by partaking of the goods of our society. Locke even attempted to make us believe that we have volunteered for military service, if need be, by not leaving our country for another. And he is followed in this by "social contract" thinkers to this day.

But even Locke's implied consent to the duties of military service was tied to something prior and more important than individual choice. By rooting the duty of military service in allegiance (express or implied) to a particular state, he admitted that we are obliged by our membership in the body of the nation to sacrifice ourselves to it if need be. Indeed, Locke's demand for self-sacrifice was more all-encompassing than that of Western religious tradition, dismissing as it did without comment the possibility of conscientious objection to an unjust war. Because the individual could not survive without his state, for Locke, he owes the state his life.

Even liberals recognize that the old liberal reliance on self-interest, however well understood, in the end is self-defeating. It is rare to find men willing to go to war out of self-interest. And mercenaries make notoriously bad warriors, all too willing to retreat or surrender. Liberal regimes have found it increasingly difficult to convince their citizens that they must die for their self-interest. The regimes must supplement self-interest arguments with the claim that the state is not merely the source of security and worldly goods but is itself something sacred. The state is made out to be the embodiment of God's will. For example, in calling on his troops in World War I to "make the world safe for democracy," Woodrow Wilson was arguing that democracy was the only just and proper form of government. He was arguing that Americans had a sacred duty to die if necessary to see their form of government and ideology succeed and spread.

But ideology is a mere shadow, or caricature, of what is needed for self-sacrifice to remain possible over time. When Alexis de Tocqueville coined the phrase "self-interest properly understood," he included within proper understanding not mere ideology but religious beliefs that bind individuals to a common morality. And that common morality held the bonds of family, the rights of property, and other fundamental institutions sacred. Not merely useful or necessary, but sacred.

Self-interest helped maintain property rights in particular. Ownership was widespread, and thus many Americans had a stake in the sanctity of property. But it was the often unexpressed belief that one betrayed God by betraying the marriage vow or stealing another's property (or otherwise breaking divine commandments) that protected the community's fundamental institutions from being undermined by individual self-indulgence.

We have dispensed with such notions of a transcendent sacred. The result? Public life has been reduced to competition among self-interested groups vying for governmental favors. Politics now constitutes the very form of servile despotism Tocqueville feared.

Commitments that are subject to abandonment if the individual's self-defined goals so dictate cannot, by definition, make individuals transcend their self-interest. The very purpose of such commitments is to help the individual better define and achieve his self-interest, to flourish more completely. Lacking a sense of the sacred and thus a willingness to bend our wills and desires to the demands of a greater good, we feel no strong obligations. We serve others only when and to the extent that such service happens to aid in our project of self-development.

Religion itself, under these circumstances, becomes merely another "thing that matters." It is reduced to just another commitment, useful in defining ourselves but by nature disposable. As such, religion cannot fulfill even its social role of sanctifying the community's fundamental institutions.

The Role of the Sacred

Valuing individual autonomy, new communitarians recognize that it must take place within a stable context. An illegitimate child, whatever we might wish for him, is likely to lead a more dangerous and less fulfilling life, whatever the economic class of his parents, than a child from a two-parent family. These and other sociological facts, now at last uncontroverted, have led communitarians to recognize the need for stability, for some kind of feeling of obligation, if the society in which individuals live is to endure and provide any decent prospect for self-fulfillment.

But can a community have true, moral obligations without a sense of the sacred? No. Those of us raised within the Western tradition often forget the fundamental, society-ordering role played by shared convictions concerning what is sacred. But without such common standards of conduct we cannot trust one another to respect what we respect or follow the rules we hold sacred.

Much of the difficulty is uniquely Western. Our civilization began with the Jews. And the Jews, unlike other peoples, did not invest their kings with priestly powers. Indeed, judges and prophets persistently criticized kings for failing to model their human laws after God's law. Thus the sphere of human action was seen as separate from, though properly modeled after, the order of the universe established by God. This conception of sacred and profane spheres passed into Western civilization through Christianity. Christ separated the things of Caesar from those of God, thus reemphasizing the distinction between political and religious authority. It was institutionalized in the often rancorous relationship between religious and political authorities during the early Middle Ages.[4]

Ironically, this separation of sacred from profane law, originally the source of religious checks on governmental power, has been transformed in modern times into an unregulated claim on power and morality by the state. Institutionally separated from state power, religion increasingly became the victim of philosophers and rulers chafing under its constraints. More and more, and with increasing ease as the people settled into comfortable hedonism, religion was pushed off the public stage, allowed to speak only when it addressed material needs and desires in a moralistic voice, eschewing religious dogma. But this separation, which relies on an often conscious refusal to consider whether political leaders are promoting the common good, merely obscures a permanent fact of life: Public order depends on mutual obligations derived from a common vision of the order of the universe and the community's role therein.

The societies belonging to Western civilization share with all others a fundamentally sacred basis. In his important work, *Twin Powers: Politics and the Sacred,* Thomas Molnar explains this permanent truth and the atomizing consequences of our practice of ignoring it. According to Molnar, for archaic peoples

> every act in life, and for that matter before and after life, took place in the sacred dimension as much as in the profane. . . . each of the ever-recurrent events of life was sacralized because it represented—or, better, *was*—part of cosmic permanence and belonged to the structure of reality. Foundations and beginnings were thus regarded as sacred, as were places, times, objects, and rites which marked the intervention of superior powers in to the course of profane existence, thereby sacralizing it.[5]

Birth and death—of peoples as well as of individuals—are in the nature of things. They are not merely specific events but also parts of a sacred order—the unchanging order of the universe decreed by a power higher than man.

Cycles of life and an ever-present but elusive beyond have, until recently, been universally recognized realities. Men often overlook this commonality because the nature of the beyond and the dependability of the cyclical here and now have been subjects of much disagreement. As Molnar notes,

> the sacred used to be present in all cultures, despite the culture's presuppositions. The thrust of Egyptian and Greek temple art was to come to terms with the cosmos, nature, and the ideal site, so as to give humanity existential security. Christian churches, on the other hand—Western, Byzantine, and Russian—were indifferent to the surrounding world from which no salvation, no existential security could be obtained. Hence the often cursory treatment of the exterior, at least in the early centuries. All efforts were re-

served for entering worshippers, who, on entering, found themselves in a different world, one of significance and splendor. Grace from God was not the same as harmony with the world outside.[6]

Again, Western religion stands out because it separates the realm of God—of all that remains constant, such as truth and love—more significantly from our changing and imperfect earthly lives than other religions. But the result was not, at least until recently, a desacralized or wholly profane culture. Molnar observes that "cultures derive their content and contours from their cosmology . . . communities form themselves in accordance with what they believe to be the transcendent reality of the cosmos." Only modern man has deluded himself into thinking he can create or remake societies out of whole cloth instead of following the dictates of God found in revelation, nature, and tradition (or the shared convictions of the people held and refined over time).

Of course, some today argue that communities "project their mundane realities into the heavens as a cosmic replica, an archetype, in order to provide some sort of otherworldly justification." But this merely proves the reality and priority of the sacred: "If social and other mundane forms *are* in need of a cosmic or transcendental confirmation in order to acquire stability and credibility, then the cosmological picture is in fact first in order of importance."[7]

Unfortunately, reality as we know it in the mundane world is a series of disappointments. Society and its authorities often fail to live up to the demands of the sacred vision. Judges are not just. Holy men are not holy. Rulers abuse their trust. And this inevitable disjunction between divine command and human performance at times calls authority into question. A figure of authority or an entire regime may fall into disrepute and even be replaced because the people have lost confidence that he or it is acting as required by the moral standards of sacred law.

Increasingly, however, we have chosen to accept the failings of democratic institutions and to call the demands of the sacred order themselves into question. Most religions hold that their sacraments are effective (e.g., the marriage ceremony forms a sacred union, complete with sacred obligations) even if the priest who performs the rite makes mistakes or is in a state of sin. Obligations and standards of performance remain, even when individuals fail to live up to them. Modern democracies, however, sanctify individual choice, essentially rejecting moral standards other than the equality and toleration derived from their own procedures.

But man is a moral and religious creature. Thus the construction of an amoral politics has set up worse and deeper conflicts than the inevitable one between transcendent standards and human practice. And the most important binding force of modern society—law—itself has fallen victim to the demands of men seeking to free themselves from the constraints of the sacred.

Law and the Sacred

The problem of law is at heart a problem of authority. Free societies in particular cannot exist without law. Unless the people know the rules by which they must live and unless they see obedience to these rules as more important than their own interests, a war of all against all will ensue. Mutual trust will be destroyed and the state either will impose its will through force or will crumble altogether. Public peace rests on prevalent obedience to the laws. Ironically, it is liberalism, that ideology most devoted to freedom, that most effectively undermines the authority and sanctity of law.

Western societies did not attribute all laws and sole lawmaking authority to God. Instead they invested rulers with most lawmaking powers. But the rulers were held answerable to God for their just or unjust pronouncements. This produced an important check on political power because criticism from religious figures could delegitimize the regime. It also allowed political philosophers and rulers to exaggerate the necessary distance between divine ideal and human performance. Some philosophers (most prominently Machiavelli and Hobbes) began to argue that transcendent standards have no proper existence or at any rate no proper guiding relationship with human laws.

So useful was the argument that transcendent standards should not bind political practitioners that it quickly spread far and wide. At first a residual Deity remained, as the clockmaker who had set nature in motion and had given it laws discoverable by man. Then this God faded into irrelevance as nature herself came to be seen as the fount of proper laws and authority. Rousseau even claimed that men were naturally good, corrupted only by society and its inhuman laws.

At each stage in this process, the authority of the laws diminished. Laws seen as the direct will of God, the infinite creator of all that is seen and unseen, were upheld as fundamentally moral and sacred, binding no matter what their consequences. The Christian tradition weakened this authority by placing God above law, thereby providing men the means by which to question the laws and even, when they violated the common good, declare them null and void. This allowed some to push God into the background and treat "natural" laws as mere facts of human nature, to be addressed through purely human laws imposed by the state and changed according to their utility and convenience. As God receded, law became increasingly a matter of self-interest. Men came to see laws as subject to their wills and not vice versa. The result? The current, insane presumption, shared by communism, fascism, and democracy alike, that man can create his own moral authority, changing and dispensing with it at his will, and continue to live in peace and prosperity.

Before dismissing this claim out of hand, consider the extent to which our judicial rulers have cut themselves off from the religious bases of their own authority. Perhaps the most telling example of this in recent years was the ruling by an Alabama federal court judge that a different Alabama federal court judge could no longer display the Ten Commandments in his courtroom. The ruling judge thereby sought to deny public recognition of the sacred legal code—the code on which Judaism, Christianity, Islam, and all the legal codes arising therefrom rely.

The Ten Commandments, handed down to Moses by God, formed a sacred pact between Him and the Jews, providing them with His favor and a common code by which to live in exchange for their obedience to that code. The Judaic civilization, and from it the Christian and Islamic, all base their legal codes on and judge their rulers by the sacred command never to murder, steal, perjure, blaspheme, or violate the other fundamental precepts considered holy because declared by God.

Today not only political forms and general legal codes but even our most basic laws lack sacred justification. The Ten Commandments have for years been banned from our schools, along with any other recognition of society's sacred bases and obligations. Even the natural law observation that the Code of Hammurabi and other codes of the ancient Near East, along with essentially every society, shared the same basic rules was reduced to a quaint anthropological fact devoid of prescriptive power. In maintaining their authority, the laws must stand on their own. They either "work," that is, provide peace and prosperity, or they are bad. And each individual, when his immediate self-interest conflicts with the law, must determine for himself whether the potential harm to him brought about by breaking that law would outweigh the potential benefits, again, to him. Even constructing legal codes has become merely a matter of enforcing the majority's calculations of what is in its best interest. This is a recipe for chaos. As Molnar observes:

> If power and the laws it erects absolutely lack the sacred in their origin and motivation, if legislators merely carry out the clauses of ever-changing contract, . . . then modern citizens find themselves weighed down by superimposed layers of arbitrariness. Their conclusion must necessarily be that anarchy . . . is rational: I give the law to myself by means of my own sovereignty yet I find I must bear the burden of a huge bureaucratic apparatus that is unable to justify itself. Well then, why not discard it? Why not bypass the entire bureaucratic machinery—which in any case claims to register and

> execute my own will—and give the law directly to myself? . . . What is important enough now to deny or delay the citizens' rush for instant satisfaction?[8]

This is precisely the dilemma that we face. The new communitarians seek to solve it through a measured, tolerant rebirth of the sacred. New communitarians like Taylor recognize the problems that arise from a lack of obligation, particularly in the area of social policy. They see in illegitimacy, crime, and welfare dependency great dangers to the liberal state they support. Committed to a political system in which no one need fear hunger or deprivation, regardless of his choices, they must encourage people not to choose crime or dependence on government, lest government go bankrupt and the undeniable social and individual dangers arising from dependence tear society apart and lead individuals to short, brutish, unfulfilled lives.

Crime, declining in some areas, continues to escalate in the formerly safe and comfortable suburbs. And rashes of senseless killings, including those of newborn babies by their mothers, repeatedly shatter the illusion of moral progress. All this as sexual deviation, drug use, and moral illiteracy flourish. Faced with the consequences of liberal skepticism, even the liberal new communitarians have come to see the need for a return of authority and obedience to our society.

Rebuilding the Sacred?

New communitarians, from Taylor to Galston to Bellah, seek to resuscitate a sense of obligation among the people so that we will again lead lives that do not undermine liberal society. But rather than reestablish the primacy of transcendent standards, to be followed by lawmakers and citizens alike, they seek to make democratic politics itself appear sacred. The theory: Men who feel that democratic politics embody justice and the good life will be more likely to choose to act responsibly and cease using up the economic resources and undermining the social and political solidarity on which their political system depends. Thus it is not the true sacred and not true obligation that liberal communitarians seek to resuscitate. They remain as hostile as ever to "authoritarian" religious groups that insist on a common code of virtuous behavior.

Faced with the fact that man cannot create and re-create societies at will, remaining ever peaceful and comfortable, intellectuals now must determine, in Molnar's words, "how to endow humanity with faculties of generating its own sacred, its own cohesive communities. The (reformulated) sacred ought to have some function in the community, but preferably on a reduced scale and with a low intensity."[9] This new, self-generated sacred is the democratic civil religion.

New communitarians seek to generate a semireligious reverence for democratic forms and procedures. They wish to make us see the democratic way of life, characterized by toleration and individual self-fulfillment, as not just in keeping with our self-interest but also inherently right, as the only form of life that does full justice to man. The people's religious zeal will be moderate because their religion's goods are fundamentally individualistic and self-serving. But the people will subscribe to a democratic creed according to which their way of life is inherently good, just, and holy. Only in this way will we see democracy as worthy of our support, worthy even of our forgoing immediate pleasures so that we will not undermine it. Only in this way will we, as Brad Stone points out, come to see virtue as essentially political in nature.

The basis for this semireligious awe toward democracy cannot be found in a new deity. The French Revolutionaries tried that, even turning Christian churches into temples to the goddess of reason. The result was millenarian frenzy and mass murder. The basis for a peaceful awe toward democracy must be found in the individual himself and in the fact that through democratic forms he is the author of his own moral code. In effect, man must worship himself by worshiping democracy as a collective expression of his own will.

As Taylor puts it,

> every political society requires some sacrifices and demands some disciplines from its members: they have to pay taxes, or serve in the armed forces, and in general observe certain restraints. In a despotism, a regime where the mass of citizens are subject to the rule of a single master, or a clique, the requisite disciplines are maintained by coercion. In order to have a free society, one has to replace this coercion with something else. This can only be a willing identification with the polis on the part of the citizens, a sense that the political institutions in which they live are an expression of themselves.

According to Taylor, free citizens will serve only what they themselves have created. Citizens must participate in government, shaping day-to-day policies, if they are to see it as their own and support it. But to govern responsibly the citizens must be loyal and productive. If it is to be free, then, the state must see to it that its citizens are capable of directing their own actions in a way that upholds the regime.[10]

The new communitarian state must train good democratic citizens—citizens habituated to the virtues necessary to support liberal democracy. Most important, as Galston argues, public education must both maintain and teach "civic tolerance." Parents may rear their children in their traditional way of life. But the state must guarantee that parents will not impede "the normal physical, intellectual, and emotional development of their children. Nor may they impede the acquisition of civic competence and loyalty."[11] Parents must allow teachers to grade their children according to how well they learn and practice liberal values—values that go against and may even destroy small, traditional, particularly religious communities such as, for example, the Old Order Amish.

The state must see to it that children are taught liberal virtues, and toleration in particular. Children must be given the "critical distance" necessary to judge their parents' way of life by liberal standards of openness, rationalism, and material comfort. The state need not take over all the family's functions in order to undermine the authority of the old order because "every child will see that he or she is answerable to institutions other than the family—institutions whose substantive requirements may well cut across the grain of parental wishes and beliefs." The child will be taught to question the tolerance and justice of his parents' way of life by a public school system that does not hold religious authority and faith sacred.[12]

But moral argument itself cannot be eliminated. We need communities to fulfill ourselves, and a people cannot have a real community without a common vision of what is good. Thus Galston urges us to reopen the public square to moral arguments—arguments concerning what it means and what it takes to lead a good life. We must, for example, pay greater respect to individuals' religious visions than we do now.

Galston also argues, however, that we cannot allow religious arguments into public debates unless they are phrased in instrumental terms. For example, religious folk may defend the family but should do so only on the grounds that it is a useful tool in promoting "the successful functioning of a liberal community"—because intact families rear more productive citizens. *Religious* arguments concerning the sanctity of marriage vows, let alone the sacred character of traditional sex roles, sexual orientation, and so on, should not be allowed because they foster doubts concerning the primacy of egalitarianism and tolerance.[13]

Old religious and cultural loyalties are to give way to a democratic faith and way of life. The form, though not the substance, of toleration will be maintained by allowing families to retain much of their child-rearing function. But the family's continuing role is strictly one of utility. The family is one useful tool for the molding of citizens capable of upholding democratic society. More important are the schools and the democratic creed they teach.

Unfortunately for the new communitarians, and for the liberal democratic society they seek to protect, their creed undermines the very sense of obligation they wish to preserve. Liberal "critical distance" and restrictions against religious arguments in the public square strip religion of any public authority by which to bind individuals to its precepts. In public discussions the religious believer must say "it would be useful to do *x*" or "the public well-being demands *x*." These are moral arguments, but they are left to stand without any fundamental basis. We do not know, for example, why "the public well-being" should be valued, let alone how it should be defined, without further discussion. But liberal rules of toleration demand that we not engage in this further discussion. The public is left, then, with lowest common denominator, liberal goods: material well-being (money and other goods are useful, no matter what one's ultimate goal), toleration (which allows each of us to pursue his own goals), and equality (which ensures that no one is punished for pursuing his particular goals)—all tools to help construct individual fulfillment.

Of course these goods are not, in fact, universal. Material well-being is of little use to those who seek a spiritual life. And, as currently practiced, toleration and equality are merely liberal tools by which to keep religious belief and practice out of the public square. Both "goods" in effect close off consideration of what is best for man in the name of conflict avoidance. In the end, when, inevitably, the people's individual desires are left unfulfilled, they come to doubt the value of peace itself. They have been taught to see their self-chosen ends as inherently good and the achievement of these ends as their inherent right. Thus anything that prevents their achievement is, at best, morally suspect.

What is more, communitarian civil religion undermines any concept of public authority by turning true religion into a private hobby. One can say "I happen to desire that we do *x*" but not "proper respect or fear of God requires that we do *x*." By stripping religion of its prescriptive power, new communitarians seek to eliminate the possibility of intolerant religious actions. But, if one can look to religion only for personal, individual rewards, as a fulfilling emotional commitment to be engaged in during one's private time, then one cannot look to religion as a source of sacred rules. Religion no longer has any public authority by which to bind individuals to its morality, let alone its particular dogma. Legal codes degenerate as "victimless crimes" come to encompass the entire realm of public morals. Even public shame, so valued by many on utilitarian grounds, becomes impossible because there is no authoritative moral rule to be shamefully violated.

The only shameful actions left are transgressions against the majority's will of the moment or against the dogma of equality. And because equality itself is enforced through largely political means (progressive taxation, antidiscrimination laws, and so on), politics becomes the sole sphere in which moral judgments are made. In effect, the state becomes the sole (semi-) religious authority. By attaching religious awe to the state, new communitarians make politics, the natural realm of bargaining, the center of human existence. And objects of bargaining cannot be held holy for long; they cannot be subjects of obligation but only of fleeting emotional commitment. The civil religion cannot bind because it lacks unchanging sacred content. In the end it merely further undermines our ability to recognize the sacred and thus form lasting ties of mutual obligation.

Triumph of the Intellectual

The new communitarians cannot achieve, construct, or even maintain true community. Given their commitment to individual autonomy, it seems unlikely that they really want strong communities at all.

The new communitarians demand material equality. They put a high price on public argument made in rational fashion. But more than anything, they value the life of the intellectual. Peter Lawler argues that for Galston, "liberalism is really the protection of liberated reason, the way of life of the philosopher, from popular prejudice or traditionalism." The same might be said of all new communitarians.

Galston claims that our Founders, and George Washington in particular, felt that "only a relatively small number of citizens can be expected to understand and embrace liberal principles on the basis of purely philosophic considerations. For most Americans, religion provides both the *reasons* for believing liberal principles to be correct and the *incentives* for honoring them in practice."[14] While Washington's adherence to such views is, to say the least, open to question, modern intellectuals like Galston clearly hold them. As Molnar points out, however, it is the intellectuals who have created for themselves a number of dangerous delusions. Freudian psychology, Marxism, and Nietzschean dreams of a world "beyond" good and evil build on ancient millenarian fantasies the early church took great pains to expose as arrogant attempts to replace God's will with the intellectuals'. Each fantasy claims that the weaker shall overthrow the stronger in the foreseeable future, each condemns the past as the source of injustice, and each promises an earthly paradise that man himself will create.[15]

But intellectual paradises are for intellectuals, not mankind. They are characterized by the activities intellectuals value, and they preclude the peace and daily fellowship most men find necessary for decent lives.

New communitarians seek to transcend the pursuit of material goods and follow their intellectual desires. To do this, however, they must acquire material and political security. This is best done through an egalitarian "opportunity society" in which credentials from intellectual institutions are highly valued. In exchange for bestowing needed credentials, then, intellectuals will be supported and allowed to pursue their own ends, as they return the democratic masses to a Rousseauean state in which individuals quietly pursue their wants of the moment, leaving philosophers to their higher form of life. This is not to say that new communitarians constructed our current social order. Markets and older notions of human nature and freedom had more to do with that. But liberal communitarians are benefited by current structures and seek to preserve them.

The only problem with this system, from a liberal point of view, is that it cannot work. Liberal intellectuals are left with no fundamental ties and no sense of the sacred. Their profession holds all truths in principle open to constant questioning. And such rationalism is catching. Those who receive their intellectual credentials will themselves come to question the fundamental bases of their society. As a result, and as has happened in our own civilization, the sacred is profaned.

And once the sacred is profaned, even the intellectuals' narrow vision of reason comes into question. The limits of God and nature are no longer recognized. The people, taking their cue from their intellectual teachers, demand construction of paradise on earth. Totalitarian movements, led by a deified Hitler or Stalin (or Mao or Pol Pot, or all too many others) work the people into a pseudorational, pseudoreligious frenzy of expectation that their revolution will overthrow oppressive forces that have been preventing the inevitable establishment of perfect justice and prosperity.

In most liberal societies, rejection of the transcendent is spawning a different movement: resurgent paganism. Unwilling to subscribe to any vision according to which man must change nature, modern day pagans—many of them open worshipers of the earth goddess Gaiea—reject civilization altogether (in theory if not in practice) as an unjust imposition on Mother Nature. Unlike ancient pagans, however, whose religion stemmed from fear of unfathomable natural forces, modern pagans seek personal godhood. Not only modern-day tree worshipers but a vast number of modern men, including the religiously skeptical, see the universe and everything in it as in a sense holy. Because nothing is better than anything else, they reason, everything is good. As themselves a part of this holy whole, these individuals become holy themselves. Everything becomes sacred, in theory. But the truly sacred, that which cannot be questioned, is individual choice—the actions of the enlightened ones who recognize their own godhood.

Nature abhorring a vacuum, superstition has come into public life to replace the religion chased out by intellectuals. And society continues to disintegrate as selfish hedonism and millenarian movements compete with each other to win over a new generation. That new generation has literally sunk into barbarism, complete with grotesque body markings and piercings. Its members revel in meaninglessness. Their public life is a veritable theater of the absurd in which sexual preference and identity, lifestyle, profession, good, evil, and life itself are all up for grabs in a sea of self-relating anarchy. All that remains constant is a cynicism that sees itself as wisdom because it questions the permanence of everything, and in a time of chaos is often proved right.

Even these dancers on the edge of oblivion recognize their predicament, if only half-consciously. They have been abandoned by parents who rejected the burden of raising them in favor of self-fulfillment. But without a stable community there is no viable self for the young to fulfill. They re-create tribal life in their desperate search for community, and they disdain their elders for being shocked at the consequences of selfish acts: they are a generation straight from William Golding's *Lord of the Flies.*

The Possibility of Community

Is community, then, impossible? Are traditionalist scholars, in this volume and elsewhere, merely pining for an irrecoverable past? Perhaps one that never actually existed?

This book is predicated on the conviction that real community once existed and can be revived. Its essays argue that a number of elements are necessary for community and that each of them is potentially within our grasp. Local control over political and social life (George Carey), respect for a common authority not subject to our own will (Wilfred McClay), strongly and commonly held religious beliefs underlying a public code of conduct (Barry Alan Shain): All these are necessary to bind us to one another and make us recognize our sacred obligations.

Traditionalists also recognize that true community requires freedom as well as order. If every personal relation is directed in all its particulars by law or force, there is no room for personal responsibility or the character-shaping lessons of self-directed experience. Neither is there room for the voluntary assent to religious creed and economic, political, and social institutions on which alone a sane adult life can be led.

If one who has been brought up in a particular religion nonetheless cannot see its moral force, he may still be able to lead a decent public life. Then again, he may not. The conflict between his beliefs and his actions may bring untold pain and perhaps a breakdown of his sanity, leading to evil acts. For example, a Christian living among pagans practicing ritual cannibalism can be neither a good Christian nor a good cannibal if he chooses to retain his beliefs while remaining where he is and raising no objection to the local customs. No one who values every human life as an inalienable gift of God can voluntarily witness the reduction of other men to the status of carrion without damage to his character as well as his soul. No self-respecting cannibal can stomach a squeamish moralizer who "accepts" his rituals without partaking of them. Someone must leave, change his beliefs, or be eaten.

Toleration would save neither Christian nor cannibal culture. It would destroy both. Differences in minor ceremonial practices may not produce conflict. But differences in essentials must conflict or they will cease to be essential, as the religions lose all coherence and motive force.

No society can exist long while tolerating both Christians and cannibals. Closer to home, even our Supreme Court has recognized that our society cannot tolerate polygamy and maintain its moral coherence. Only in communities where men's religious practices and morality are the norm or, at a minimum, compatible in their essentials with other established practices, can men be free to lead the lives that their beliefs dictate. Only then can their beliefs and practices reasonably well coincide. Thus, as Norman Barry points out, true freedom is achieved not through a toleration that elevates disinterest to a virtue but through recognition of man's need to leave a community with which he is in fundamental disagreement to find, or found, one in which his religious vision is closely matched by public practice.

To recognize that men are moral agents is to recognize that at some level religions and their moral codes conflict. Although peace may be possible, it may require a certain distance between communities, even if they remain within the same nation. Such was the problem federalism once addressed with great success in America.

One is obligated to the nation in ways different from and less intimate than one's obligations to family, religion, or local community. One has less in common and has fewer ties of reciprocal obligation with a fellow American than a sibling or a neighbor. Likewise, one can tolerate more diversity of viewpoint among religions than within a single religion. If this were not true, if a single religion could encompass the doctrine of Christ's virgin birth, life, death, and resurrection along with belief in the gods of Mount Olympus, religion would lose all meaning. The closer bonds of religion require more closely shared beliefs than mere common citizenship.

But citizenship requires real bonds rooted in a common culture. And culture comes from the cult, or religion, and the moral habits that religion inculcates in the people. Shared altars and participation in common ceremonies give rise to common moral practices providing a common point of reference regarding the nature and content of our obligations.

Unless we recognize that society as a whole is held together by sacred obligations, the ties will no longer bind us to anyone or anything. Unless we allow our more intimate attachments to teach us to accept the looser attachments (the less intimate but still ultimately sacred friendship) of society, we will revert to mere tribalism or lose all sense of obligation. We will abandon one another in empty pursuit of our ever changing and insatiable wants of the moment.

New communitarians want individuals to find fulfillment here on earth through philosophical and political argument. But experience shows that there can be no fulfillment here on earth. Disappointment and tragedy are integral parts of life because our desires are rarely matched by reality. What is more, what fulfillment we can achieve in this life is found not in fleeting material successes nor even in commanding our own will, or that of others. Such fulfillment as we can achieve is to be found in service, in fulfilling our obligations to those around us. Growing up within a community, we not only derive much of our character from our experiences with family, church, and local associations but we also acquire obligations to the people who have helped shape our lives—obligations rooted in our sacred duty to accept the Creator's gift to us of our life, with the people and circumstances that come with it.

The notion that we can find fulfillment by developing our own strengths and capacities, without seeking to serve others, is nonsensical. Just because one would make a good murderer does not mean that it would be properly fulfilling to do so. A good murderer is even worse than a bad one because he is more likely to succeed and continue murdering. Just because one has talented hands and the skills to draw affecting pictures does not mean that it would be proper or fulfilling for him to abandon his family, lead a boorish personal life, and use his abilities to intentionally offend others in the name of art. That would not be meaningful creativity, it would be selfishness.

So long as we see our connections with others as spawning, at most, emotional commitments that must give way to our individual talents and desires, we will fail to recognize our true, sacred obligations. We will be unable to serve others, to provide the daily contact and good deeds from which friendship comes. And friendship, whether the distant form of fellow feeling between strangers who live in the same society or the intimate sort born of family ties, is both the basis of community and the most constant joy we can know.

Self-interested contracts that are entered into from and for the advantage of each individual party do not found societies, and if they are allowed to supplant friendship, they undermine societies. The fundamental insight is that of the great eighteenth-century philosopher and statesman Edmund Burke. The liberals of Burke's day sought to reduce society to the status of an everyday contract. In response Burke declared that society is a contract, but it is not a mere contract in goods

> to be taken up for a little temporary interest, and to be dissolved by the fancy of the parties. It is to be looked on with other reverence, because it is

> not a partnership in things subservient only to the gross animal existence of a temporary and perishing nature. It is a partnership in all science; a partnership in all art; a partnership in every virtue and in all perfection. As the ends of such a partnership cannot be obtained in many generations, it becomes a partnership not only between those who are living, but between those who are living, those who are dead, and those who are to be born.[16]

God created man a social creature needing companionship with his fellows both to survive and to lead a good life. It is in the nature of things, in God's eternal contract with man, that societies form and be supported by their members. Only in society can man develop his character—learn his obligations and strive to fulfill them. In the process of fulfilling his obligations man develops the habits of heart, head, and hand necessary to lead a good life. To provide all this requires continuity. We must know the rules of our arts and sciences, the standards of virtue by which we will be judged. We must know the rules before we can follow them, let alone hold them sacred. And, as Burke argued, societies are held together by obligations—to the neighbors among whom one lives, to one's children, to whom one owes a stable future within which they may find a place, and to one's ancestors, who have given one a life and a way of living that it would be impious to reject.

Religion and Tradition

Obligations are enforced by the fear of God. Not mere fire and brimstone, but much more the fear of showing ingratitude to man's creator and greatest benefactor causes most men to seek to fulfill their fundamental obligations and to feel profound guilt when they fail to do so. Such is the nature of things. However, the nature of things, in particular of man's limited knowledge, attention span, and consciousness, is such that few keep God and their obligations in the forefront of their minds. Rather, most of us most of the time rely on tradition as our guide to right conduct.

The community survives because most of its members most of the time follow their accustomed ways. Rules of conduct, standards of right and wrong that have been passed down for generations, often lack the status of law. But they have great force nonetheless. The force of history, the aura of ancient, ancestral origins causes men to look on tradition with filial reverence.

Ironically, it was to escape the bonds of tradition that liberals threw society into its current chaos, in which laws backed by the force of the state scarcely command assent where once voluntary adherence to common standards was considered normal. Tradition involved less coercion than state action, and in fact was once looked upon as a significant check on governmental power. Tradition embodied the wisdom of the ages, tested over time and in changing circumstances. Its acceptance by the people gave them the power to rule even tyrants by chaining them to accepted practice in most areas of life. A king might execute a courtier for the slightest misstep, but in few cases would he dare trespass on the common law rights of even the weakest of his subjects.

But tradition did not have the status of a religion. Religion itself, the proper belief and worship of God, has its own stature and role to play in community. Burke and his allies saw that religious institutions provide a source of authority separate from the state; they provide rules even rulers must follow. The officials of the church had authority among the people and so could withstand the attacks of a wayward state. Because the people believed and because the church was accepted as a fundamental institution with a standing independent of political power, would-be tyrants feared the clergy.

It was to eliminate a powerful check on his power that Britain's great tyrant, Henry VIII, slaughtered the priests, sacked the monasteries, and set up his own church, with himself at its head. It was to wipe out the last vestiges of religious authority that Hobbes sought to make of the government a "living God." Both paths led to tyranny by way of mass destruction.

Religion would not have been so powerful an opponent had it not been supported by tradition. Until recently, people generally worshiped as their parents had and were thankful for the structure religious ceremonies gave to their lives. Christenings, marriages, and funerals were ceremonies by which religion gave its sanction and a promise of eternal meaning to human events. Unfortunately, intellectuals in particular have declared that such structure is in fact the primary benefit of religion. By reducing religion to a tool of public peace and private comfort, they have undermined its sacred character and thus its ability to provide even these secondary goods. If religion and its traditions are not sacred, they are meaningless impositions on our self-expression, and they will be abandoned. Religion's primary role is to prepare man for judgment; only by recognizing this can we recognize and uphold religion's authority in this life.

Freedom from moral constraints, the freedom to delude ourselves that we control our own destinies, is the undoing of community. Centralized governments, the usurpation of charity and other social functions by the state, and other innovations taking away the functions of the local community have sapped its strength. But the source of these innovations is also the true source of our loss of community: pride. The foolish belief that our plans of today need not recognize the authority of experience, the wisdom embodied in tradition, has led us to abandon our neighbors in pursuit of a perfection that exists only in our own flawed minds.

It will take far longer to reorder our communities than the few decades involved in throwing them into anarchy. But the process begins with the simple acceptance of our need for our friends, families, neighbors, ancestors, and God if we are to build a meaningful and decent life. We must recognize that the twin evils of tyranny and anarchy are not avoided through servile democratic absolutism but through the sacred contract of society in which tradition, religion, and prudent statesmanship aim to provide an ordered community in which we are free to pursue a life of friendship and mutual obligation.

Notes

Introduction

1. Alexis de Tocqueville, *Democracy in America,* ed. J. P. Mayer, trans. George Lawrence (Garden City, N.Y.: Doubleday, 1969), 511.
2. Tocqueville, *Democracy*, 511.
3. Alexis de Tocqueville, *The Old Regime and the French Revolution*, trans. Stuart Gilbert (Garden City, N.Y.: Doubleday, 1955), 47.
4. Tocqueville, *Old Regime*, 148.
5. Bertrand de Jouvenel, *On Power* (Indianapolis: Liberty Press, 1993), esp. chap. 7.
6. Herbert Croly, *The Promise of American Life* (New York: Macmillan, 1911), 22.
7. Croly, *Promise*, 418.
8. Croly, *Promise*, 196.
9. Robert Nisbet, *The Quest for Community* (San Francisco, Institute for Contemporary Studies, 1990).
10. Nisbet, *Quest*, 139.
11. Croly, *Promise*, 280.
12. Croly, *Promise*, 280
13. Croly, *Promise*, 418.
14. Robert Nisbet, "Still Questing," *Intercollegiate Review* 29 (Fall 1993): 44–45.
15. Tocqueville, *Democracy*, 692.
16. Tocqueville, *Democracy*, 692.
17. Nisbet, *Quest*, 18.
18. Nisbet, *Quest*, 171–72.
19. Croly, *Promise*, 284.
20. Croly, *Promise*, 283.

Chapter 1

1. Jean Bethke Elshtain, "Catholic Social Thought, the City, and Liberal America," in *Catholicism, Liberalism and Communitarianism: The Catholic In-*

tellectual Tradition and the Moral Foundations of Democracy, ed. Kenneth L. Grasso, Gerard V. Bradley, and Robert P. Hunt (Lanham, Md.: Rowman & Littlefield, 1995), 97.

2. The standard starting point for discussions of our declining social solidarity is Robert D. Putnam's "Bowling Alone: America's Declining Social Capital," *Journal of Democracy* 6 (January 1995): 65–78.

3. Michael J. Sandel, "Freedom of Conscience or Freedom of Choice?" in *Articles of Faith, Articles of Peace*, ed. James Davison Hunter and Os Guiness (Washington, D.C.: Brookings Institution, 1990) 76, 75.

4. Alasdair MacIntyre, "A Partial Response to My Critics," in *After MacIntyre: Critical Perspectives on the Work of Alasdair MacIntyre,* ed. John Horton and Susan Mendus (Notre Dame: University of Notre Dame Press, 1994), 302.

5. MacIntyre, "Partial Response," 302–3.

6. Robert A. Nisbet, *The Quest for Community* (London: Oxford University Press, 1953). We draw heavily on this and a later work, *The Twilight of Authority* (New York: Oxford University Press, 1975), in which Nisbet examines many of the earlier work's themes in light of events of the previous quarter century. For purposes of convenience, citations of these works will be given parenthetically and their titles abbreviated as, respectively, QC and TA.

7. Mary Ann Glendon, *Rights Talk: The Impoverishment of Political Discourse* (New York: Free Press), 136.

8. Michael Sandel, "Morality and the Liberal Ideal," *New Republic*, 7 May 1984, 16.

9. Christopher Lasch, *The Revolt of the Elites and the Betrayal of Democracy* (New York: Norton, 1995), 101.

10. Lasch, *Revolt of the Elites*, 103–4.

11. Lasch, *Revolt of the Elites*, 104–5.

12. Robert N. Bellah, "The Invasion of the Money World," in *Rebuilding the Nest: A New Commitment to the American Family*, ed. David Blankenhorn, Steven Bayme, and Jean Bethke Elshtain (Milwaukee: Family Service America, 1990), 236.

13. Robert N. Bellah, Richard Madsen, William M. Sullivan, Ann Swidler, and Steven M. Tipton, *The Good Society* (New York: Knopf, 1992), 6.

14. See Sandel, *Democracy's Discontent*, 65–66.

15. See William M. Sullivan, "Bringing the Good Back In" in *Liberalism and the Good*, ed. R. Bruce Douglass, Gerald M. Mara, and Henry S. Richardson (New York: Routledge, 1990), 7–8.

16. Michael Walzer, "The Communitarian Critique of Liberalism," *Political Theory* 18 (February 1990): 22.

17. Walzer, "Communitarian Critique," 16–17.

18. Bruce Frohnen, *The New Communitarians and the Crisis of Modern Liberalism* (Lawrence: University Press of Kansas, 1996), 42.

19. Frohnen, *New Communitarians*, 24.

20. Frohnen, *New Communitarians*, 22–24.

21. R. Bruce Douglass and Gerald M. Mara, "The Search for a Defensible Good: The Emerging Dilemma of Liberalism," in *Liberalism and the Good*, 257.

22. Douglass and Mara, "The Search," 257–58.

23. Walzer, "Communitarian Critique," 14. For a superb account of the influence of liberalism's epistemology and metaphysics on the history of liberal political thought, see Thomas A. Spragens Jr., *The Irony of Liberal Reason* (Chicago: University of Chicago Press, 1981). Spragen focuses on how the gradual recognition of the revolutionary implications of liberalism's conceptions of reason and nature have shaped the history of liberal political theory.

24. Francis Canavan, *The Pluralist Game: Pluralism, Liberalism and the Moral Conscience* (Lanham, Md.: Rowman & Littlefield, 1995), 118.

25. Canavan, *Pluralist Game*, 119.

26. Canavan, *Pluralist Game*, 121.

27. Canavan, *Pluralist Game*, 121.

28. Canavan, *Pluralist Game*, 121.

29. Carl Schneider, "Moral Discourse and the Transformation of American Family Law," *Michigan Law Review* 83 (1985): 1859.

30. Roberto Mangabeira Unger, *Knowledge and Politics* (New York: Free Press, 1975), 81.

31. Glendon, *Rights Talk*, 137.

32. Elshtain, "Catholic Social Thought," 109.

33. Stanley Hauerwas, "Symposium," *Center Journal* 1, #3 (Summer 1982): 44–45, quoted in Canavan, *Pluralist Game*, 98.

34. Elshtain, "Catholic Social Thought," 100.

35. Glendon, *Rights Talk*, 143, 120, 136.

36. Lasch, *Revolt of the Elites*, 97–98.

37. Hauerwas, "Symposium," 45.

38. Glendon, *Rights Talk*, 111.

39. Thomas A. Spragens Jr., *Reason and Democracy* (Durham, N.C.: Duke University Press, 1990), 7–8.

40. Clarke E. Cochran, "The Thin Theory of Community: The Communitarians and their Critics," *Political Studies* 32 (1989): 432, 434.

41. Cochran, "Thin Theory," 434.

Chapter 2

1. Russell Kirk, "Humane Sociologist: Remembering Robert Nisbet," *University Bookman* 36 (Winter 1996): 31.

2. Aristotle *Politics* 1280b.

3. Edmund Burke, *Reflections on the Revolution in France,* ed. J. G. A. Pocock (Reprint; Indianapolis: Hackett, 1985), 85.

4. Rowland Berthoff, "Peasants and Artisans, Puritans and Republicans: Personal Liberty and Communal Equality in American History," *Journal of American History* 69 (December 1982): 590.

5. James A. Henretta, "Morphology of New England Society in the Colonial Period," *Journal of Interdisciplinary History* 2 (Autumn 1971): 394.

6. Forrest McDonald, *E Pluribus Unum: The Formation of the American Republic 1776–1790* (1965; reprint, Indianapolis: Liberty, 1979), 201, 221.

7. Thomas Jefferson, "Letter to Joseph C. Cabell," in *Writings,* ed. Merrill D. Peterson (New York: Literary Classics of the United Sates, 1984), 1380–81.

8. Thomas Jefferson, "Letter to Samuel Kercheval," *Writings,* 1399.

9. Kenneth A. Lockridge, *New England Town—the First Hundred Years: Dedham, Massachusetts, 1636–1736,* exp. ed. (New York: Norton, 1985), 184–85.

10. Bernard Moeller, *Imperial Cities and the Reformation: Three Essays,* trans. and ed. H. C. Erik Middleford and Mark V. Edwards Jr. (Philadelphia: Fortress, 1972), 73.

11. Max Weber, *Protestant Ethic and the Spirit of Capitalism,* trans. Talcott Parsons (New York: Scribner's, 1958), 242.

12. Samuel Benninger, cited by Gregory H. Singleton, "Protestant Voluntary Organizations and the Shaping of Victorian America," *American Quarterly* 27 (December 1975): 551.

13. Bernard Bailyn, *Ideological Origins of the American Revolution* (Cambridge: Harvard University Press, 1967), 204.

14. The Federal Farmer, "Letter XVII," in *The Anti-Federalist,* ed. Herbert J. Storing and sel. Murray Dry (Chicago: University of Chicago Press, 1985), 92.

15. Herbert Croly, *Promise of American Life* (1909; reprint, Indianapolis: Bobbs-Merrill, 1965), 31.

16. Gouverneur Morris, in *Records of the Federal Convention of 1787*, ed. Max Farrand, 4 vols., rev. ed. (New Haven: Yale University Press, 1937), 1:551–53; Alexander Hamilton, "Remarks and Speeches at the New York Ratifying Convention," in *Selected Writings and Speeches of Alexander Hamilton,* ed. Morton J. Frisch (Washington, D.C.: AEI Press, 1985), 219.

17. Luther Martin, "Genuine Information," in *Records of the Federal Convention*, 3:197.

18. George Bryan, cited by Herbert J. Storing, *What the Anti-Federalists Were For* (Chicago: University of Chicago Press, 1981), 9.

19. Edward Countryman, *American Revolution* (New York: Hill and Wang, 1985), 78.

20. Oscar Handlin and Lillian Handlin, *Liberty and Power, 1600–1760* (New York: Harper & Row, 1986), 91.

21. Perry Miller, "Puritan State and Puritan Society," in *Errand into the Wilderness* (Cambridge: Harvard University Press, 1956), 143.

22. Abraham Williams, "Massachusetts Election Sermon," in *American Political Writing during the Founding Era,* 1760–1805, ed. Charles S. Hyneman and Donald S. Lutz, 2 vols. (Indianapolis: Liberty, 1983), 1:3–4.

23. Nathaniel Niles, "[First of] Two Discourses on Liberty," in *American Political Writing,* 1:260–63.

24. Francis Canavan, "Relevance of the Burke-Paine Controversy to American Political Thought," *Review of Politics* 49 (Spring 1987): 166.

25. John Brown, *Thoughts on Civil Liberty, on Licentiousness, and Faction* (London: J. White & T. Saint, 1765), 12–13.

26. Preceptor, "Vol. II. Social Duties of the Political Kind," in *American Political Writing*, 1:176–77.

27. Joseph Lathrop, "A Miscellaneous Collection of Original Pieces," in *American Political Writing*, 1:670–71.

28. Michael Zuckerman, "Social Context of Democracy in Massachusetts," *William and Mary Quarterly* 25 (October 1968): 538–39.

29. "Pennsylvania Declaration of Rights," in *Roots of the Bill of Rights: An Illustrated Source Book of American Freedom*, ed. Bernard Schwartz, 5 vols. (New York: Chelsea House, 1980), 2:274.

30. Paul K. Conkin, "Freedom: Past Meanings and Present Prospects," in *Freedom in America*, ed. Norman A. Graebner (University Park: Pennsylvania State University Press, 1977), 209.

31. George Lee Haskins, *Law and Authority in Early Massachusetts: A Study in Tradition and Design* (Lanham, Md.: University Press of America, 1960), 224.

32. Richard Hofstadter, *America at 1750: A Social Portrait* (New York: Vintage Books, 1971), 281.

33. William E. Nelson, "Eighteenth Century Constitution as a Basis for Protecting Personal Liberty," in *Liberty and Community: Constitution and Rights in the Early American Republic* (New York: Oceana, 1987), 28.

34. Alexis de Tocqueville, *Democracy in America*, ed. Phillips Bradley, 2 vols. (New York: Vintage Books, 1954), 2:275.

35. Cited by Daniel T. Rodgers, *Contested Truths: Keywords in American Politics since Independence* (New York: Basic Books, 1987), 110.

36. David H. Flaherty, "Law and the Enforcement of Morals in Early America," *Perspectives in American History* 5 (1971): 248.

37. Kenneth A. Lockridge, *Settlement and Unsettlement in Early America: The Crisis of Political Legitimacy before the Revolution* (Cambridge: Cambridge University Press, 1981), 46–47.

38. Christine Leigh Heyrman, *Commerce and Culture: The Maritime Communities of Colonial Massachusetts, 1690–1750* (New York: Norton, 1984), 143.

39. Timothy H. Breen, "Persistent Localism: English Social Change and the Shaping of New England Institutions," *William and Mary Quarterly* 32 (January 1975): 4.

40. Lockridge, *Settlement and Unsettlement*, 36–37.

41. Lockridge, *Settlement and Unsettlement*, 7.

42. Lockridge, *New England Town*, 16.

43. David Hackett Fischer, *Albion's Seed: Four British Folkways in America* (New York: Oxford University Press, 1989), 232–33.

44. D. B. Rutman and A. H. Rutman, *Place in Time: Middlesex County, Virginia 1650–1760* (New York: Norton, 1984), 59–60.

45. John J. Waters, "From Democracy to Demography: Recent Historiography on the New England Town," in *Perspectives on Early American History*, ed. Alden T. Vaughan and George Billias (New York: Harper & Row, 1973), 248.

46. Gregory H. Nobles, *Divisions throughout the Whole: Politics and Society in Hampshire County, Massachusetts, 1740–1775* (New York: Cambridge University Press, 1983), 10–11, 185–86.

47. A. D. Chandler Jr., *Visible Hand: The Managerial Revolution in American Business* (Cambridge: Harvard University Press, 1977), 17. Not until 1920 would more than 50 percent of Americans live in cities or towns of more than 2,500 people.

48. See United States Bureau of the Census, *Historical Statistics of the United States, Colonial Times to 1957* (Washington, D.C.: U.S. Government Printing Office, 1960).

49. See John M. Murrin, "Review Essay," *History and Theory* 11 (1972): 248, 256.

50. Thomas Bender, *Community and Social Change in America* (New Brunswick: Rutgers University Press, 1978), 12.

51. Heyrman, *Commerce and Culture,* 203–4.

52. Michael Zuckerman, *Peaceable Kingdoms: New England Towns in the Eighteenth Century* (New York: Knopf, 1970), 140.

53. W. H. Nelson, *American Tory* (Oxford: Oxford University Press, 1961), 53.

54. Clinton Rossiter, *First American Revolution: The American Colonies on the Eve of Independence* (New York: Harcourt Brace Jovanovich, 1956), 121.

55. See Charles S. Sydnor, *American Revolutionaries in the Making: Political Practices in Washington's Virginia* (New York: Free Press, 1952), 111.

56. Donald S. Lutz, *Popular Consent and Popular Control: Whig Political Theory in the Early State Constitutions* (Baton Rouge: Louisiana State University Press, 1980), 159–60.

57. Carl Bridenbaugh, *Myths & Realities: Societies of the Colonial South* (New York: Atheneum, 1963), 184–85.

58. Judith M. Diamondstone, "Government of Eighteenth-Century Philadelphia," in *Town & County: Essays on the Structure of Local Government in the American Colonies,* ed. Bruce C. Daniels (Middletown, Conn.: Wesleyan University Press, 1978), 243–44.

59. Bender, *Community and Social Change in America,* 68.

60. Patricia Bonomi, "Local Government in Colonial New York: A Base for Republicanism," in *Aspects of Early New York Society and Politics,* ed. Jacob Judd and Irwin H. Polishook (Tarrytown: Sleepy Hollow Restorations, 1974), 50.

61. Waters, "From Democracy to Demography," 225–26, and see Withington, *Toward a More Perfect Union* (New York: Oxford University Press, 1991), 228.

62. Sydney V. James, *People among Peoples: Quaker Benevolence in Eighteenth-Century America* (Cambridge: Harvard University Press, 1963), 332–33.

63. Fischer, *Albion's Seed,* 821.

64. Robert A. Gross, *Minutemen and Their World* (New York: Hill & Wang, 1976), 174–75.

65. Robert V. Hine, *Community on the American Frontier: Separate but Not Alone* (Norman: University of Oklahoma Press, 1980), 118.

66. Fischer, *Albion's Seed,* 827.

67. Samuel Eliot Morison, *Oxford History of the American People* (New York: Oxford University Press, 1965), 212–13.

68. Edward Everett, "History of Liberty," in *Orations and Speeches on Various Occasions*, 4 vols. (Boston: Charles C. Little and James Brown, 1850–64), 1:161–62.

69. Keith Thomas, *Religion and the Decline of Magic* (New York: Scribner's, 1971), 561–63.

70. Jack P. Greene, *Pursuits of Happiness: The Social Development of Early*

Modern British Colonies and the Formation of American Culture (Chapel Hill: University of North Carolina Press, 1988), 77.

71. Daniel Walker Howe, *Making the American Self: Jonathan Edwards to Abraham Lincoln* (Cambridge: Harvard University Press, 1997), 108.

72. Heyrman, *Commerce and Culture*, 414.

73. Gross, *Minutemen and Their World*, 153.

74. Robert H. Wiebe, *Opening of American Society: From the Adoption of the Constitution to the Eve of Disunion* (New York: Knopf, 1984), 3.

75. Bender, *Community and Social Change in America*, 86.

76. James Bryce, *American Commonwealth,* 2 vols. (1910; reprint, New York: Macmillan, 1910), 2:340.

77. Croly, *Promise of American Life,* 31.

78. John P. Roche, "Curbing of the Militant Majority: A Dissent from the Classic Liberal Interpretation of Civil Liberties in America," *Reporter,* 18 July 1963, 34.

79. See James West [Carl Withers], *Plainville, U.S.A.* (New York: Columbia University Press, 1945), 162.

80. Wiebe, *Opening of American Society*, 383–84.

81. Wiebe, *Opening of American Society*, 383–84.

Chapter 3

1. Alexis de Tocqueville, *Democracy in America*, trans. Henry Reeve, with an introduction by Erik von Kuehnelt-Leddihn, 2 vols. (New Rochelle, N.Y.: Arlington House, n.d.), 2:144.

2. *Foundations of Colonial America: A Documentary History*, ed. W. Keith Kavenagh, 3 vols. (New York: Chelsea House, 1983), 1: pt. 1, 352.

3. *Foundations*, 1: pt. 1, 352.

4. *Foundations*, 1: pt. 2, 553.

5. *Foundations*, 1: pt. 2, 498.

6. *Foundations*, 1: pt. 2, 498.

7. *The Founders' Constitution*, ed. Philip B. Kurland and Ralph Lerner, 5 vols. (Chicago: University of Chicago Press, 1987), 1:215.

8. *Founders' Constitution*, 1:23.

9. *Founders' Constitution*, 1:26.

10. *Founders' Constitution*, 1:10.

11. *Documents Illustrative of the Formation of the Union of the American States*, ed. Charles C. Tansill (Washington D.C.: Government Printing Office, 1927), 297.

12. *Documents Illustrative*, 235.

13. *Documents Illustrative*, 390.

14. Alexander Hamilton, James Madison, and John Jay, *The Federalist,* ed. George W. Carey and James McClellan (Dubuque: Kendall/Hunt, 1990), 41.

15. Hamilton, Madison, and Jay, *The Federalist*, 198.

16. I borrow the phrase "inert legalism" from William McClay's fine article,

"Communitarianism and the Federal Idea," *The Intercollegiate Review* 32 (Spring 1997): 39.

17. Much of what I have to say about the origins and nature of the subsidiary principle is taken from Kenneth L. Grasso's as yet unpublished essay, "The Common Good, the State and the Principle of Subsidiarity in Catholic Social Thought." I am indebted to Professor Grasso for providing me with a copy of this article.

18. Hamilton, Madison, Jay, *The Federalist*, 238.

19. Hamilton, Madison, Jay, *The Federalist*, 119.

20. Hamilton, Madison, Jay, *The Federalist*, 289.

21. Hamilton, Madison, Jay, *The Federalist*, 44.

22. Hamilton, Madison, Jay, *The Federalist*, 47.

23. Hamilton, Madison, Jay, *The Federalist*, 48.

24. Hamilton, Madison, Jay, *The Federalist*, 325.

25. *American Political Writing during the Founding Era, 1760–1805*, ed. Charles S. Hyneman and Donald Lutz, 2 vols. (Indianapolis: Liberty, 1983), 2:1177.

26. Hamilton et al., *The Federalist*, 45.

27. Albert Jay Nock, *Our Enemy, the State* (Delavan, Wis.: Hallberg, 1994), 24.

28. For this debate, see *Annals of Congress*, 4th Congress, 2d Session, 1712–27.

29. Nock, *Our Enemy*, 24.

Chapter 4

1. "A Modell of Christian Charity," in *Winthrop Papers*, 6 vols. (Boston: Massachusetts Historical Society, 1929–92), 2 (1931):282–95. Except in the title, I have altered archaic spellings for greater clarity and accessibility.

2. See Mary Ann Glendon, "Religion and the Court: A New Beginning?" in *Religious Liberty in the Supreme Court*, ed. Terry Eastland (Washington, D.C.: Ethics and Public Policy Center, 1993), 471–82; and Mary Ann Glendon and Raul F. Yanes, "Structural Free Exercise," *Michigan Law Review* 90 (December 1991): 477.

3. Thomas Jefferson, "Report of the Commissioners for the University of Virginia," in *Thomas Jefferson: Writings*, ed. Merrill Peterson (New York: Library of America, 1984), 461.

4. David Riesman et al., *The Lonely Crowd: A Study of the Changing American Character* (New Haven: Yale University Press, 1950).

5. Alexis de Tocqueville, *Democracy in America*, trans. Henry Reeve, 2 vols. (New York: Knopf, 1945), 2:98–99.

6. Toqueville, *Democracy*, 2:131.

7. Daniel Walker Howe, "The Evangelical Movement and Political Culture in the North during the Second Party System," *Journal of American History* 77 (March 1991): 1216–39, esp. 1220.

8. William Ellery Channing, "Self-Culture," cited in Daniel Walker Howe, *Making the American Self: Jonathan Edwards to Abraham Lincoln* (Cambridge: Harvard University Press, 1997), 132.

9. Horace Bushnell, *Views of Christian Nurture; and of Subjects Adjacent Thereto* (Hartford: Edwin Hunt, 1847), 5–22.

10. Charles Grandison Finney, in *Lectures on Revivals of Religion*, ed. William G. Loughlin (Cambridge: Harvard University Press, 1960), 9–15.

11. Tocqueville, *Democracy*, 2:310–11.

12. Ralph Waldo Emerson, *The Portable Emerson*, ed. Carl Bode and Malcolm Cowley, new ed. (New York: Viking, 1981), "Circles," 232; "The Over-Soul," 226; and "Self-Reliance," 141–42.

13. Walt Whitman, "Song of the Open Road," in *Complete Poetry and Collected Prose*, ed. Justin Kaplan (New York: Simon & Schuster, 1982), 305.

14. Elizabeth Cady Stanton, "The Solitude of Self," in *The American Intellectual Tradition*, 3d ed., ed. David A. Hollinger and Charles Capper (New York: Oxford University Press, 1997), 2:49.

15. Emerson, "The American Scholar," 70.

Chapter 5

1. Charles Taylor, "Atomism," in *Philosophical Papers* 11 (Cambridge: Cambridge University Press, 1985), 188.

2. Charles Taylor, *Multiculturalism and the Politics of Recognition* (Princeton: Princeton University Press, 1992), 32–34.

3. Taylor, *Multiculturalism*, 34.

4. Taylor, *Multiculturalism*, 33.

5. Charles Taylor, *Sources of the Self* (Cambridge: Harvard University Press, 1989), 43–44.

6. Taylor, *Multiculturalism*, 28.

7. Taylor, *Multiculturalism*, 58.

8. Taylor, *Multiculturalism*, 61.

9. Taylor, *Multiculturalism*, 52–61.

10. Taylor, *Multiculturalism*, 70.

11. Taylor, *Multiculturalism*, 64 (emphasis in original).

12. Taylor, *Multiculturalism*, 68–69.

13. Taylor, *Multiculturalism*, 72.

14. Taylor, *Multiculturalism*, 68–69.

15. Taylor, *Multiculturalism*, 66.

16. Taylor, *Multiculturalism*, 73.

17. Taylor, *Multiculturalism*, 73.

18. Charles Taylor, *The Ethics of Authenticity* (Cambridge: Harvard University Press, 1992), 45, 49.

19. Charles Taylor, "Liberal Politics and the Public Sphere," *Philosophical Arguments* (Cambridge: Harvard University Press, 1995), 262, 115.

20. Taylor, *Authenticity*, 110.

21. Taylor, *Authenticity*, 110.

22. Nathan Glazer, *The Limits of Social Policy* (Cambridge: Harvard University Press, 1988), 7.

Chapter 6

1. Robert Bellah, Richard Madsen, William Sullivan, Ann Swidler, and Steven Tipton, *The Good Society* (New York: Knopf, 1991), 6. Emphasis added.

2. See Ronald Beiner, *What's the Matter with Liberalism?* (Berkeley: University of California Press, 1992); Amitai Etzioni, *The Spirit of Community* (New York: Simon & Schuster, 1993); Roberto Unger, *Knowledge and Politics* (New York: Free Press, 1984); Michael Walzer, *Spheres of Justice* (New York: Basic Books, 1983).

3. See Robert Nisbet, *The Quest for Community* (New York: Oxford University Press, 1953); Peter Berger and John Neuhaus, *To Empower People: The Role of Mediating Structures in Public Policy* (Washington, D.C.: AEI Press, 1977); Charles Murray, *In Pursuit of Happiness and Good Government* (New York: Simon & Schuster, 1988); Michael Novak, *Free Persons and the Common Good* (Lanham, Md.: Madison Books, 1989).

4. See Novak, *Free Persons,* 121–37, for a description of the indifference shown by statist communitarians to contemporary advocates of natural community. Novak reports in his endnotes, 210, that Bellah told him in a phone conversation of his conscious decision to exclude discussion of "conservative" and "neoconservative" communitarians from his works.

5. See Robert Nozick, *Anarchy, State, and Utopia* (New York: Basic Books, 1974); John Rawls, *A Theory of Justice* (Oxford: Oxford University Press, 1971).

6. Marx is an additional influence on Bellah. See Robert Bellah, *Beyond Belief* (New York: Harper & Row, 1970), xii-xix, for Bellah's characterization of Marx's influence on his life and thought. The evidence of Durkheim's influence is clear in virtually everything Bellah has written.

7. Robert Bellah, Richard Madsen, William Sullivan, Ann Swidler, and Steven Tipton, *Habits of the Heart,* updated ed. (Berkeley: University of California Press, 1996), xxviii, xxiii, xxviii, xxx. After the introduction and preface, the pagination of this edition is identical to previous editions.

8. Robert Bellah, "Civil Religion in America," in *Beyond Belief* (New York: Harper & Row, 1970), 171, 179, 184, 186.

9. Robert Bellah, editor's introduction to *Emile Durkheim on Morality and Society,* ed. Robert Bellah (Chicago: University of Chicago Press, 1973), xxxv.

10. Robert Bellah, "The Revolution and the Civil Religion" in *Religion and the American Revolution,* ed. Jerald C. Brauer (Philadelphia: Fortress, 1976), 62, 65–66.

11. Bellah, "Revolution," 68–69, 71–72.

12. Jean-Jacques Rousseau, "The Social Contract," in *The Basic Political Writings of Jean-Jacques Rousseau,* trans. Donald Cress (Indianapolis: Hackett, 1987), 222–23.

13. Jean-Jacques Rousseau, *Emile,* trans. Allen Bloom (New York: Basic Books, 1978), 213.

14. Jean-Jacques Rousseau, "The Discourse on Inequality," in *The Basic Political Writings,* 55.

15. Rousseau, *Emile,* 214, 93.

16. Rousseau, "The Discourse on the Sciences and the Arts," in *Basic Political Writings,* 7.

17. Allen Bloom, "Rousseau—The Turning Point," in *Confronting the Constitution,* ed. Allen Bloom (Washington, D.C.: AEI Press, 1990), 214.

18. Rousseau, "Social Contract," 163.

19. Rousseau, "Social Contract," 223, 226.

20. Robert Bellah, "editor's introduction," x.

21. This is the thesis of Durkheim's *The Elementary Forms of the Religious Life,* trans. Joseph Ward Swain (New York: Free Press, 1965). For a summary of this work in Durkheim's own words, see "The Dualism of Human Nature and Its Social Consequences," in *Morality and Society,* 149–63.

22. Emile Durkheim, "Individualism and the Intellectuals," in *Morality and Society,* 51, 47.

23. Emile Durkheim, *The Division of Labor in Society,* 2d ed., trans. George Simpson (New York: Free Press, 1964), 24–28; Regarding his view of educators, see Durkheim, *Moral Education,* trans. Everett Wilson and Herman Schnurer (New York: Free Press, 1961).

24. Durkheim, *Division of Labor,* 24, 10.

25. Bellah, "Civil Religion in America," 183; *Beyond Belief,* xix.

26. Bruce Frohnen, "Robert Bellah and the Politics of 'Civil Religion,' " *The Political Science Reviewer* 21 (Spring 1992): 151. Frohnen, inspired by Tocqueville, deems Bellah "a pantheist." Durkheim's socialization of the law is evident in each of his works, but it is perhaps in *Professional Ethics and Civil Morals,* trans. C. Brookfield (London: Routledge & Kegan Paul), 110–20, that his attack on natural law is most explicit. For Rousseau's critique of natural law see the preface to "Discourse on Inequality," 33–36.

27. James Madison, "Is Universal Peace Possible?" in *The Forging of American Federalism,* ed. Saul Padover (New York: Harper & Row, 1965), 260–61.

28. Bellah, "Comment," *Sociological Analysis* 50, no. 2 (Spring 1989): 147.

29. Bellah, "Normative Framework," 369–70.

30. Bellah et al., *Habits of the Heart,* 152–63, 80, 286–90.

31. Ibid., 65–71, for the earlier discussion of vocation. See Emile Durkheim, *Division of Labor,* 1–31, for Durkheim's conception of corporatism.

32. Alexis de Tocqueville, *Democracy in America,* trans. George Lawrence (New York: Doubleday, 1969), esp. 506–24, 690–702.

33. These sorts of statistical comparisons are available from a number of sources. My sources are the following: The Jewish/gentile and Irish-American Catholic/Irish-American Protestant comparisons are from Christopher Jencks, *Rethinking Social Policy* (New York: Basic Books, 1992), 28. The American-born Asian/white comparison is from Lawrence Harrison, *Who Prospers?* (New York: Basic Books, 1992), 165. The African immigrant/American average comparison is from Linda Chavez, "Immigration Politics," in *Arguing Immigration,* ed. Nicholas Mills (New York: Touchstone, 1994), 35. The final two comparisons are from Thomas Sowell, *Civil Rights: Rhetoric or Reality* (New York: Morrow, 1983), 77–79, 81.

34. On the effects of commerce, see Montesquieu, *The Spirit of the Laws*, trans.

Anne Cohler, Basia Miller, Harold Stone (Cambridge: Cambridge University Press, 1989), 328–53; David Hume, *Essays: Moral, Political and Literacy* (Indianapolis: Liberty, 1985), 253–80; Adam Smith, *An Inquiry into the Nature and Causes of the Wealth of Nations* (Indianapolis: Liberty, 1981), passim; Adam Ferguson, *A History of Civil Society* (New Brunswick, N.J.: Transactions, 1980), passim.

35. Bellah et al., *Habits of the Heart,* xiv.

36. For a discussion of the effect of fatherlessness on income, see Sara McLanahan and Gary Sandefur, *Growing Up with a Single Parent* (Cambridge: Harvard University Press, 1994).

37. Sylvia Ann Hewlett, *When the Bough Breaks* (New York: Basic Books, 1991), 92.

38. James Collier, *The Rise of Selfishness in America* (New York: Oxford University Press, 1991), 255.

39. Barbara Defoe Whitehead, "Dan Quayle Was Right," *Atlantic,* April 1993, 77; David Popenoe, *Life without Father* (New York: Free Press, 1996), 63.

40. David Blankenhorn, *Fatherless America* (New York: Basic Books, 1995), 55–56, 35.

41. For a discussion of the physical and sexual abuse of children, see Popenoe, *Life without Father,* 64–73. The Canadian study is cited in Barbara Defoe Whitehead, "Dan Quayle Was Right," 72.

42. Bellah et al., *Habits of the Heart,* xxvii.

43. Regarding studies of material resources, see William Bennett, *De-Valuing America* (New York: Summit Books, 1992), 55. Bennett reports on 150 cases but the figure is more like 200.

44. For a discussion of the academic achievement of one-parent and two-parent children, see Daniel Patrick Moynihan, *Family and Nation* (San Diego: Harcourt Brace Jovanovich, 1986), 92–93.

45. Laurence Steinberg, *Beyond the Classroom* (New York: Simon & Schuster, 1996), 86, 87, 97.

46. Adam Smith, *The Theory of Moral Sentiments* (Indianapolis: Liberty, 1982), 227–34; Edmund Burke, *Reflections on the Revolution in France* (London: J. M. Dent, 1960), 44.

47. Edmund Burke, "Letter to a Member of the French National Assembly," in *Works,* 8 vols. (London: John C. Nimmo, 1899), 4:26.

48. Nathan Tarcov, *Locke's Education for Liberty* (Chicago: University of Chicago Press, 1984), 3.

Chapter 7

1. William A. Galston, *Liberal Purposes: Goods, Virtues, and Diversity in the Liberal State* (Cambridge: Cambridge University Press, 1991), 304.

2. William A. Galston, "Socratic Reason and Lockean Rights: The Place of the University in Liberal Democracy," in *Essays on the Closing of the American Mind,* ed. Robert Stone (Chicago: Chicago Review Press, 1989), 121.

3. Galston, *Liberal Purposes,* 16.

4. Galston, *Liberal Purposes*, 250.
5. Galston, *Liberal Purposes*, 304.
6. Galston, *Liberal Purposes*, 243–44, 265.
7. Galston, *Liberal Purposes*, 265–66.
8. Galston, *Liberal Purposes*, 59.
9. Galston, *Liberal Purposes*, 13–14.
10. Galston, *Liberal Purposes*, 17–18.
11. Galston, *Liberal Purposes*, 295.
12. Galston, "Socratic Reason," 121.
13. William A. Galston, "What Is Living and What Is Dead in Kant's Practical Philosophy?" in *Kant and Political Philosophy,* ed. Ronald Beiner (New Haven: Yale University Press, 1993), 208–9.
14. Galston, "Socratic Reason," 122–23.
15. William A. Galston, "Cosmopolitan Altruism," *Social Philosophy and Policy* 10 (Winter 1993): 118–34.
16. Galston, *Liberal Purposes,* 254–55.
17. William A. Galston, "False Universality: Infinite Presonality and Finite Existence in Unger's *Politics*," *Northwestern Law Review* 81 (Summer 1987): 759.
18. Galston, "What Is Living," 219.
19. Galston, *Liberal Purposes,* 6.
20. William A. Galston, "Equality of Opportunity and Liberal Theory," in *Justice, Equality, Here and Now,* ed. Frank Lucash (Ithaca, N.Y.: Cornell University Press, 1986), 93.
21. Galston, *Liberal Purposes*, 268, 272–73.
22. *Liberal Purposes*, 267–68.
23. *Liberal Purposes*, 267–68.
24. *Liberal Purposes*, 273, 292.
25. *Liberal Purposes*, 279.
26. *Liberal Purposes*, 280–81.
27. *Liberal Purposes*, 293.
28. *Liberal Purposes*, 292.
29. *Liberal Purposes*, 258.
30. *Liberal Purposes*, 294.
31. Galston, "False Universality," 763–64.
32. William A. Galston, "Tocqueville on Liberalism and Religion," *Social Research* 54 (Autumn 1987): 517.
33. Galston, "What Is Living," 225–32.
34. Galston, "What Is Living," 225.
35. Galston, *Liberal Purposes,* 301, 296.
36. Galston, "Cosmopolitan Altruism," 118–28.
37. Galston, "Cosmopolitan Altruism," 131–32.
38. Galston, "Socratic Reason," 121.

Chapter 8

1. Charles Taylor, *The Ethics of Authenticity* (Cambridge: Harvard University Press, 1991), 52.

2. Charles J. Reid Jr., "The Canonistic Contribution to the Western Rights Tradition," *Boston College Law Review* 33 (December 1991): 86.

3. Barbara Dafoe Whitehead, "Dan Quayle Was Right," *Atlantic Monthly*, September 1993, 16.

4. An excellent discussion of this history is provided in Russell Kirk, *The Roots of American Order* (Washington: Regnery, 1987). See in particular chapters 1–2.

5. Thomas Molnar, *Twin Powers: Politics and the Sacred* (Grand Rapids, Mich.: Eerdmans, 1988), 4.

6. Molnar, *Twin Powers*, 117–18.

7. Molnar, *Twin Powers*, 69.

8. Molnar, *Twin Powers*, 90–91.

9. Molnar, *Twin Powers*, 128–29.

10. Taylor, *Ethics*, 165, 171–74.

11. William A. Galston, *Liberal Purposes: Goods, Virtues, and Diversity in the Liberal State* (Cambridge: Cambridge University Press, 1991), 254.

12. Galston, *Liberal Purposes*, 255.

13. Galston, *Liberal Purposes*, 280.

14. Galston, *Liberal Purposes*, 265 (emphasis in original).

15. Galston, *Liberal Purposes*, 265.

16. Edmund Burke, *Reflections on the Revolution in France*, ed. J. G. A. Pocock (Indianapolis: Hackett, 1987), 84–85.

Index

Adams, John, 88, 91
Albany Plan, 67–68, 70, 73
Alcott, Bronson and Louisa May, 85
Althusius, Johannes, 18
American communitarianism: breakdown of, 49–50, 58–62, 82–83; key elements of, 39–41; localism of, 42–43, 45–49, 51–53, 57–58; Protestant influences on, 41, 43–45, 47–48, 50–51, 55–57, 89–90, 91. *See also* Community
Anti-Federalist, 61, 72, 92, 94, 113
Appleby, Joyce, 59
Aristotle, 41, 144, 145, 150, 154, 163
Articles of Confederation, 68–69, 73
Atwater, Jeremiah, 78

Bancroft, George, 57
Barry, Norman, 16, 182
Beiner, Arnold, 125
Bellah, Robert, 16, 18, 29, 30, 175; on civil religion, 128–29, 133–34; influence of Durkheim upon, 131–33; influence of Rousseau upon, 129–31; materialistic approach of, 135–37; statist views of, 134–35
Bellow, Saul, 116
Bender, Thomas, 54, 60
Berger, Peter, 125, 126
Berlin, Isaiah, 118
Bill of Rights, 72, 114, 156
Bismarck, Otto von, 10
Blankenhorn, David, 136–37
Bloom, Allan, 143, 144, 148, 150, 153, 154, 163
Bonomi, Patricia, 54
Breen, Timothy, 50
Bridenbaugh, Carl, 53
Brown, John, 47
Bryce, James, 60
Burke, Edmund, 18, 25, 41, 126, 135, 138, 139, 183–84, 185
Bushnell, Horace, 95–96

Caesar, 170
Canavan, Francis, 32, 33–34, 47
Carey, George, 15, 181
Chandler, Alfred, 52
Channing, William Ellery, 95, 96, 97
Charles I, 4
Christ, 90, 99, 170, 182
Cochran, Clarke, 36–37
Code of Hammurabi, 174
Community: conceptions of 28–30; contemporary classifications of, 125–27; historical character of, 3–5; nature of 1–2, 63–64; as source of virtue, 75–78
Conservatism: in early American thought, 39–41; place of obligation in, 181–84; possesses sense of sacred, 170–73; tradition and religion, foundations of, 184–86; and traditional communitarianism, 138–40.

See also American communitarianism
Constitution, 5, 15, 45, 60, 64, 65, 68, 72, 73, 76, 77, 81, 83, 85, 91, 92, 98, 113, 156
Constitutional (Philadelphia) Convention: on balancing state and national powers, 70–71; and compromises, 71–73
Cotton, John, 96
Croly, Herbert, 16, 45; as progressive theoretician, 8–9; vision of national community, 10–14, 60–61

Declaration of Independence, 39, 69, 88, 91, 98
Declaration of Rights (France), 132
Declaration of Rights (Pennsylvania), 48
Dewey, John, 30
Douglas, Stephen, 49
Dukakis, Michael, 149
Durkheim, Emil, 18, 25, 126–35, 140

Edwards, Jonathan, 96, 97
Eighteenth Amendment, 81
Elshtain, Jean Bethke, 17, 34
Emerson, Ralph Waldo, 85–87, 97, 99, 100–101
Etzioni, Amitai, 125
Everett, Edward, 58

Federalism: decline of, 65, 79–83, 113–14; emerges in Constitutional Convention, 71–73; as outgrowth of colonial experience, 65–68; and the principle of subsidiarity, 73–75; restoration of, 83–84
Federalist, 42, 62, 69, 76, 77, 78; and the problem of virtue, 75–78, 92
Ferguson, Adam, 126
Finney, Charles Grandison, 96
First Amendment, 82, 92
Fisher, David Hackett, 51, 56, 57
Fitzgerald, F. Scott, 86
Fourteenth Amendment, 65, 84
Franklin, Benjamin, 67–68
Frohnen, Bruce, 16, 31
Fundamental Orders of Connecticut, 66

Gaiea (earth goddess), 180
Galston, William, 16, 175–76, 179; affinity to the traditionalist position, 153–54; and the American moral tradition, 154–56; and Aristotelian approach, difficulties with, 144–47; on civil rights movement, 156–57; on the "divided self," 161–62; on efforts to save liberalism, 143–44; and Enlightenment liberalism, nature of, 147–48; and "functional traditionalism," 158–59; on "moral pluralism," 159–61; on moral relativism and modern liberalism, 148–50; on secular humanism and Christian fudamentalism, 159–61. *See also* American communitarianism, Liberalism
German Federal Republic, 83
Glazer, Nathan, 122
Glendon, Mary Ann, 28, 33, 34, 36, 92
Goethe, Johann, 88
Golding, William, 181
Grasso, Kenneth, 14
Great Awakening, 91
Great Compromise, 71
"Great Society," 79
Green, T. H., 30
Greene, Jack, 59
Gross, Robert, 60

Habermas, Jurgen, 143
Hamilton, Alexander, 45, 72, 74
Handlin, Oscar and Lillian, 46
Harrington, James, 58
Hauerwas, Stanley, 34, 35
Hawthorne, Nathaniel, 85, 100
Hegel, Georg, 88, 137
Henry VIII, 185
Heyrman, Christine, 50, 52, 60
Hine, Robert, 57
Hitler, Adolf, 180
Hobbes, Thomas, 173, 185

Howe, Daniel Walker, 59, 95
Hume, David, 126
Hutchinson, Anne, 96

Intermediate assocations: role and importance of, 22–24, 37–38, 42

James II, 4
Jefferson, Thomas, 30, 43, 61, 91, 92–93, 96
Jencks, Christopher, 134
Johnson, Lyndon, 48
Johnson, William, 70
Jouvenal, Bertrand de, 7

Kant, Immanuel, 150, 151
Kirk, Russell, 41
Kristol, Irving, 143, 160

Lasch, Christopher, 29–30, 34–35
Lathrop, Joseph, 48
Lawler, Peter, 16, 179
Lemon, James, 55
Liberal (new) communitarianism: fundamental tenets of breed cynicism, 179–81; reject transcendent, consequences of, 173–175; reliance on civil religion, weaknesses of, 175–79; sense of sacred obligation, need for, 166–73
Liberalism: and communitarianism, 28–31, 165–66, 168–70; and individualism, 31–36, 87–88, 103–4. *See also* Galston, William; Liberal communitarianism; Taylor, Charles
Locke, John, 30, 57, 58, 88, 150, 152, 158, 168–69
Lockridge, Kenneth, 50
Louis XIV, 4
Lutz, Donald, 53

Machiavelli, Niccolò, 173
MacIntyre, Alasdair, 105, 154; on communitarianism, 17–18
Madison, James, 30, 69, 72, 73–74, 133; and the problem of factions, 76–77
Mann, Horace, 95, 96
Mao Tse-tung, 180
Martin, Luther, 45
Marx, Karl, 18, 42, 126
May, Henry, 60
McClay, Wilfred, 15, 181
McDonald, Forrest, 45
Michelangelo, 86
Molnar, Thomas, 171–72, 174–76, 179
Mondale, Walter, 155
Montesquieu, 45, 122, 126, 135, 139
Morison, Samuel, 57
Morris, Gouverneur, 45
Mother Earth, 167
Mother Nature, 180
Mount Olympus, 182
Murray, Charles, 125

Neuhaus, John, 125
New Deal, 8, 65, 79, 80, 83
New England Confederation, 67, 70, 73
New Jersey Plan, 70
Niehbur, Reinhold, 100
Niles, Nathaniel, 46–47
Ninth Amendment, 72
Nisbet, Robert, 13, 23, 24, 37, 125, 126; community and pluralism, 10; on fiction of national community, 11–12; on the need for community, 18–20; pluralistic tradition, character of, 25–28; on Rousseau and statism, 20–22. *See also* Bellah, Robert
Nobles, Gregory, 51
Nock, Albert Jay, 79–80, 81
Novak, Michael, 125, 126
Nozick, Robert, 126

Paine, Thomas, 57, 91
Pluralists: and mediating institutions, 5–6
Pol Pot, 180
Preston, Captain, 57
Price, Richard, 45 Protestantism: and communitarianism, 89–93; and individualism, 93–97; modern transformation of, 97–101
Proudhon, Joseph, 25
Publius, 42

Rawls, John, 105, 110, 126
Reisman, David, 93
Right of exit (secession), 112–13; and Charles Taylor's view on, 113–14
Roche, John, 61
Rodgers, Daniel, 49
Rorty, Richard, 162–64
Rossiter, Clinton, 53
Rousseau, Jean-Jacques, 10, 11, 14, 18, 20, 21, 107, 109, 110, 121, 126–33, 135, 138, 140, 150, 151, 153, 163, 164, 173. *See also* Bellah, Robert; Nisbet, Robert
Rowe v. Wade, 120
Rutman, Darrett and Anita, 51

Sandel, Michael, 17, 30, 37, 134, 161
Schneider, Carl, 32
Shain, Barry, 14, 181
Sidney, Algernon, 58
Smith, Adam, 126, 129, 138
Socrates, 147, 149, 150
Spragens, Thomas A., 36
Stalin, Joseph, 180
Stanton, Elizabeth Cady, 98
Steinberg, Laurence, 137
Stone, Brad, 16, 176
Storing, Herbert, 61
Subsidiary principle, 73–75; disregard of, 81–83
Sullivan, William, 30
Supreme Court, 6, 182; and federalism, 82–83, 84
Sydnor, Charles, 53

Tarcov, Nathan, 141
Taylor, Charles, 16, 165, 167, 175, 176; and conservative aspects of, 119–20; and cultural relativism, 115–19; and distrust of markets, 122, 123–24; on the good life, 106–7, 110; on liberal pluralism, 115; on the politics of multiculturalism, 107–8, 110; on the problem of Quebec, 111–12; and rejection of philosophical liberalism, 104–6, 110; and rejection of Rousseau, 109–10; and similarities to liberal communitarianism, 120–23
Ten Commandments, 174
Tenth Amendment, 72–73
Thomas, Keith, 58–59
Thoreau, Henry, 48, 85
Tocqueville, Alexis de, 18, 25, 49, 64, 65, 66, 88, 96, 126, 129, 143, 147, 155–56, 159–62, 164, 169, 170; on dangers of individualism, 93–94; on debilitating effects of omnipotent state, 12–13, 134–35; on decline of communities, 2–4
Tolstoy, Leo, Count, 116
Tower of Babel, 100

Unger, Roberto, 33, 125, 148

Virgnia Plan, 70, 71, 73

Waltzer, Michael, 31, 32, 37, 125, 126
Washington, George, 91, 146, 179
Waters, John, 51, 55
Weibe, Robert, 60
Whitman, Walt, 97
Williams, Abraham, 46
Wilson, Woodrow, 169
Winthrop, John, 89–90, 96, 99
Wolfe, Alan, 29

Zuckerman, Michael, 48

About the Contributors

Norman Barry is professor of politics at the University of Buckingham. He specializes in analytical political philosophy, welfare theory, and business ethics. His books include *Hayek's Social and Economic Philosophy, An Introduction to Modern Political Theory* (3d edition), *On Classical Liberalism and Libertarianism, The New Right, Welfare,* and *Business Ethics.*

George W. Carey is professor of government at Georgetown University where he has taught courses in American political theory for over twenty years. Among his works is *The Federalist: Design for a Constitutional Republic.* He has been editor of *The Political Science Reviewer* since its inception in 1973.

Bruce Frohnen, speechwriter for U.S. Senator Spencer Abraham, has taught politics at Reed College, Cornell College, Emory University, and Oglethorpe University. He is the author of *The New Communitarians and the Crisis of Modern Liberalism* and *Virtue and the Promise of Conservatism: The Legacy of Burke and Tocqueville.*

Kenneth L. Grasso is associate professor of political science at Southwest Texas State University. He is coeditor of *Catholicism, Liberalism and Communitarianism: The Catholic Intellectual Tradition and the Moral Foundations of Democracy.* His articles have appeared in journals including *First Things, Interpretation,* and the *Review of Politics.*

Peter Augustine Lawler is professor of political science at Berry College. Among his books are *The Restless Mind: Alexis de Tocqueville on the Origin and Perpetuation of Human Liberty, Community and Political Thought Today* (coeditor), and the forthcoming *Postmodernism Rightly Understood: The Return to Realism in American Thought.*

Wilfred M. McClay is associate professor of history at Tulane University. His book, *The Masterless: Self and Society in Modern America,* won the Organization of American Historians' Merle Curti Award for 1995. During the 1998–99 academic year he will occupy the Royden B. Davis, SJ, College Chair at Georgetown University.

Barry Alan Shain is associate professor of political science at Colgate University. He is the author of *The Myth of American Individualism* and the forthcoming *Revolutionary America's Declaration: The Nature of Rights at the Founding.*

Brad Lowell Stone is professor of sociology and director of American studies at Oglethorpe University. He is the author of numerous reviews and articles and recently received Oglethorpe's award for teaching excellence. He has also served as a visiting professor at the University of Iowa and at Emory University.